KU-821-840

JUST

SO MUCH

HONOR

ESSAYS COMMEMORATING

THE FOUR-HUNDREDTH ANNIVERSARY

OF THE BIRTH OF JOHN DONNE

Edited by

PETER AMADEUS FIORE

THE PENNSYLVANIA STATE

UNIVERSITY PRESS

University Park and London

[library stamp]

Library of Congress Cataloging in Publication Data
Fiore, Peter Amadeus, 1927–
  Just so much honor.
  Includes bibliographical references.
  1. Donne, John, 1573–1631—Addresses, essays,
lectures. I. Title.
PR2248.F5   821'.3   79–157768
  ISBN 0–271–00554–8

Copyright © 1972 by The Pennsylvania State University
All Rights Reserved
Library of Congress Catalog Card Number: 79–157768
International Standard Book Number: 0–271–00554–8
Printed in the United States of America
Designed by Lawrence A. Krezo

*JUST
SO MUCH
HONOR*

THE FLEA

Marke but this flea, and marke in this,
How little that which thou deny'st me is;
It suck'd me first, and now sucks thee,
And in this flea, our two bloods mingled bee;
Thou know'st that this cannot be said
A sinne, nor shame, nor losse of maidenhead,
　　Yet this enjoyes before it wooe,
　　And pamper'd swells with one blood made of two,
　　And this, alas, is more then wee would doe.

Oh stay, three lives in one flea spare,
Where wee almost, yea more then maryed are.
This flea is you and I, and this
Our mariage bed, and mariage temple is;
Though parents grudge, and you, w'are met,
And cloysterd in these living walls of Jet.
　　Though use make you apt to kill mee,
　　Let not to that, selfe murder added bee,
　　And sacrilege, three sinnes in killing three.

Cruell and sodaine, hast thou since
Purpled they naile, in blood of innocence?
Wherein could this flea guilty bee,
Except in that drop which it suckt from thee?
Yet thou triumph'st, and saist that thou
Find'st not thy selfe, nor mee the weaker now;
　　'Tis true, then learne how false, feares bee;
　　Just so much honor, when thou yeeld'st to mee,
　　Will wast, as this flea's death tooke life from thee.

FOR JOSEPH, MY BROTHER

WITH ALL THE THOUGHTS
A DEDICATION IMPLIES

CONTENTS

ABBREVIATIONS

EA
ÉTUDES ANGLAISES

ELH
A JOURNAL OF
ENGLISH LITERARY HISTORY

MLR
MODERN LANGUAGE REVIEW

MP
MODERN PHILOLOGY

PMLA
PUBLICATIONS OF THE MODERN
LANGUAGE ASSOCIATION OF AMERICA

PQ
PHILOLOGICAL QUARTERLY

SEL
STUDIES IN ENGLISH LITERATURE

SP
STUDIES IN PHILOLOGY

SR
STUDIES IN THE RENAISSANCE

RES
REVIEW OF ENGLISH STUDIES

UTQ
UNIVERSITY OF TORONTO QUARTERLY

PETER AMADEUS FIORE

JOHN DONNE
TODAY

It was not long after the death of John Donne that the literary
world began to realize that he was a master of language both in
verse and in prose, a poet whose posthumously published works
were to exercise a forceful influence on the world of English letters. Thomas Carew recognized him as the "King, that rul'd as
hee thought fit / The universal Monarchy of wit," while Ben
Jonson saw this wit as such that "no 'affection praise enough can
give!" Dryden praised him for his deep thoughts in common
language, and spoke of him as "the greatest Wit" in the nation's
history. Pope agreed that Donne had as much wit as any poet
could possibly have and proceeded, as he did with Horace, to
rewrite his satires. Johnson, by singling out the "discordia con-
cors" or the "occult resemblance in things apparently unlike" as
the distinctive mark of the poet's wit, gave direction to much of
Donne criticism.

   The great Romantics, as Helen Gardner has pointed out,
struck a new and different note in Donne criticism. For them,
Donne was valued more for the passionate personality suppressed beneath the surface of his poetry than for his wit. But it
was the twentieth century that witnessed the most serious revival of interest in Donne. H. J. C. Grierson's edition of the Poetical Works in 1912 gave critics one of the first comparatively

definitive texts to work with, and Donne soon became one of the major authors in college and university catalogs. Critics cannot be indebted enough to Grierson for this remarkable edition, especially considering that Donne was a poet who did not supervise the publication of his poems. Grierson had to cope with problems of variant readings, had to investigate innumerable manuscript collections, and had to single out any number of poems attributed to Donne that were simply not his. Grierson's work stimulated T. S. Eliot to share in the rediscovery of Donne and, his essays on the poet aside, his reference to "a mechanism of sensibility which could devour any kind of experience" is certainly at the core of Donne's works. Before this century was very far advanced, many critics, a number of them represented in this volume, went on to place Donne in his rightful position next to Chaucer, Shakespeare, and Milton.

It seems significant that the four-hundredth anniversary of the birth of John Donne should occur during an age in which the prose and poetic output of the poet is probably more popular than in any other age. I know of no other poet from the past, save Shakespeare, who is so akin to the twentieth century mentality than Jack Donne turned Dean of St. Paul's. The reasons are obvious. Everyone is fascinated with the libertine youth "gone straight," so reminiscent of Augustine. The outlaw psychology of Donne's sermons, which so attracted many St. Paul's churchgoers, has much the same attraction today. His compulsion to make explicit in language what was implicit in his deepest and most anguished experience typifies our own present day problem of communication. The love of reason, argument, and debate is evident in his poetry; his use of the Socratic technique, reflecting a background in law and scholastic philosophy, certainly appeals to a generation that takes very little for granted. The ever-recurring microcosm-macrocosm conceit in his poetry appeals greatly to an age concerned with world community, equality, and the dream of an eventual celestial city. And when

Gosse observed at the end of his account of Donne's life that "No one, in the history of English Literature, as it seems to me, is so difficult to realise, so impossible to measure, in the vast curves of his extraordinary and contradictory features," he pointed out that which gives Donne part of his perennial attraction: his complex and contradictory nature. He was sinner and saint, he could be sublime and profane in the same instance, he could be a rakish contemplative and a buffoon theologian, he was a passionate lover and a calculated cynic, in him God and the Devil were always striving for mastery of his soul. All of us can see in him some aspect of our own nature; all of us can sympathize with one or the other of his moods.

Two aspects of Donne's style come to mind particularly when I speak of the poet's appeal to the present age: the remarkable subtlety with which he achieves an effect in a poem, and the grotesque images and metaphors which he uses at the most unlikely moments. His subtlety lies in his technique of connecting diverse elements of a poem by the slightest manipulation of words and images which result in a development of sensibility. In "A Valediction: Forbidding Mourning," the "gold to Ayery thinness beate" simile has its proper effect only when we realize that the maleability of gold has been suggested lines earlier by "refin'd" and "let us melt." In "The Apparition," the lover returns to threaten his mistress who is in bed with another lover. The whole idea of ghostly apparition in the poem is supported by such images as "fain'd vestall," "False sleep" and "veryer ghost." But there is further support for the argument of the poem in the use of "aspen wretch." The aspen, the quivering leaf, referred also, in the seventeenth century, to the talkative woman, the chattering female with the wagging tongue. The narrator in the resolution of the poem refuses to reveal to her what he will say so that she will not repent for fear of his threats, no matter how intense the protestations of this inquisitive yet faithless woman are. Furthermore, acting in a

3

submerged metaphorical sense, the aspen, the quivering leaf, also evokes the idea of an asp, a tiny and quivering serpent. The movement in the images of "stirre" and "cold quicksilver" gives further support to the idea, and the reference brings home all the more strongly the fierce and cumulative hate the narrator now feels for the "murdresse." In "A Valediction: of Weeping," the small tear with its overall design of roundness grows by stages into coins, fruits, a round ball, a globe, a world, a world overflowed, a moon, even a sphere. Contained in these images is the underlying theme of the two loves intermingling, and this idea reaches its fullness in the final stanza. His tear has mingled with her image and has been stamped by it; his tears have become pregnant of her; her image in his tear creates a world; their tears together overflow the world; they are both in the same sphere; finally, their union, their intermingling, within this sphere is so complete that when they sigh, they actually sigh each other's breath with the power to destroy each other. This theme of union, so central to so many of Donne's love-poems, is presented here by contrasting images. The poem speaks of weeping as drowning their love, of the danger of sighing each other out of existence, of the possible death from over-indulgence in tears, and all of this is illustrated by the opposite images of pregnancy, fruit, and growth. The subtlety of effect comes when we realize that they are not really such opposites after all. In fact, the whole thing illustrates a vision of life that Donne never questioned, that life is actually an intermingling of such diverse things. Even more important, the poem in its total context says that good things, as well as bad, must be controlled in their growth, that by excessive indulgence in these things we ourselves give them the power to destroy.

Donne's use of grotesque is unique. No other poet in the English language could take a traditional Christian concept and intertwine it with such intellectual ingenuity and theological ingeniousness. One is horrified yet dazzled by his treatment of the life-death paradox in "Death's Duell." He says that we have a "winding sheete in our Mothers wombe, which grows with us from our conception, and we come into the world, wound up in that winding sheet, for we come to seek the grave." The winding sheet in the mother's womb is the substance which not only protects the embryo but nourishes it and prepares it for the miraculous moment of birth, the moment of embarkation on the journey to the final shroud. For Donne, so united is death to life that birth is a prefiguring of death, the womb a prefiguring of the grave. Elsewhere, he says the womb is a "grave, a putrid prison" in which "wee are dead so, so that wee doe not know wee live . . . we have eyes and see not, eares and heare not." He notes that just as worms are bred by the corpse and then fed on it, so too is the child bred by the mother and then feeds on her. In another instance, to illustrate the reality that birth, suffering, and death are all one, Donne notes that the child comes head-first from the mother's womb, prefiguring that "headlong falling into calamities which it must suffer after." Suffering is not only a part of life but a prerequisite for salvation, and after using the usual Biblical example of Job, Donne quite graphically proceeds to use Christ as the primary example for man, in that Christ became "the Sewer of all the corruption, of all the sinnes of the world, no Sonne of God, but a meere man, as no man, but as a contemptible worme." The little ironies of life are ever present in Donne's works because he could not eradicate from his mind the most tremendous irony of all, death. Furthermore, as Miss Doebler has observed, grotesque images and morbid digressions in Donne's sermons support the great paradox that life must die to itself to live in the fullest sense. If the great life-death paradox with its supporting macabre images appears incongruous, even absurd, in the context, it is simply because life for Donne, with all its moments of sublime ecstasy, has its corresponding inner anguish and revolting aspects. Life is one in all its aspects: ugly and beautiful, revolting and enchanting, profane and sublime, and the poet projects this vision through corresponding macabre-sublime images. The reality behind the "Batter my Heart" sonnet is that the soul is captive to God's enemy and it begs for freedom to become imprisoned by God. Like the ascetics of old, who described their most contemplative experiences in terms of sex, Donne manifests this sacred wish in terms of "enthrall mee" and "ravish mee" (expressions of rape) so that the soul might finally be "ever chast." Curiously enough, the poet re-echoes this in one of his later sermons when he says that God shook "this house, this body with agonies and palsies, and set this house on fire, with fevers and clanetures, and frightened the Master of the house, my soule, with horrors, and heavy apprehensions, and so made an entrance into me." The shock of surprise (and shock theology is fashionable today), which Evelyn Simpson observed in Donne's use of metaphors from the theater and gaminghouse to illustrate some profound truth of religion, is much the same here.

In each case, however, the reader will notice in the sermons that death, and all the death-like images, almost always serve as a preface to a discourse on the resurrection; or, in the meditations, as a desire to fill the listener with humility, a necessary condition for the contemplation of great mysteries. Being a master poet, Donne knows how to manipulate literary effects with all the variety he feels is necessary for his own and his listeners' spiritual needs. He wanders from conventional paths to produce startling descriptions. But the context of the entire sermon from which grotesque passages are singled out reveals that his objective is to arouse the imagination of his hearers, to make them sense the horror of death. When he presents his listeners with a glorious vision of the resurrection, he helps them to accept this under the influence of emotions rather than of mere pious faith. Again and again, Donne uses images of violence, disease, and suffering. His basic view of existence is on the surface pessimistic: he describes vividly the absolute wretchedness of man and of the world in which he lives, and disease and decay run throughout his work. But paradoxically his message is one of hope: his motive is to bring the listener down to the very depths of agony and despair only to raise him to the promise of a glorious resurrection. In Sermon XXII, he notes that although he has described in gross detail the horror and misery of life and death, so high above us is the glory that God holds for us, that he (Donne) is unable to offer a word to describe it. Since he cannot really describe this state of glorification, he can best prepare himself and others for the attainment of salvation by concentrating in detail, no matter how grotesque it may be, on the utter lowliness of man. Hopefully realising what we are, and what we would be without God, a "worme of the grave," we will grow in appreciation of God's love for and mercy towards us. Donne expresses this quite beautifully when he says in Sermon XLVII, "No metaphor, no comparison is too high, none too low, too trivial, to imprint in you a sense of God's everlasting goodnesse towards you."

The contributors to this volume have graciously submitted these original essays on Donne in commemoration of the four-hundredth anniversary of the poet's birth. I regret that it was impossible for various reasons to include many more fine scholar-critics in this collection; but Donne criticism has flourished to such an extent in our time that a single volume cannot do justice to it all. The principle of eminence and excellence in the world of Donne criticism was the prime basis for my choice of contributors. All of them are universal scholars in the international community of learned people; all are known for their verve and sensitivity of critical perception; above all, all are known for their exemplary scholarship.

I am deeply grateful to the Glens Falls Foundation for a grant which allowed me to return to London to work more closely with the British contributors. I wish to acknowledge with gratitude the painstaking and excellent work done by Mrs.

Mary Monfred and Mrs. Ann Dwyer in typing the manuscript. I am particularly grateful to Professor Arthur Brown for his advice and ripe criticism, always strict but always selfless and generous; also to B. A. Wright, Merritt Y. Hughes, Lore Metzger, Finian Kerwin, O.F.M., Alban Maguire, O.F.M., Kathleen and Jane Lester-Cheney, Hilda Lester-Jackson, Roger Fink, and Louis Andreatta. Above all, I am deeply indebted to my contributors and to my publisher.

EDWARD LE COMTE

꙰

JACK DONNE

FROM RAKE TO HUSBAND

Women were the *sine qua non* of Jack Donne's poetry, and he gave vivid attention to lust in his sermons, right up to the end. Sounding and looking like a skeleton, he transfixed the courtiers of Whitehall with a shocking comparison between the kiss of Judas and the kiss of a woman. "About midnight" Jesus "was *taken* and *bound with a kisse*, art thou not *too conformable* to him in that? Is not that *too literally*, too exactly *thy case? at midnight* to have *bene taken* and *bound with a kisse?*"[1] But the sensuality of the poems, the *mea culpa* of the sermons (above all, the Lincoln's Inn sermons on the sins of youth, to an audience that included some of Donne's boon companions) are by themselves easily discounted as conclusive evidence.[2] The *Songs and Sonets* and the *Elegies* could be flights of erotic fancy, or satires on various love poets of the past, or didactic pieces[3] that furnish no clue to the personal life or even to the personality of the poet. It was not an age given to autobiography,[4] and no genius needs to be as literal as Gosse, eager for missing facts, thought Donne was. As for the first-person beating of the breast in the sermons, preachers were supposed to elicit a feeling of shared sin. "Objective observers report that religious converts commonly exhibit a tendency to exaggerate the darkness of the deeds they did before they entered into light." Donne, looking back, could have thought, like Justice Shallow, that he was carnally bolder than he was.[6] Nevertheless, the sixteenth-century poet does show a preoccupation with sensuality, and non-literary evidence of this is not lacking. If he was not a rake, he gave a good imitation of one.[7]

Was it a pose or was it real? Cleanth Brooks[8] has warned us against our "either-or" way of thinking; maybe it was "both-and." Let us start with the pose of an earlier John Donne, who was contemporary with, though known not to be, the great-great grandfather (unidentified) of the poet and was of the same tribe of the Donnes of Kidwelly, Carmarthenshire, South Wales, whose coat-of-arms was adopted by the poet. The Donne Triptych by Hans Memlinc, now in the National Gallery, London,[9] was painted in Bruges in 1468. This Donne, one of the first of the Donnes to migrate from Wales to London,[10] had come to Flanders for the marriage of Charles the Bold of Burgundy to Margaret of York, sister of Edward IV. Sir John (as he is proleptically called, since he was knighted in 1471 for his services at the battle of Tewkesbury) kneels to the left of the enthroned, baldachined Virgin and Child, gazing out past; his fair wife Elizabeth and their small daughter kneel on the right. The whole secular family exudes self-satisfaction and worldly success; the pious postures have been assumed not for worship, but for portraiture. Sir John, who is handsome in a determined sort of way, has suffered the loss of hair above his brow, but has compensated by a careful overlapping of strands from the back.

We skip to the last decade of the sixteenth century for pictures of the young poet. Until recently we had only one, the William Marshall engraving for the 1635 *Poems*. This image, coarsely at odds with portraits of Donne in later life and carved unskillfully by the same engraver who botched Milton ten years later (and whom Milton satirized)[11] has received a surprising amount of praise, perhaps in the spirit of making the most of all we had for this decade of the 1590s. In any case, it features the warrior, though it is not, perhaps, without hints of the lover.[12]

In 1959 John Bryson uncovered the lost Lothian portrait that Helen Gardner hails as "the most striking portrait we have of any English poet."[13] The pose that it strikes is that of Donne the melancholy lover. It refutes at last and forever any skepticism as to whether the poet acted out his poems. Here are the folded arms, the broad-brimmed hat (ready to be pulled down in despondency), the Byronic open collar, the blasphemous change in the Latin collect from Lord to mistress, *Domine* to *Domina*: *Illumina nostras tenebras, Domina.* At the end of his life, Donne still had this hanging in his deanery. He could at least have had the decency to black out the inscription.[14] Still, one remembers that on the threshold of entering the ministry he was barely dissuaded from flaunting his "false mistresses" by publishing an edition of his secular poems.

Ambiguous words characterize what Walton called "his irregular youth."[15] Tobie Mathew put him among the "libertines."[16] But what did he mean by that? This may have been a criticism of such daring thought as went into *Biathanatos*,[17] without reference to behavior, in contrast to Walton's comment: "All which time was employed in study; though he took great liberty after it."[18]

There is the famous reminiscence from Sir Richard Baker:[19] "Mr. *John Donne*, who leaving Oxford, lived at the Inns of Court, not dissolute, but very neat; a great *Visiter* of Ladies, a great frequenter of Plays, a great writer of conceited Verses." At least we understand the last phrase. As for play-going, I have shown that Donne evidently went to see *The Taming of the Shrew*.[20] But what is meant by "not dissolute, but very neat"? Professor Sprott welcomes this "direct denial of dissoluteness."[21] I take it in conjunction with "neat" as a comment, not on conduct, but on dress: Donne was not (*Oxford English Dictionary*

[1961], obsolete definition 3): "loose, lax, slack, careless, negligent, remiss." The open collar was planned.

We are left with "a great *Visiter* of Ladies," about which Professor Sprott remarks: "Perhaps it is fanciful to see in the italics in which *Visiter* is printed an indication of emphasis on the limited meaning of that word."[22] But Sprott is quoting from an edition printed 51 years after Baker's death; the first edition (1643) does not have the italics. Even if they had been the author's, one could just as well see a euphemism, an irony, meant to be understood—*verbum sapientibus*—by the more knowing, who would also savor Walton's comparison of Donne to "a second St. *Austine,* for, I think, none was so like him before his Conversion."[23] Mrs. Evelyn Simpson, in volume 10 of the *Sermons,* quotes a description of Augustine as "obsessed with the ravages which unbridled sexuality produces in human beings."[24]

We come, finally, to what Walton called "the remarkable error of his life,"[25] Donne's secret marriage. What exactly were its circumstances? We do not even know its exact date. In 1601 the author of *The Progresse of the Soule* made a personal reference to "beauties nets,"[26] and that was the year he became "irremediably"[27] committed to Ann More, Francis Wolley's cousin and the favorite niece of his employer's second wife. They probably met as early as 1598, when she was 14, he 26. The love had ample time to ripen throughout 1599, with the two of them under the same roof, for the girl was a more or less permanent guest at Sir Thomas Egerton's official residence at York House in the Strand. Her father could spare her: Sir George had had nine children by his wife who died in 1590. He himself found it convenient to visit York House when he was in town.

But things changed in 1600. On 20 January the girl's aunt, the lord keeper's wife, died. He remarried 21 October. Sometime between these dates, Sir George grew suspicious of Donne, "and knowing prevention to be a great part of wisdom, did therefore remove her with much haste from that to his own house"[28] thirty miles to the southwest at Loseley Park, near Guildford, in Surrey. "But too late," adds Walton, for Jack and Ann exchanged "faithful promises" before a parting that was to last more than a year.

The chance to meet in the city again finally came with the convening of Elizabeth's last parliament on 27 October 1601. Sir George More sat in that parliament; so did Donne, who in due course wrote to inform Sir George of a secret reunion, which must have been full of what Walton calls "passion"[29] after such long separation. "At her lyeing in town this last Parliament, I found meanes to see her twice or thrice."[30] The next sentence of Donne's letter reads: "We both knew the obligacions that lay upon us, and we adventured equally, and about three weeks before Christmas we married." The word "adventured" contains a romantic consciousness of going against the law. In marrying a 17-year-old girl (legally an infant) without her parent's or guardian's consent Donne was violating both the canon and the civil law, and he did not have to be the lawyer that he was to know this. He also was committing another breach, clandestinity. He had hoped all this would not have the consequences it in fact did have; thus his letter was carefully phrased, if ultimately rather tactless. He persuaded an intermediary, the earl of Northumberland, to carry the missive to his unwitting father-in-law who, having been rendered uneasy by rumors, at last had to be told.

The most curious word in the letter is "about": "about three weeks before Christmas we married." The new husband is writing "From my lodginge by the Savoy, 2 Februa" 1602; he has been married barely two months, if that, but he cannot remember what day? Surely it was a time for precision, for being definite in announcing a *fait accompli* that it was hoped all parties concerned would accept. We are used to husbands forgetting their anniversaries after some years, but the author of

13

"The Anniversarie" is disappointing with his "about," as if he were dealing with a matter of no particular importance.

However, at that time, dates were often vague, even in legal depositions. When in 1613 Frances Howard petitioned for a nullification of her marriage to Robert, the third earl of Essex, the word "about" was used repeatedly: "That the afore-said Robert, at the time of the pretended Marriage, was about 14, and is about 22 or 23 at this time."[31] When the earl "put in his answer" he sounded just as shaky with regard to the same primary facts: "he thinketh that at the time of his Marriage, he was full 14 years, and is now 22 and upwards."[32] Did he not *know*? From John Milton the elder, the scrivener, we have nineteen legal depositions made between 1604 and 1635 that indicate birthdates for him ranging anywhere from 1562 or 1563 to 1569. "In the five earliest depositions he is 'aged 40 years or thereabouts'; seven years later he is '45 years or there-abouts.' "[33] John Milton the poet, despite his scholarly bent, entered into his family Bible a tantalizing note regarding his brother Christopher's birth: "Christofer Milton was born on Friday about a month before Christmass at 5 in the morning 1615."[34] In dating his first wife's death, this poet also uses "about." If Milton and many others were so casual, there is no reason to cross-examine Donne.

But Donne, writing so soon after the event he is an-nouncing, may have chosen his "about" with care. He may, for one conjecture, have wished to leave it open as to whether Ad-vent had or had not come, since if it had, that would be another count against the marriage. The first Sunday of Advent (29 November in 1601) ushered in a closed season for marriages (un-less a special license was obtained) that lasted until the Octave of the Epiphany (13 January), a restriction that William Shake-speare and another Ann had had to reckon with nineteen years before.[35]

For another conjecture, Donne's "about" may signal a

strong hope that no one will press him too hard, under oath, as to the exact date of the ceremony. For a document has survived that gives no countenance whatsoever to Donne's December date. Yet he has been taken unswervingly at his word, even by the latest and most definitive biographer, R. C. Bald. And perhaps he should be, for the document, like everything else we have been dealing with, is somewhat ambiguous. In this case it seems that Donne was not only ambiguous himself, but the cause of ambiguity in others, for one, a judge of the Court of Audience of Canterbury.

What occurred first, however, was court action by Sir George More, the outraged father-in-law, who did not react to Donne's letter of 2 February 1601/2 in the way Donne had hoped. More intended to challenge the marriage and punish those who had taken part in it. In Bald's words, he "insisted that the culprits should be brought before the High Commission."[36] This is a fair inference, though the records of the Court of the High Commission were apparently destroyed by Parliament during the Civil War. Donne refers in subsequent letters to "the Commissioners,"[37] and a similar case had been brought before the court in 1601.[38]

Punishment was not long in coming. Next time Donne writes to Sir George it is "From the Fleete, 11 Febr."[39] The two Brooke brothers were thrown into two other prisons, Christopher for having given the bride away, the Reverend Samuel for having officiated. These two friends and abettors of the poet remained confined longer than he, who was released after three or four days on grounds of health. Sir George remained far from pacified, and all that Donne could express in a letter to Goodyer of February 23 was "hopes." He offered a pretty paradox: "The Commissioners by imprisoning the witnesses and excommunicating all us, have implicitly justified our marriage."[40] In other words, if it were not a valid marriage, why would the authorities be taking such extreme steps to punish it? They must be upset about something, not nothing, a nullity, an empty ceremony. This is an ingenious hope, as compared to the ingenuous hope, in the same missive, of Sir George's "good nature."

The marriage of John Donne and Ann More was eventually validated, though nobody knows on what grounds. We have nothing from the Court of the High Commission. We do have a copy of a decree of another court, to which little or no attention has been paid. This document has had a checkered history. Sir George More kept it among his papers at Loseley House. A. J. Kempe neglected it when he printed a selection of *The Loseley Manuscripts* in 1836. It was cataloged, but inaccurately, in the Appendix to the *Seventh Report of the Royal Commission on Historical Manuscripts*, 1879.[41] Donne scholars, as Lady Mary Clive remarked in her 1966 biography, *Jack and the Doctor*, left this tome "apparently unopened."[42] Sir Edmund Gosse, in 1899, mentioned the document, but evidently did not read it.[43] This is understandable, for it is in a formidable secretary hand. It is now among the Donne papers at the Folger Shakespeare Library, Washington, D.C. Following the lead of Lady Mary's book, I requested a xerox and published a preliminary note, drawing conclusions that Mr. W. Milgate[44] disagreed with in print. Through him I learned that Professor Bald, who died in 1965, had, as would be expected, examined the document. He gives it passing mention in his *John Donne— A Life*, edited by Mr. Milgate, which appeared in 1970. "It is not a very informative document," commented Professor Bald, "though its purport is clear."[45] I must beg to differ. At a major point its purport is *not* clear, and I find it *very* informative.

For one thing, it clears up a mysterious statement by Izaak Walton who does not mention the High Commission nor any suit by Sir George More. He does mention one by Donne, to win back his wife: "he . . . was forced to make good his title, and to get possession of her by a long and restless suit in Law."[46] When I was writing my life of Donne, published in 1965, I as-

16

sumed Walton had become confused here, as he so often had. But he had not.[47] Donne did sue to have his marriage validated and to get back his wife. Richard Swale, who may also have sat in February on the Court of High Commission, sat for the case as the Court of Audience of the province of Canterbury. Dr. Swale rendered his judgment in favor of the plaintiff on 27 April 1602.

Sir George More is not mentioned, though he was the force that came between man and wife: Walton discreetly employs the passive—the "wife was (to her extream sorrow) detained from him."[48] Donne said in his letter of 23 February to Goodyer, "Sir George will, as I hear, keep her till I send for her: and let her remain there yet, his good nature and her sorrow will work something."[49] Days passed, but Ann remained sequestered. When further letters of petition failed,[50] Donne took the matter to court, the same court that had looked into the hasty and overprivate marriage of Sir Edward Coke and the Lady Hatton in 1598.[51] Donne's suit was promulgated or "promulged" on 2 March. It dragged on for eight weeks.

*IN DEI NOMINE AMEN: Auditis visis et intellectis ac plenarie et mature discussis per nos Richardu*m *Swale legu*m *doctorem Curie audient*em *Cantuar*iensis *causaru*m *et negotioru*m *auditore*m *legit*ime *constitutu*m . . ."[52] This judge, this assessor, repetitiously and with the full panoply of legal jargon recognizes that the parties have long been kept in suspense as to whether they were legally married. Having consulted with others, he renders his final decree (*hoc nostrum finale decretum*):

> . . . *cum consilio Jurisperitoru*m *cum quibus in hac p*art*e communicavimus prenom*inatos *Johanne*m *Dun*num *et Anna*m *Moore a*lias *Dun*num *mense Januarij Anno do*mini *1601 in hac p*arte *libellato*s *ab omni contractu matrimoniali et ab om*nibus *sponsalijs (except*is *inter eundem Johanne*m *et Anna*m*) liberos et immunes atqu*e *in huius libertate et im*munitate *notarie existentes matri-*

*monium verum et purum inter sese contraxisse et solem-
nizari procurasse matrimoniumque verum et purum
fuisse et esse inter dictos Annam Moore alias Dunnum
et Johannem Dunnum rite initum necnon solemnizatum
per presbiterum ad effectum predictum habilem et com-
petentem et in praesentijs testium fidedignorum dic-
tosque Johannem Dunnum et Annam Moore alias Dunnum fuisse et esse legitimum virum et uxorem et legitimo
in matrimonio copulatos proque viribus et valore matri-
monij predicti inter eos solemnizati pronunciamus.*

The only date in the body of the decree is January 1602 (New Style), not Donne's December 1601. What is Swale saying? Is he saying what Bald interprets him as saying, "that in January 1601/2 John Donne and Ann Donne alias More were free from all marital contracts or obligations except those into which they had entered with one another, and that their marriage, duly celebrated by a priest, was good and sufficient, and that they were therefore lawful man and wife"?[53] Or is Swale saying what the cataloger of 1879 and Donne's biographer of 1966, Mary Clive, find him saying, that the Donnes married in the month named?

Mr. Milgate, Bald's editor, while granting that "Swale's judgment is . . . ambiguous in phrasing," supports Bald: "The document does not say that the marriage *took place* in January 1601/2, but that in that month Donne and Ann *were* free of any other marital obligations and *had* been properly married. . . . As far as the court was concerned, this was apparently as true of January 1st as of January 31st, and it seems reasonable to interpret the words to mean that by January 1601/2 the marriage *had* taken place."[54] If Swale meant to state that during that month the couple were free of any marital obligations except to each other, I should think he would have used, instead of the ablative of point of time, the accusative of duration, not *mense*, but *mensem*. In any case, any who favor the Bald-

Milgate interpretation should explain why Swale plucks out of the air the month of January.[55] At the same time, one has to wonder why, if Swale was pointing to the time of marriage, he did not give the day, why he was even airier than Donne about that.

Possibly nothing should be made of the discrepancy. For one thing, court records of the time could be incredibly sloppy and careless. For a famous instance, it seems that the clerk, in preparing Shakespeare's marriage license, wrote "Whately" instead of "Hathaway."[56] Would one learn anything by finding a document parallel to Swale's decree, as in the case of John Kidder, weaver, who in a London allegation dated 25 November, 1598 "allegeth that he hath commenced a suite in the Court of Audience against . . . Catherine Draycott uppon a contract of marriadge and hath had a sentence deffinitive passed on his side in the said Court, wherein she is adjudged to be his lawfull wyfe"?[57] Perhaps there are students of antiquarian or ecclesiastical law who could clarify the *mense Januarij* as routine. It would be the beginning of a new year only in the popular, not the legal or ecclesiastical reckoning (as witness the 1601 date). Would it be likely that Swale had no interest in dating except to antedate More's action of February? It seems perverse to be so casual at the finale of a long and what purports to be a most carefully considered case. Could it be a slip of the copyist, despite the attestation of Deputy Registrar Thomas Gibson that this is a true and faithful copy—a slip that More himself left uncorrected?

I cannot see the document as making sense except as dating the marriage of Donne and Ann. As Professor David Novarr comments (in a letter): "If they were married in December, just what is proved about the legality of a *December* marriage (and I gather that this is what is at stake) by saying that in *January* they were free to marry?"

Pending a plausible alternative explanation, I am left

19

with the conclusion that Donne did not tell the truth to his father-in-law, for a reason that has to be conjectured. Donne concealed many things from More; the letter in which he finally told him something not only has the word "about" in it but fails to recollect exactly how often Donne and the daughter had met ("twice or thrice")[58] the preceding fall. Within a sequence of three sentences Donne explains the situation and declines to name those present at the important ceremony. It can be said that this last was for the protection of friends. Any predating of the marriage would have been mainly for the protection of Ann More, a gallant gesture. "I humbly beg of you that she may not to her danger feele the terror of your sodaine anger."[59] Clement of Alexandria had remarked that a good man usually speaks the truth, but that, for one of a number of allowable exceptions, a physician may further the healing of his patient with a lie.[60] Donne obviously regarded the headstrong man with whom he was dealing as one who could not be asked to swallow too much truth at once.

As I see the sequence of events, Ann and John, after a separation of many months, found each other irresistible when at last they met again several times in the fall of 1601. They had made solemn promises to each other, and looked forward to marrying. Physical union was not an evasion of, but a way into, marriage: it strengthened their legal claims on each other.[61] So, with the dissolution of Parliament on 19 December, Ann was taken back by her father to Loseley, neither a virgin nor a bride. In January, it probably was, the girl sent word to her lover in London that she had reason to believe she was pregnant. Thereupon, perhaps on the occasion or pretext of a visit to her former host, the avuncular Egerton, she escaped from her father long enough for a secret ceremony. Egerton's secretary, when at last he had to inform Sir George More, predated the marriage so that the couple's first child, Constance, would be born nine months afterwards, not seven or eight.[62] Constance's birth or baptismal date is, alas, unknown[63] because the Pyrford records were lost.

Perhaps the actual ceremony occurred in late January, but Swale, though of course he could not conspire to falsify the month, gave the couple as much leeway as possible by refraining from naming the day. He was, after all, pronouncing what amounted to a *sanatio in radice*, and in law the child, no matter how soon born, would be legitimate. By 27 April it would have been very apparent indeed that Ann was with child, a *fait accompli* bound to influence both the court and her father.

Towards the end of his first letter[64] to his father-in-law, Donne uncomfortably anticipated the ill things that Sir George had heard about him. Specifically, as Donne's letter of 13 February brings out, there were the two accusations "of having deceived some gentlewomen before, and that of loving a corrupt religion."[65] I do not know whether the latter charge included embracing the doctrine of mental reservation, but I think I know what "deceived" means. Surely the charge was not that Donne had secretly married other women before, nor, like Mr. B with Pamela, plotted to lead them through a fraudulent ceremony. "Deceived" must mean seduced.

In contrast to the rhetoric[66] he used with Sir George, Donne was straightforward with Dean Morton in 1607, when that future bishop offered him a benefice if he would "enter into holy Orders": "I dare make so dear a friend as you are my Confessor; some irregularities of my life have been so visible to some men," that the "sacred calling," despite post-marital reform, might be brought into "a dishonour."[67]

Walton, as usual, is not to be pinned down. In the final version of his narrative of this period he moralizes over "a passion! that carries us to commit *Errors* with as much ease as whirlwinds remove feathers, and begets in us an unwearied industry to the attainment of what we desire. And such an Industry did, notwithstanding much watchfulness against it, bring them secretly together (I forbear to tell the manner how) and at last to a marriage too, without the allowance of those friends, whose approbation always was, and ever will be necessary, to make even a vertuous love become lawful."[68] Donne's secretiveness has been repeated.[69] What is meant by "even a vertuous love"? Does "at last" point to a considerable break in time between the unsanctified union and the sanctified (though unsanctioned) union, the clandestine meetings that led finally to the clandestine marriage? Does "at last" have any flavor of "high time"?

Whatever the details of the scandal, it was big enough for King James, who was in Scotland at the time, to recall it and use it as a reason for not advancing Donne seven years later. Donne's phrasing (in a letter to his would-be patron, Lord Hay) about this blot in his past is piquant: "the worst part of my historie . . . my disorderlie proceedings . . . that intemperate and hastie act of mine."[70] The last sounds remarkably critical, as stern as the line in *Comus* (67) about "fond intemperate thirst," which in turn sends us back to Donne's own sonnet on his wife's death: "A holy thirsty dropsy melts mee yett." What began as "disorderlie" and "intemperate" ended as a longing for a saint in heaven.

The usual apology constructed for Will Shakespeare and Ann Hathaway, whose daughter Susanna was born six months after the wedding ceremony, is that they had plighted their troth before witnesses. This gave them something like marital rights.[71] But there is no evidence for such an engagement, and Walton is careful to deny it for our later couple: "These promises were only known to themselves."[72] The apology for Jack and Ann, if perchance their daughter Constance was born a little early (say, around September first[73] in 1602), is love. I do not doubt it was mutual and true and lasting unto the grave and beyond. Ann, as well as God, was to be thanked for delivering Jack "from the Egypt of lust, by confining my affections."[74] Whatever "lover-like"[75] poems Donne addressed to Lucy, countess of Bedford, or Mrs. Magdalen Herbert, it just does not fit the total later picture to postulate, as Yeats did,[76] a Donne unfaithful to his wife or even her memory. This husband has been criticized, in a way that is historically unfair, for having worn out his wife with repeated pregnancies.[77] But this signifies that he continued to find her, or they each other, irresistible, even when he was 45, which in those days was the threshold of old age. As he wrote in a letter of 1614, "We had not one another at so cheap a rate, as that we should ever be weary of one another."[78]

I am even hesitant about calling the young man a rake, in any place more sober than a title, for there is the Aristotelian problem of definition: how many acts make a man such and such? As a character in a John O'Hara story[79] says, "I did some raking, but I don't think I was a rake." In gazing at the fascinating Lothian portrait, one agrees with a contemporary who said of Donne: "neither was it possible that a vulgar Soul should dwell in such promising Features."[80] The works, by and large, bear that out.

State University of New York at Albany

Notes

1. John Donne, "Death's Duel," *Sermons*, ed. George R. Potter and Evelyn M. Simpson, 10 vols., (Berkeley, 1953–62), 10:246.

2. *See* the early part of my *Grace to a Witty Sinner: A Life of Donne* (New York, 1965). The present article is an addendum to that book and to my note (which contains some details not repeated here), "The Date of Donne's Marriage," *EA*, 21 (1968): 168–69.

3. N. J. C. Andreasen, *John Donne: Conservative Revolutionary* (Princeton, 1967).

4. But a change was coming, and it would be like Donne to be in the vanguard. See Joan Webber, *The Eloquent "I": Style and Self in Seventeenth Century Prose* (Madison, 1968).

5. S. Ernest Sprott, "The Legend of Jack Donne the Libertine," *UTQ*, 19 (1950): 343.

6. This is T. S. Eliot's conclusion. "It is pleasant in youth to think that one is a gay dog, and it is pleasant in age to think that one *was* a gay dog." Theodore Spencer, ed., *A Garland for John Donne* (Cambridge, Mass., 1931; reprint ed., Gloucester, Mass., 1958), p. 10.

7. "Although to try to connect particular lyrics with particular ladies and write a *Vie Amoureuse de John Donne* out of the Elegies and 'Songs and Sonnets' seems to me to be to chase a will-of-the-wisp, I cannot believe that Donne's poetry had no relation to the development of his moral, intellectual, and emotional life, and that his readers in our century were wholly astray in finding in his poetry the revelation of a very powerful individuality." Helen Gardner, ed., *John Donne: A Collection of Critical Essays* (Englewood Cliffs, N.J., 1962), pp. 11–12.

8. *The Well Wrought Urn* (New York, 1947).

9. R. C. Bald, *John Donne—A Life* (Oxford, 1970), p. 21, puts the painting "at Chatsworth," but it passed from the collection there of the Duke of Devonshire in 1956.

10. The first may have been John Don the elder, mercer, whose will, dated 28 August, 1480 and proved in December, is summarized in the *Transactions* of the Carmarthenshire Antiquarian Society (vol. 25, part 60 [1935], p. 63. I owe this reference to Mr. W. H. Morris of Sunnymead, Kidwelly, Carmarthenshire, South Wales). Prosperous but childless, Don was called "the elder" because he had a younger brother also named John (just as, for another instance of a bygone practice, Martin Luther's father and one of his brothers were baptized respectively Gross-Hans and Klein-Hans).

11. In the four lines of Greek iambics, "In Effigiei Eius Sculptorem." This frontispiece of the 1645 *Poems* was dropped in 1673. It was galling to the author of *Eikonoklastes* that Marshall did better by the martyred Charles I in *Eikon Basilike*, and his caricature of the sectaries drew a pun in *Tetrachordon*: "for which I do not commend his marshalling." *The Works of John Milton*, ed. Frank Allen Patterson, 18 vols. (New York, 1931–38), 4:69.

12. John Donne, *The Elegies and the Songs and Sonnets*, ed. Helen Gardner (Oxford, 1965), Appendix E: "The Marshall Engraving and the Lothian Portrait" (p. 266), cites the "love-locks" and the motto based on "the protestation of a fickle mistress."

13. Ibid., p. 269.

14. Cf. Mary Clive, *Jack and the Doctor* (London, 1966), p. 10.

15. Izaak Walton, *Lives of John Donne* . . . (London, 1936), p. 52.

16. Sprott, "Legend of Jack Donne," p. 339.

17. Ibid., pp. 339–41; George Williamson, "Libertine Donne: Comments on *Biathanatos*," *PQ*, 13 (1934): 276–91. The date of Mathew's reference is 1608, when Donne was already the father of four. If any activity other than conversation is meant, it may be the meetings of the "Sireniacal" drinking fraternity of which Donne was a member. But it does nothing for his reputation that Mathew pairs him with Richard Martin, described by Bald (p. 190) as "frivolous," "the acknowledged leader in all revels within the [Middle] Temple," who "never lost an opportunity for convivial gaiety" and was the putative father (p. 249) of an illegitimate child.

18. Walton, *Lives*, p. 67.

19. In *A Chronicle of the Kings of England*, quoted by Sprott, p. 341, from the "9th impression" of 1696. Bald, p. 72, quotes the first edition, 1643 (part 2, p. 156), which I have checked.

20. Le Comte, *Grace to a Witty Sinner*, p. 255.

21. Sprott, "Legend of Jack Donne," p. 341.

22. Ibid.

23. Walton, *Lives*, pp. 47–48.

24. *See* 10: 348, from J. N. D. Kelly, *Early Christian Doctrines* (London, 1958), p. 365. Later, Mrs. Simpson was to remark that Donne "found in Augustine's *Confessions* a striking parallel with his own stormy and licentious youth." *John Donne's Sermons on the Psalms and Gospels*, ed. Evelyn Simpson (Berkeley, 1963), p. 5.

25. Walton, *Lives*, p. 60.

26. Stanza 5, line 6.

27. His own word in his first letter to Sir George More, p. 444 of John Hayward's edition of Donne's *Complete Poetry and Selected Prose* (New York, 1936).

28. Walton, *Lives*, p. 27.

29. Ibid.

30. Donne, *Complete Poetry*, ed. Hayward, p. 444.

31. T. B. Howell's *A Complete Collection of State Trials* (London, 1816), 2: 785.

32. Ibid., 787. Donne was more precise when he testified for a case on

17 June 1618 that he was "aged 46. yeres or nere thereaboutes" (Bald, *John Donne—A Life*, p. 335).

33. William Riley Parker, *Milton—A Biography* (Oxford, 1968), 2:684.

34. Ibid., p. 705. *See* the flyleaf of Milton's Bible reproduced as the frontispiece of this volume; also note the entry that the blind poet instructed Jeremy Picard to enter on the death of Mary Powell Milton. In the allegation concerning his third marriage, "Milton gave his age as 'about 50 years' (he was actually 54)" (p. 1095).

35. See *The Reader's Encyclopedia of Shakespeare*, ed. Oscar James Campbell and Edward G. Quinn (New York, 1966), p. 503.

36. Bald, *John Donne—A Life*, p. 135.

37. Roland G. Usher, *The Rise and Fall of the High Commission* (Oxford, 1913), pp. 36–37, gives examples of the late sixteenth-century usage and comments: "Such usage . . . makes it clear that contemporaries employed 'Commission' and 'Commissioners' as the equivalents of 'court' and 'judges,' and understood them to connote a permanent institution of so settled a character that it could properly be spoken of in the singular number. . . . The great bulk" of the resulting decrees were "issued in matrimonial and testamentary cases" (p. 102).

38. Bald, *John Donne—A Life*, pp. 132–133.

39. Donne, *Complete Poetry*, ed. Hayward, p. 445–46.

40. Sir Edmund Gosse, *The Life and Letters of John Donne* (New York, 1899; reprint ed., Gloucester, Mass., 1959), 1: 109.

41. Le Comte, "The Date of Donne's Marriage," p. 168.

42. Despite the fact that the volume is listed as a source in the English *Dictionary of National Biography* article on Donne (p. 1138). This article, by Augustus Jessopp, unfortunately slips or misprints in giving the year of the marriage: "about Christmas 1600" (5: 1130), an error for 1601 that is still copied: e.g., Beatrice White, *Cast of Ravens: The Strange Case of Sir Thomas Overbury* (London, 1965), pp. 193, 203. Jessopp knew better. *See* his *John Donne, Sometime Dean of St. Paul's* (London, 1897), pp. 22–23.

43. Gosse, *Life and Letters*, 1: 117.

44. W. Milgate, "The Date of Donne's Marriage—A Reply," *EA*, 22 (1969): 66–67.

45. Bald, *John Donne—A Life*, p. 139.

46. Walton, *Life*, p. 29.

47. For some of his hits and misses *see* David Novarr, *The Making of Walton's Lives* (Ithaca, 1958); R. C. Bald, "Historical Doubts Respecting

EDWARD LE COMTE

Walton's *Life of Donne*," in Millar MacLure and F. W. Watt, eds., *Essays in English Literature from the Renaissance to the Victorian Age Presented to A. S. P. Woodhouse* (Toronto, 1964), pp. 69–84.

48. Walton, *Life*, p. 29.

49. Gosse, *Life and Letters*, 1: 109.

50. Those in Gosse, *Life and Letters*, 1: 112–15, the first day of March, to More and to Egerton.

51. *See* Catherine Drinker Bowen, *The Lion and the Throne* (Boston, 1957), pp. 123–24, 295. Mr. Milgate (of the Australian National University, Canberra) provided me by letter with a quotation from John Godolphin, *Repertorium Canonicum* (London, 1678), p. 106, citing Sir Edward Coke (I gathered from W. S. Holdsworth, *A History of English Law*, London, 1903, 1: 371, that this is 4th Instit. 337) as saying that "this Court . . . meddleth not with any matter between party and party of any contentious Jurisdiction, but dealeth with matters *pro forma* . . . and with matters of voluntary Jurisdiction, as the granting of the Guardianship of the Spiritualities *Sede vacante* of Bishops, . . . dispensing with Banns of Matrimony, and such like." Nevertheless, while omitting any reference to that "contentious" third party, Sir George More, Swale's decree is presented as the issue of an adversary proceeding between Donne, the plaintiff, *partem agentem sive querelantem*, and Ann More, alias Donne, the defendant, *ream sive querelatam*, both with legal representatives or procurators— Price and Milberne respectively. The proceedings took place in London.

After our public disagreement of 1968–69 I started a correspondence with Mr. Milgate, who proceeded to share with me the pertinent contents of Professor Bald's book, then as yet unpublished. Mr. Milgate also provided me with his own knowledge and further reflections, thus helping me with the utmost generosity to develop an article at odds with (but, I trust, cautiously so) this well-known Donne specialist's own views.

How difficult fathers could be is seen in the 1599 case of a former Lord Mayor of London: "Our Sir John Spenser of London was the last week committed to the Fleet for a contempt, and hiding away his daughter, who they say is contracted to the Lord Compton, but now he is out again and by all meanes seekes to hinder the match, alledging a precontract to Sir Arthur Henninghams sonne: but upon his beating and misusing her, she was sequestered to one Barkers a proctor and from thence to Sir Henry Billingsleyes where she yet remains till the matter be tried." John Chamberlain, *Letters*, ed. N. E. McClure 2 vols. (Philadelphia, 1939), 1: 73. This case may be reflected in *The Shoemaker's Holiday*. *See* D. Novarr, "Dekker's Gentle Craft and the Lord Mayor of London," *MP*, 57 (1960): 233–39.

52. Friends and colleagues came to my assistance in making out the handwriting. Professor Robert O. Fink, Latin paleographer at the State

27

University of New York at Albany, made a transcription of most of the document. Mr. Milgate passed on to me, as a check, Professor Bald's transcription (not printed in his book). The unitalicized expansions are mine.

53. Bald, *John Donne—A Life*, p. 139.

54. Milgate, "The Date of Donne's Marriage—A Reply," p. 66.

55. Mr. Milgate's next sentence read: "The specifying of this month rather than December 1601 might simply be due to Donne's having brought the suit late in January, or to his, or Swale's wish to make clear that the suit antedated that brought by Sir George More before the High Commission after receiving his son-in-law's confession (in a letter dated 2 February, 1601/2)." However, he has withdrawn this on noticing the pro*mulgata fuit . . . secundo Marci* appendage to Swale's final decree.

Professor David Novarr of Cornell, on reading a draft of the present article, asks, "Would Swale have avoided December because of Advent?" But he adds, "Why, then, not use November?" In reply to my question concerning Swale's lack of interest in dating except to antedate More's action of February, my colleague Professor Francis Sypher suggests that if the Latin means that the couple was married *as of* January 1601/2, Swale was deliberately postdating to avoid placing the marriage in the forbidden season. He could not predate because they were not married in November. Furthermore, the litigation was brought to decide the validity of the marriage, not its date. Professor Sypher posits that "the judge avoids and *closes* the possibility of further objections on any ground connected with the date or circumstances of the marriage." I lack the knowledge of law to have an opinion on this.

56. Campbell and Quinn, *Encyclopedia of Shakespeare*, p. 941, s.v. "Whately, Anne." Unless it was another William Shakespeare or another Anne. For similar errors *see* Joseph William Gray, *Shakespeare's Marriage* (London, 1905), p. 26.

57. Gray, *Shakespeare's Marriage*, p. 194. Irene J. Churchill, *Canterbury Administration: The Administrative Machinery of the Archbishopric of Canterbury Illustrated from Original Records* (London: S.P.C.K., 1933), 1:470–99 gives some Latin formulae used by the court in the Middle Ages, but Act Books of the Audience seem not to exist.

58. He probably does not use "twice or thrice" as a literal statement, but rather as an idiom meaning "a few times" (*see* the *Oxford English Dictionary* [1961], s.v. "twice" 1d). Mr. Milgate points out this same usage in the opening of "Aire and Angels": "Twice or thrice had I loved thee . . ."

59. Donne, *Complete Poetry*, ed. Hayward, p. 444.

60. This, from the *Stromata*, was entered by Milton in his Commonplace Book under "De Mendacio" (*Works of John Milton*, 18: 141). This poet, whose honor has not been questioned in our century except by obscure

Continental scholars and Hilaire Belloc, went on to state in his *De Doctrina Christiana*: "No rational person will deny that there are certain individuals whom we are fully justified in deceiving. Who would scruple to dissemble with a child, with a madman, with a sick person, with one in a state of intoxication, with an enemy, with one who has himself a design of deceiving us, with a robber?" (17:299). *See* Ruth Mohl, *John Milton and his Commonplace Book* (New York, 1969), pp. 71 ff.

61. "A valid but clandestine marriage might be made merely by sexual intercourse preceded by promises to marry; but all such unions were stigmatised by public and ecclesiastical opinion." C. L. Powell, *English Domestic Relations, 1487–1653* (New York, 1917), p. 6. Although his *Treatise of Spousals* was not printed until 1686 Henry Swinburne wrote around this time that "albeit there be no Witnesses of the Contract, yet the parties having verily (though secretly) Contracted Matrimony, they are very Man and Wife before God; neither can either of them with safe Conscience Marry elsewhere, so long as the other party liveth." *Spousals*, p. 87, quoted by Powell, *Domestic Relations*, p. 17. Thus Donne may have used "married" in one sense while allowing it to be understood in another. His two crucial sentences require interpolation: "We both knew the obligacions that lay upon us, and we adventured equally, and about three weeks before Christmas we married [without benefit of clergy]. And as at the doinge, [which extended into the formal ceremony performed by the Reverend Samuel Brooke in January] there were not usd above fyve persons, of which I protest to you by my salvation, [*this* he is willing to swear to] there was not one that had any dependence or relation to you, so in all the passage of it [hint of an extensive period of time?] did I forbear to use any suche person, who by furtheringe of it might violate any trust or duty towards you." He could say, as Claudio did, "She is fast my wife, / Save that we do the denunciation lack / Of outward order." *Measure for Measure*, act 1, scene 2, lines 151–53. But, to repeat, the couple, however right they might seem to each other (Clay Hunt thought that the girl in bed in "The Goodmorrow" was Ann More) risked opprobrium—*see Donne's Poetry: Essays in Literary Analysis* (New Haven, 1954), pp. 68, 232. "And when matrymony is thus laufully made / yet the man maye not possesse the woman as his wyfe / nor the woman the man as her husbonde . . . afore suche tyme as that matrymony be approued and solempnysed by oure mother holy chyrche /and yf they do in dede they synne deedly." William Harrington, *Commendacions of Matrymony* (1528), quoted by Powell, p. 233. In very obvious cases the marriage register could bear the notation "By necessity" or pointedly substitute "Singlewoman" for the word "maiden." Gray, *Shakespeare's Marriage*, p. 188, cites an instance where "maiden" was written, then cancelled. For percentages on prenuptial pregnancies, *see* Peter Laslett, *The World We Have Lost* (New York, 1965), p. 139.

The misogynist Joseph Swetnam was to recommend in 1615 that if a man was bent on marrying, a maid of seventeen (Ann's age) would be "flexible and bending, obedient and subiect to doe anything." Quoted by Louis B. Wright, *Middle-Class Culture in Elizabethan England* (reprinted in Ithaca, 1958), p. 487. Shakespeare's child-brides are not typical: as Swetnam implies, even seventeen was exceptionally young for a bride—*see* Laslett, *World We Lost*, p. 82.

62. Mr. Milgate remarked ("A Reply," p. 67), "It is, moreover, difficult to see what difference the antedating of the wedding by a few weeks could have made to Ann's reputation." On reading this I came to the conclusion that Mr. Milgate must be a bachelor, which he is. To my pressing argument, Mr. Milgate replied (in a letter): "In the circles in which Donne and the Mores and most of Donne's friends moved, 'reputation' doesn't seem to me (*pace* Legouis, a reference to the *jugement de Salomon* pronounced on the controversy by Editor Pierre Legouis as an appendage to "A Reply," p. 67) to have been assessed in mid-Victorian terms (and so much of these as survive today); that the indiscretion of the marriage itself would have been the chief scandal." I agree that the elopement would have been the greater scandal, but because of this beginning, and what with contention and lawsuits, there would have been those in the social circles referred to—and Donne would have feared there would be—who would have counted the months on their fingers. The country folk took "country matters," along with their "accidents," in stride; at the opposite extreme in drawing attention were the prominent courtiers and lords and the pregnant maids of honor, Raleigh-Throckmorton, Southampton-Vernon. Still, one can imagine the passing comment a gossip like Chamberlain would have bestowed on the Donnes, if they had come to his attention; one can imagine it from his actual comment on a prominent case four years earlier: "Mistris Vernon is from the court, and lies in Essex House; some say she hath taken a venew [thrust] under the girdle and swells upon yt, yet she complaines not of fowle play but sayes the erle of Southampton will justifie yt: and yt is bruited underhand that he was latelie here fowre dayes in great secret of purpose to marry her and effected yt accordingly." Chamberlain, *Letters*, ed. N. C. McClure, 1:43–44. It was still, even in 1602, the reign of the Virgin Queen. Under the Stuarts, Chamberlain deplored that Donne persisted in his youthful vice of writing poetry. "I send you here certain verses of our Deane of Paules upon the death of the Marquis Hamilton, which though they be reasonable wittie and well don yet I could wish a man of his yeares and place to geve over versifieng." *Letters*, 2: 613.

The remainder of Mr. Milgate's objection ("A Reply," p. 67) was: "Such a lie would, however, have been particularly fatuous, since Donne knew that the circumstances of the marriage would be fully investigated, partly at his own instigation, by two important Courts; and it can hardly be supposed that the other persons present at the marriage could have been persuaded to lie also." I cannot see at all that "Donne knew" what was going to happen, though he knew what *could* happen. He hoped for the best, the acceptance of the marriage (and his word), *fait accompli*. He did not foresee that he would be thrown into gaol, that there would be lawsuits, his or anyone else's. When he learned that nothing was going to be glossed over, as he had hoped, he may promptly have expanded—or retracted—his own "gloss" on the date. But he had counted, as he says, on "good nature"; (he was blithe as late as February 23, even after these consequences descended upon those concerned: letter in Gosse, *Life and Letters*, 1: 109).

63. As Mr. Milgate wittily comments, "to the flourishing of scholarship"!

64. "If any take advantage of your displeasure against me, and fill you with ill thoughts of me, my comfort is, that you know that fayth and thanks are due to them onely, that speak when theyr informacions might do good; which now it cannot work toward any party. For my excuse I can say nothing, except I knew what were sayd to you." Donne, *Complete Poetry*, ed. Hayward, pp. 444–45.

65. Gosse, *Life and Letters*, 1:106.

66. Donne argues that the charges "are vanished and smoked away (as I assure myself, out of their weakness they are), and that as the devil in the article of our death takes the advantage of our weakness and fear, to aggravate our sins to our conscience, so some uncharitable malice hath presented my debts double at least." Ibid. For references in Bald to Donne's equivocations, *see* my review in *JEGP*, 70 (1971): 155–56.

67. Walton, *Lives*, p. 34.

68. Ibid., pp. 27–28. His first version, *The Life and Death of Dr. Donne, Late Dean of St. Paul's* (London, 1640), read: "Their love (a passion which of all other Mankind is least able to command and wherein most errors are committed) was in them so powerful that they resolved and did marry without the approbation of those friends that might justly claim an interest in the advising and disposing of them." Mary R. Mahl, ed. *Seventeenth-Century English Prose* (Philadelphia, 1968), p. 318. Had he received any new information in the interim, or was he stretching out his style with what he himself calls "some double expressions"? (Walton, "The Epistle to the Reader" *Lives*, p. 6). Novarr, *The Making of Walton's Lives*, p. 70, comments: "He did not have a single important fact to add to this account in 1658, but he would expand this section showing the secular Donne to preserve the relative equilibrium between it and the expanded later life. He therefore rewrote it in more leisurely fashion and added many wise saws which tend to justify the behavior of the principal actors." "Secretly," "the manner," and "at last" were not added until 1675.

69. To quote Grierson, "It was, one suspects from several circumstan-

ces, a little Donne's way in later years to disguise the footprints of his earlier indiscretions." Donne, *Poems*, ed. Grierson (Oxford, 1912), 2:xviii.

70. Bald, *John Donne—A Life*, p. 161.

71. Cf. the latter part of the third scene of the first act of Webster's *The Duchess of Malfi* and such statements from the heroine as, "I have heard lawyers say, a contract in a chamber/*Per verba [de] presenti* is absolute marriage" and "How can the church build faster? / We now are man and wife, and 'tis the church/ That must but echo this."

72. Walton, *Lives*, p. 27.

73. ". . . the christening, perhaps in August," says the Clive biography, slyly (p. 65), after stating on p. 56 that "the wedding ceremony took place in January." If I am casting wanton aspersions on Ann, I feel better for having been preceded by two ladies, of whom one, Lady Mary Clive, had looked at (though I gather from p. 61 not too carefully) the Swale decree, and the other, Evelyn Hardy (*Donne: A Spirit in Conflict* [London, 1943], p. 83), was making a guess based on her view of Donne. Then there are the modern critics: for a review *see* Pierre Legouis, "Donne, L'Amour et Les Critiques," *EA*, 10 (1957): 115–22. Theodore Redpath, ed., *The Songs and Sonets* (London, 1959), p. xviii uses the word "liaison."

74. Donne's *Essays in Divinity*, ed. Evelyn M. Simpson (Oxford, 1952), p. 75.

75. Donne, *Poems*, ed. Grierson, 2:xxii.

76. *Letters of William Butler Yeats*, ed. Allan Wade (New York, 1955), pp. 571, 710, 902. Cf. Donaphan Louthan apropos of "Twicknam Garden," *The Poetry of John Donne* (New York, 1951), pp. 149–50.

77. See the quotations and discussion in my *Grace to a Witty Sinner*, pp. 171–73.

78. Gosse, *Life and Letters*, 2:48.

79. "Mrs. Stratton of Oak Knoll," *The O'Hara Generation* (New York, 1969), p. 122.

80. John Hacket, *Scrinia Reserata* (Savoy, 1693), p. 63.

ROGER SHARROCK

✺

WIT, PASSION
AND IDEAL LOVE

REFLECTIONS ON

THE CYCLE OF DONNE'S REPUTATION

Donne's reputation as a poet has never stood higher than it does
now in the third quarter of the twentieth century. It is so firmly
consolidated as no longer to need fostering by the legend of a
former total neglect. Donne and the tradition of verbal wit to
which he gave the impetus were indeed eclipsed by the revolution in poetic style associated with the names of Waller and
Denham; after seven seventeenth-century editions there was
only one in the eighteenth, that of Tonson in 1719. But he can
never have lacked discerning readers prepared, like Johnson
when editing Shakespeare's comedies, to look beyond the limits
prescribed by the Augustan temper, however committed to it
they were, and ready to forgive the verbal "clenches" while recognizing his "wit" or intellectual power. That Pope should have
adapted and modernized the satires is evidence of this continu-
ity of respectful recognition; so is Johnson's concession in his
Life of Cowley, as a tailpiece to his disquisition on the false wit
of the metaphysical poets, that to write in Donne's manner it
was at least necessary to read and think.

However, the legend of neglect and revival concerns not so much the earlier period as it does the nineteenth century and after. Grierson's edition of 1912 may have marked an epoch, but it was preceded by a century of steadily growing interest in Donne that began with the eulogies of Coleridge and Lamb and continued with the tributes of successive men of letters in essays and anthologies. Nineteenth century Donne criticism has been charted and described by Helen Gardner and, very fully, by Kathleen Tillotson.[1] It is almost all characterized by warm appreciation and a sense of personal discovery; if Francis Turner Palgrave had not been prevented by his own editorial principles from including any of Donne's poems in *The Golden Treasury*, the early twentieth-century opinion that Donne's passion and intelligence were not appreciated by Victorian readers would have been far less easily formed. Broadly speaking, two lines of interpretation may be detected in the attempts of these Victorian critics to analyze their emotional involvement (mainly with the *Songs and Sonnets* but also with some of the *Divine Poems*). The poet is commended for psychological truth, for his sincerity and directness in achieving the true language of passion; or for the blend of feeling and wit obtained by his "union of opposite qualities."

The two approaches are not necessarily incompatible: they tend to separate when a writer suggests that Donne's personal intimate note is achieved *in spite* of his conceits; they come together when he is recognized for achieving some sort of reconciliation of passion and complexity. As Helen Gardner has pointed out, the germ of the twentieth century Donne revival is already present in Johnson's notion of the enforced interconnection of heterogeneous experiences, "a combination of dissimilar images, or discovery of occult resemblances in things apparently unlike." But what Johnson had criticized as perverse in the combination was to be proclaimed after Eliot's essay "The Metaphysical Poets" as especially indicative of true poetic creativity. On the other hand, the critical view of Donne expressed in Grierson's introduction to his edition often seems to favor the first approach, the view of the poet as the exponent of "the true language of passion," a phrase used in 1838 by G. H. Lewes,[2] and with this goes a recognition of Donne as an explorer of the psychology of sexual love. Grierson writes of the poet's "justification of love as a natural passion in the human heart." Yet Grierson's great edition chiefly influenced those who inclined to the second conception, as in the case of Yeats, to whom the critic sent a copy; or of the young Rupert Brooke who wrote two essays on Donne and declared that "when passion shook him . . . expression came through intellect." Critics after 1912 and especially after the critical revolution of Pound, Eliot, and Leavis, sought the subtle union of discordent qualities in Donne and were less ready to see simplicity, passion and a truthful recording of the emotions of sexual love.

Much of this development from the personal, honest, curious Donne of the Romantics and the Victorians to the major poet of ambiguity and "felt thought" was due to a fashionable and often uncritical tendency to amplify the stray remarks of T. S. Eliot into a systematic orthodoxy. The idea of complexity and the idea of simplicity and passionate honesty involve contrary dispositions that are still with us in our attitude toward Donne and toward poetry generally. They are not inevitably linked to the historical phenomenon of the myth of "felt thought" and unified sensibility, but represent permanent opportunities of choice. In the older view Donne was an exceptional minor poet who saw some particular thing very clearly and focused it in an unforgettable phrase:

> *A bracelet of bright haire about the bone.*

> *. . . her pure and eloquent blood*
> *Spoke through her cheeks and so distinctly*
>   *wrought . . .*

These and lines like them, quoted on countless occasions throughout the nineteenth century, consecrate the image of Donne as a poet who condensed single intensely perceived moments of experience.

The Donne of the critical textbooks of the day before yesterday had transmuted all experience: love, death and the detritus of cosmology and theology into the life of language. Fulfilling the demands of postsymbolist aesthetic, he was not so much seeing any facet of life clearly, but looking through and beyond it. In retrospect the peculiar excitement of that aesthetic lies in its disregard of the surface of life united to a passionate apprehension that the poet's images were able, as were the symbols of the hermetic tradition, to plumb the depths of an interior reality: "Poetry should be a miracle; not a hymn to beauty, nor beauty's mirror; but beauty itself, the colour, fragrance and form of the imagined flower, as it blossoms again out of the page."[3] Professor Kermode has made us familiar with the historical development of a body of critical opinion about the romantic image and its reliance on an ideology of cultural crisis or decay; but there comes a stage in our thinking about poetry, even if we are students of literature, when the attribution of historically conditioned motives will no longer serve for full explanation. They may assist us to explain away the theories of others, but we still have to make our own choices. Especially in regard to Renaissance poetry, we have to decide on the delicate balance between personality and convention, between rhetorical dexterity and language as a reflection of experience. We are probably in a much better position than we were even twenty years ago to understand Donne's poetry in the light of the habits of thought he shared with his contemporaries, and to appreciate his technique as the exponent of an international style and not a lonely rebel. Many scholars were never deceived by the too easy formula of dissociation of sensibility, but it would be a pity if a new generation were to substitute for it a paler but no less unprovable orthodoxy. So personal a poet as Donne cannot be treated as an exemplar of the handbooks of rhetoric.

In the history of Donne's reputation the wheel has now come full circle; what began as praise of sheer wit, the ingenuity of trope detected by his contemporaries particularly in "The Storm" and "The Calm," seems likely to return to a similar position after the revolutions of more ambitious judgments. A recent critic, Mr. A. S. Smith, writing on "Air and Angels," has declared: "It is not then the novelty of its attitudes or insights that makes the poem worthwhile. They are stock—there is no direct enlargement of perception or addition to knowledge. . . . These [expressions of emotion, intention] far from being the central impulses, are only pegs of plot on which the various plays are hung: they are likely to have generated less feeling than did the sheer pleasure of writing well. . . . There was a poetry of wit, as there has been a poetry of the passions, or of vision, or of the unconscious, or what you will; and to that poetry the assumptions of our own day make frail guides."[4]

The writer distorts his case by overstatement. The statement about other chronological kinds ("of the passions . . . of vision . . . of the unconscious") does not assist us to give sympathetic recognition to the standards of an age of hard, unsubjective rhetorical poetry (which is presumably what is intended). The mimesis of emotion or the communication of mystical vision must, in literary terms, demand the mediation of language: a rhetoric must be constructed if it is not there already. The corollary of this is that it is impossible to conceive of a rhetoric without something or some attitude to communicate. The well-bred indifference to autobiography or metaphysics leaves unanswered the yawning gap of question as to what this poetry is about. It is perhaps fair however to refer to the posi-

tive quality which this critic indicates in the poem in attempting to re-expound the monarch of wit for the later twentieth
century: "There is a fineness, a pungent elegance about all this,
that holds the imagination like a good fugue. Nor is an age conscious of its own hysteria likely to undervalue Donne's adult detachment, the cool forensic sanity of his tone." (p. 178). The notion that readers may compensate for deficiencies in the mental
climate of their own age by immersing themselves in the taste
of a contrary period is perhaps a doubtful one: after all, a nostalgic retreat from our hysteria (displayed perhaps in some
global sense in "our wars and broken skies," but certainly not
in the cool tone of much contemporary English verse) is in itself
one of those "assumptions of our own day" that make frail
guides. But the weakness of this argument does not invalidate
the main case for treating "Air and Angels" and other poems of
Donne as brilliant exercises in argument in which the common-
places of amatory compliment are polished and rearranged. At
least this critic has supported his case by a full and convincing
exposition of the dialectic of the poem in all its stages. Doubt
begins to intrude when we ask what is carried by the rhetoric
and the mock-academic definition: the idea that in the final
proposition the woman's (technically inferior) love provides the
sphere that the male love informs,—like a cosmic intelligence
that controls, but yet must move within, its sphere—implies that
the lover has ingeniously led up to asking for his love to be returned so that it may be completed.

This is acceptable and enlightening as commentary on
the difficult last stanza; however the view that the only load of
meaning sustained by the framework of wit is a message of civilized, faintly ironic courtship, suitably cool and forensic, is be-
lied by the tone and emphasis of the first twenty lines of the
poem. One cannot ignore the reverentially slow and precisely
modulated movement induced by the mixture of tetrameter and
pentameter lines:

Twice or thrice had I lov'd thee,
Before I knew thy face or name;
So in a voice, so in a shapelesse flame,
Angells *affect us oft, and worship'd bee* . . .

If it be objected that the deduction of mood from meter is always too impressionistic, there is the serious, even solemn, implication of that philosophy of love which is in the forefront of the poem as interpreted by the new rhetorical critic. For the theory according to which the lovers have met in a previous existence, or are severed parts of an original hermaphroditic whole, the doctrine running through the first stanza, can bear on the emotional effect of the lover's address in two quite different ways. Mr. Smith sees only that in the Elizabethan and Caroline period ideas like this, plentifully endowed with opportunities for paradox, were employed in the academic debates of the Inns of Court; he therefore concludes that we should read Donne's lines in the spirit of learned wit. As support he invokes the "marvellously complex and consistent play of figure," and presumably he might add the sheer extravagance of the ideas in the poem. But the form of Donne's poem is not that of a debate, however much he may at times suggest the witty sophistry of a prolusion. It is a dialogue between two lovers with the man only overheard (as in most of the *Songs and Sonnets*). In such a context the determinist theory of love expounded is bound to cast a tone of religious awe and respectful veneration of the beloved. The tropes announcing that something has grown from nothing, or that even to concentrate on a single hair of the woman's head would still upset the balance and enjoyment of his love by sheer excess of marvelling, are surely not to be appreciated solely in terms of the play of wit:

With wares which would sinke admiration,
I saw, I had loves pinnace overfraught . . .

39

The definitions are not smart in their delivery, but simple and subdued, more like the dazed wondering that begins "The Good-morrow," but a wondering that now rests in assurance.

There is a further and still stronger objection to the purely rhetorical interpretation. It is possible to sneer at the romantic over-valuation of single suggestive phrases by nineteenth century critics and those "new critics" who were really their disciples. But how do the lines come there in the first place? Their outstanding quality was not put there by the proponents of the ideology of unified sensibility:

> *Still when, to where thou wert I came,*
> *Some lovely glorious nothing I did see.*

> *For, nor in nothing, nor in things*
> *Extreme, and scatt'ring bright, can love*
> *inhere . . .*

A philosophical gloss on "Lovely glorious nothing" may tell us that it refers to that intimation of the intangible, elusive divine beauty referred to by Ficino and his followers; but the words do their work as poetry and charge the abstract thought with a peculiar tenderness and wonder. Both statements stand out in relief against the unsensuous, dialectical development of the other lines. It is significant that the second statement, though equally striking, does not add anything to the paradoxical argument of the evocative central phrase. It is understandable that an ideology of unified sensibility was invented to explain the phenomenon of these phrases; for in them Donne uses the technique that Walter Benjamin has attributed to Baudelaire: he causes words to collapse and regroup themselves in new meanings.[5] Understandable, but wrong, for the regrouping does not create a disembodied poetic emotion but refers precisely to the dazzling brightness of a certain stage of passionate love. It is well that Mr. Smith and others should teach us to read *whole* poems by Donne, but his claim to be a great poet rather than just an influential period writer rests on this transformation of word and phrase within the context of the love debate, not simply on his refurbishing of the tradition of learned wit.

Passion and tenderness lie behind the play of wit, and it is proper to give them their due proportion in the complicated amalgam of a Donne poem. General readers have, I suspect, continued to observe this proportion under the new monarchy of wit with its scholarly administrators just as they did in earlier critical reigns when only the voice of ambiguity was heard. If the voice of natural, even simple passion can be detected in abstruse lyric like "Air and Angels" it is far more prominent in poems such as "The Good-morrow" and "The Sunne Rising" where it tends to become the dominant element of feeling. On these poems one can trust, like Johnson, "the commonsense of readers, uncorrupted by literary prejudice." Donne's critical reputation has fluctuated, but has he not always had a core of readers for a few poems unswayed by shifts of critical opinion?

The literary men who, early in this century, brought about the shift of view that accorded Donne the status of a major poet were closer to French symbolist poetry and to contemporary verse experiment than they were to the earlier seventeenth century. The new interpreters of Donne the rhetorician are scholars and their case is a stronger one, buttressed by sound learning. But both groups are united in seeing Donne as a major poet whose accomplishment is displayed through the whole range of his work. Dwelling on his skill in reproducing the tones and nuances of passion recalls an earlier tradition of appreciation. Might it not be timely to recall an even earlier one: "the best poet of the world in some things" and, one might add, in some poems; for many readers in the past, the intense pleasure involved in an encounter with a few of his poems lay in their strangeness and eccentricity, the fact that they lay off the beaten

41

track of English poetry and did not play any set literary game. To approach Donne as an eccentric and brilliant minor poet may have been easier when any conception of the main line of English poetic tradition was still governed by classical and Augustan assumption about the propriety of language. However, as with the question of his style, it may be possible to sustain the old view on different grounds. Mr. Alvarez has reminded us that Donne and his "school" were not professional poets, not even such dedicated amateurs as Sidney had been, but a group of wits and Inns of Court men to whom poetry was but one activity in a busy life of law, government, and place-hunting. Now R. C. Bald's admirably documented biography enables us to see its subject as a brilliant example of those gentry of modest fortune who could only make their way by finding a place with some great man, as Donne did with Sir Thomas Egerton. The great disaster of Donne's civil career was his secret marriage to his patron's niece; cut off from all roads to preferment, trying desperately to reconcile himself with the great, Donne seems in the first years of his century to be in a situation approaching that of those malcontents of contemporary tragedy, of Marston, or Middleton. The career was patched up by later ecclesiastical preferment and success (though not to the extent of a bishopric) but the tragedy remained that such an intelligence could not reach the highest employment in the state. Donne's literary efforts seem to me more comparable to those of Raleigh or Bacon than to those of Spenser if his relation and degree of commitment to the literary career be considered. Mr. Bald reminds us how small and passing a phase of his total activity is constituted by the lyric poems.

The best of Donne's serious and passionate love poetry is poignantly associated with the failure of his worldly career.[6] "The Sunne Rising" and "The Canonization" describe a self-sufficient world of love which has turned itself away from the

public cares of day-to-day life: the latter poem explicitly rejects
the values of the other ordinary world:

> *For Godsake hold your tongue, and let me love,*
> *Or chide my palsie, or my gout,*
> *My five gray haires, or ruin'd fortune flout,*
> *With wealth your state, youre minde with Arts*
> *improve,*
> *Take you a course, get you a place,*
> *Observe his honour, or his grace,*
> *And the Kings reall, or his stamped face*
> *Contemplate; what you will, approve,*
> *So you will let me love.*

Donne had ignored all these things by marrying Anne More.
After the romantic excesses of Gosse who discovered a highly
conjectural early love affair with a married woman, attempts to
relate the poems to Donne's biography have not been fashionable. But now we observe the cyclic movement of interpretation
in yet another direction. As R. C. Bald has pointed out,[7] these
poems must belong to the early years of Donne's married life,
because of their references to a king, and in "The Sunne Rising" to James I's favorite sport of hunting. Helen Gardner in
her edition of the *Songs and Sonnets* has likewise assigned the
group of serious love poems to these years, partly on textual
grounds and on account of the evidence of Donne's interest in
Neo-Platonic and Cabbalistic ideas, but also for explicitly biographical reasons: "In his enforced retirement he continued his
remote reading, and having lost the world for love, was attracted in authors whose speculations had already fascinated him by
a theory of love radically different from the naturalistic view
that had been the basis of much of his earlier love poetry."[8] A
poem of course stands in a complex relationship to biography

without being a transcript of life; but it may not be presumptuous to suggest that the relationship of Donne's finest love poetry to his wife and the most crucial episode of his life marks him as a poet who is not wholly committed to his art (it might be pungently elegant or passionate and profound—that would be an indifferent matter, for the extent of commitment is the whole point) like, say, Byron, for whom literary creation is a kind of extension of living and personality.

So far I am conscious that if I have challenged current opinion it is only to return with a slightly different emphasis to older views of Donne. But modern scholarship can help to focus a greater appreciation of what I have referred to as the group of serious love poems and their common characteristics: their peculiar and arcane philosophy of love which distinguishes them from those earlier *Songs and Sonnets*, which were presumably written before the end of the sixteenth century, and especially certain qualities of plainness, tenderness and dramatic immediacy. The intellectual conceits present in *all* the poems are often mistakenly used as a dominant common factor.

Few critics of Donne have considered the love poetry as a steady development from witty play on the sexual relation toward dramatic poems of high romantic passion, unless they were prepared to indulge in sentimental speculation. The division of the lyrics in Helen Gardner's great edition into two distinct groups according to manuscript authority makes a different approach possible. Her interpretation of the textual position has been keenly contested and will no doubt continue to be so; but it is to be remarked that no one so far has decisively opposed her division of the *Songs and Sonnets* into an earlier group of poems, love songs, and lyrics in monologue form dealing largely with themes and situations which are found in his *Elegies* of the same period, and a later one, written after 1600, consisting of "highly original lyrics which combine dramatic feeling and the vigour of speech with the music of song." Her rearrangement of the poems in accordance with their conjectured chronological order is bound to have a profound effect on our view of the poet and his attitude to love. The order of the 1633 edition, which ignored chronology, has been followed by all the subsequent editions including that of Grierson; it has surely helped to exaggerate the quality of virtuoso variety that so many readers find. The first six poems represent a bewildering kaleidoscope of moods: the passionate directness of a Romeo and Juliet in "The Good-morrow"; cynicism crossed with musical grace ("Song"); naturalistic libertinism ("Womans Constancy"); a quietly argumentative poem in quatrains expressing in Platonic fashion the love of a particular woman as an image of ideal virtue ("The Undertaking"); an *alba* in which the traditional form is treated dramatically and realistically to express a mood of complete harmony and maturity in sexual love comparable to that of the first poem ("The Sunne Rising"); and finally another libertine defence of promiscuity, which is suggestive of a musical air in the second stanza, but develops more purely dramatically in the third ("The Indifferent"). The metrical variety of these first six poems is as great as the differences in feeling and attitude. In the new Oxford edition the three poems expressing cynical attitudes to love come in the first section, two of them appearing together ("The Indifferent" and "Womans Constancy"). "The Good-morrow" and "The Sunne Rising" are near neighbors in the second section where they are accompanied by "The Undertaking." Thus if we can imagine a generation of readers introduced to Donne through texts accepting this arrangement, they will clearly gain the impression not of scintillating variety but of two distinct "periods" of the poet's work: in the first he wrote light-hearted and cynical erotic poems in the form of songs, or at any rate in fairly short stanzas; in the second he produced a group of highly distinctive poems celebrating faithful mutual love as a miraculous union. These latter poems tend to be in elaborate, carefully wrought stanzas which mingle slow-paced decasyllables with shorter and longer lines.

If the special individuality and integrity of the core of Neo-Platonist poems within the second group has been isolated for the first time, as I think it has, then this has bound to have repercussions on our reading of the other poems. To see a consistent doctrine of love common to a number of poems, some dramatic celebrations of union, others philosophic analyses of that state, must lead to thinking about all Donne's lyrics in terms of what they have to tell us about love rather than as exercises in wit which display to a greater or lesser extent the complex personality of the author. His work has been too exclusively discussed in terms of a personal style, while the historical and internal evidence points to the fact that the style was methodically evolved in order to communicate a certain type of content. Instead of returning to Petrarchan simplicities of phrase and image for describing a transcendent mutual love, Donne devised complex verse schemes and, for some poems but not all, a difficult, allusive style; but the difficulty of such poems as "The Ecstasy" or "A Nocturnall on S. Lucies Day" is not that of competitive wit: it expresses the exclusiveness proper to initiates in a mystery, as do the Provençal poems of the *trobar ric*.

The mystery resides in the belief that a perfect union is possible between male and female lovers who by uniting complete the divinely ordained single creature who was separated by the Fall. Helen Gardner's commentary has shown how close Donne's thought is to the formulations of sixteenth century Christian Platonists like Ficino, Sperone Speroni, and especially Leone Ebreo (Abrabanel). Such speculation tends enormously to reinforce all those elements in the medieval and Petrarchan love code which stress the exclusiveness, superiority and secrecy of courtly love; lovers who love like this are not merely outside society, they are above a fallen world. In a quite exact sense they are a cosmic hope for mankind, repairing the ruins of nature:

46

Dull sublunary lovers love
(Whose soul is sense) cannot admit
Absence, because it doth remove
Those things which elemented it.

But we by'a love, so much refin'd,
That our selves know not what it is,
Inter-assured of the mind,
Care lesse, eyes, lips, and hands to misse.

Wee for loves clergie only' are instruments:
When this booke is made thus,
Should againe the ravenous
Vandals and Goths inundate us,
Learning were safe; in this our Universe
Schooles might learne Sciences, Spheares Musick,
Angels Verse.

In this love of initiates the man represents pure actuality
and form, the woman pure potentiality; this throws further
light on the apparently inferior role woman's love is cast in at
the close of "Air and Angels," which has occasioned so much
recent discussion. As Mr. Smith's essay points out, all the authorities agree that the woman is inferior, but we might add it
is an extremely relative type of inferiority which makes her an
analogue of the universal mother. We may refer to two passages
in Leone Ebreo's *Philosophy of Love*: "God only bestows his
eternity on those that are capable of its enjoyment, and such are
the intellect, the seat of the Ideas, and first matter, which is
chaos: for the one is pure actuality and form and the other pure
potentiality and wholly formless matter, the one being the universal father of all things and the other the universal mother.
These alone could partake of the divine eternity; but their children who through the medium of their two parents are made

47

and formed by God (as is the whole universe and each of its parts) are not capable of such eternity. For every thing created is formed, that is composed of the matter of chaos and the form of the intellectual ideas, and must have a beginning and end in time. . . . Hence the work and end of the divine creation were eternal in the first parents of the world, though not in its separate creation, and are eternal in the eternal succession of many worlds."[9] But it is possible for men and women in the world of generation to take possession again of their share in eternal life, not merely by participating in a repetitive movement ("the eternal succession of many worlds") but by complete restoration of the original unity through the discovery of an ideal love; after relating the story of the androgyne and its separation by Apollo (he is paraphrasing Plato's account in the Symposium) Leone Ebreo adds: "From that time forth, love, *which heals man's wounds and restores the unity of his primeval nature*, was engendered amongst men; and by its restoration of two into one it is the remedy of the sin which led to one being made into two. Love in every man is, therefore, male and female, for each of them is but a half and not a whole man, and therefore desires to be made whole in its other half. Wherefore, according to this legend, human love was born of the division of man. And its parents were the two halves, both male and female, loving each other that they might achieve their former unity."[10] The strange gravity of Donne's lovers which sets them above the disciples of courtly love is a consequence of their being moved by a cosmic excitement and responsibility. They return from their rapt suspension of the senses to their bodies (in "The Ecstasy") not in order to copulate and provide what would satisfy some modern critics as a satisfactory balance of soul and body but in order to be an example to the world:

> *So must pure lovers soules descend*
> *T'affections, and to faculties,*

> *That sense may reach and apprehend,*
>   *Else a great Prince in prison lies.*

> *To' our bodies turne wee then, that so*
>   *Weake men on love reveal'd may looke. . . .*

In this perfect love the male and female qualities achieve a perfect balance without conflict. The language of their relationship is precise rather than fancifully hyperbolical:

> *My face in thine eye, thine in mine appears*
>   *And true plaine hearts doe in the faces rest,*
> *Where can we finde two better hemispheares*
>   *Without sharpe North, without declining West?*

Neither person is taking anything from the other because they are really one person. The permanent attraction of this metaphysical nicety is that it corresponds with the psychological facts of passionate love. "The Good-morrow" is a moment of naturalistic drama; the lovers in bed do not complain of a coming parting like the usual characters in an *alba*; they rest in assured harmony. But at each stage of the man's speech a mystery of ideal love is introduced which is at the same time a simpler statement of the feeling of identity brought by passion. They were destined to meet; their earlier loves were meaningless except as dim anticipations; love "makes one little roome, an every where": they are indeed a microcosm of the whole created world; as they look into each other's eyes and see each other reflected therein, the hemisphere metaphor comes naturally to the man as an illustration of their mutual trust. But they really are halves of a divided world; and finally the man, having the sense of immortality given by passion so strongly upon him, declares that they cannot die because they represent a mixture of equal parts: it is the unequal mixtures of created substances which are

49

corruptible;[11] they enjoy the balance of the restored perfect creature.

The symmetrical balance of the lovers as parts of a whole in these poems provides a contrast to the dynamic of love as it is reflected in the lyrics of the first, chronologically earlier group in the Oxford edition, which show no traces of Platonism. When there is no exact balance, the scale flies up; one partner is exploited by the other. What may be termed the secular love lyrics of Donne illustrate the melancholy truth classically enunciated by Stendhal: there is always some disparity in an affair so that one person is enjoying himself or herself (or suffering) more than the other to an extent which may be marginal or considerable.

The notion of exchange or unequal dealing is frequent in the libertine poems. The lover of "Loves Exchange" has gone up in the scale:

> *Onely'I have nothing which gave more,*
> *But am, alas, by being lowly, lower.*

In "The Legacie" there is an exchange of hearts between the lovers, but since she combines fickleness with coldness he finds that he has the worst of the bargain:

> *Yet I found something like a heart,*
> > *But colours it, and corners had,*
> > *It was not good, it was not bad,*
> *It was intire to none, and few had part . . .*
> *I thought to send that heart in stead of mine,*
> *But oh, no man could hold it, for twas thine.*

In "The Flea" the seducer's idea that the flea which has sucked both their bloods symbolizes their "marriage bed, and marriage temple" within its "living walls of Jet" is a kind of parody of the ideal androgynous union. The lover of "The Broken Heart" has conventionally enough surrendered his heart, but it has been shattered to pieces "at one first blow"; the conceit is developed to state that since substance cannot scholastically be reduced to nothing and nature abhors a vacuum, the broken pieces must still in some way be retained. Whatever the disparity of love there is still the obstinate retention of mental qualities represented as hearts, fears and jealousies; in fact, although the world of love in Donne's poems excludes all outer reality and other persons except as imagery for the state of passionate involvement, the non-Platonist poems contrive to make even emotions behave like objects or physical organs. So many poems are reduced to property disputes or catalogs of mental possessions (the legal imagery is significant here). Even the terrible revenge of the man's ghost on his faithless mistress in "The Apparition" can be seen as the correction of a balance. The problem of inequality in love is clearly stated in "Loves Deitie":

> *But since this god produc'd a destinie,*
> *And that vice-nature, custome, lets it be;*
>   *I must love her, that loves not mee.*

> *Sure, they which made him god, meant not so much:*
>   *Nor he, in his young godhead practis'd it.*
> *But when an even flame two hearts did touch,*
>   *His office was indulgently to fit*
> *Actives to passives: Correspondencie*
>   *Only his subject was. It cannot bee*
>   *Love, till I love her, that loves me.*

It is now possible to see an interesting relationship between the two groups of poems which modern scholarship has separated, a relation depending on the philosophy, or rather the physics of love. "Correspondencie" is a reference to the idea of

51

perfect balance, but in "Loves Deitie" and its group the principle of a mystical, balanced love is invoked theoretically as a standard by which to measure the inequality of desires devouring the lover. In the later group the mystical balance is directly experienced; even the more metaphysical, expository poems, lectures in love's philosophy like "A Lecture upon the Shadow," come after empirical knowledge had demanded theoretical analysis.

The image of equalizing debts is also often found in the sermons applied to the relations of the soul with God; here it is no doubt deeply influenced by the reformed doctrine of the Redemption. Perhaps a link between these uses and the balanced exchanges of love in the *Songs and Sonnets* is to be found in the funeral sermon when Donne attempts to strike a balance between the disparate ages of Lady Danvers and her second husband: "So that, I would not consider her, at so much more than *forty*, nor him, at so much lesse than *thirty*, at that time, but, as their *persons* were made *one*, and their *fortunes* made one, by *mariage*, so I would put their *yeeres* into *one number*, and finding a *sixty* between them, thinke them thirty a peece; for as twins of one houre, they liv'd."[12] I have referred several times to the tenderness and dramatic naturalness of the Platonic core of poems. The philosophy of love is never abstract or unreal but proved on the pulses of the lovers. One of Donne's most successful strokes of technique is to break a train of subtlety by a spontaneous burst of direct feeling. In the last stanza of "A Feaver" for instance, after a string of scholastic comparisons:

> *For I had rather owner bee*
> *Of thee one houre, than all else ever.*

In the last stanza of "A Valediction of my Name in the Window" the final turn of wit, however exaggerated, increases the poignancy:

Impute this idle talke, to that I goe,
For dying men talke often so.

Even the image of longitude and latitude in "A Valediction: of
the Booke," ll. 59–63, though complicated and drawn out, is not
strained because it offers an emotional as well as an intellectual
fitness. What begins as witty conceit ends with a dying fall, symbolic darkness succeeding brightness:

> *To take a latitude*
> *Sun, or starres, are fitliest view'd*
> *At their brightest, but to conclude*
> *Of longitudes, what other way have wee,*
> *But to marke when, and where the darke eclipses bee?*

Similarly in "A Valediction: Of Weeping" the fanciful figure of
tears destroying the image of the beloved in the eyes is given
substance by being so close a vehicle for the fear of real danger
at sea during the lover's voyage:

> *O more then Moone,*
> *Draw not up seas to drowne me in thy spheare,*
> *Weepe me not dead, in thine armes, but forbeare*
> *To teach the sea, what it may doe too soone.*

There are lighter, more playful examples of the affectionate
naturalness that permeates the imagery but is especially apparent in the climaxes of poems: the "late schoole boyes, and sowre
prentices" of "The Sunne Rising" or the witty political image
at the end of "Loves Growth":

> *As princes doe in times of action get*
> *New taxes, and remit them not in peace,*
> *No winter shall abate the springs encrease.*

The famous lines of that poem,

> *Love's not so pure, and abstract, as they use*
> *To say, which have no Mistresse but their Muse,*

may be seen in a rather different light from that in which they are usually interpreted. An esoteric and exclusive philosophy of love is united with the common, even the reassuringly homely. The first stanza of "The Good-morrow" is the supreme example: here the effort to canonize sexual love is so dramatically convincing that the Neo-Platonist scaffolding is hardly necessary. These are any two lovers in a room, but the room is "an every where" and the lovers are beginning the exploration of each other at the point Ficino and Leone Ebreo had reached by a train of fine-spun reasoning:

> *I wonder by my troth, what thou, and I*
> *Did, till we lov'd? were we not wean'd till then?*
> *But suck'd on country pleasures, childishly?*
> *Or snorted we i' the seaven sleepers den?*
> *'Twas so; But this, all pleasures fancies bee.*
> *If ever any beauty I did see,*
> *Which I desir'd, and got, 'twas but a dreame of*
> *thee.*

It is appropriate to finish here, where most of us begin our reading of Donne, at the stage which is really the conclusion of his technical revolution: here he achieved a fusion of the naturalism of atmosphere of the Latin love elegy, of dramatic verse timing and pause, and of a dynamic philosophy of love, that maintains an emotional authority unlike anything in poetry since the troubadours. It is an exclusive love poetry in which the lovers in their "every where" abolish the whole world. The external world is only a painted backcloth to them; however lively its prentices, huntsmen and gossip of plague-bills, it is only material for the thoughts of love. It may be this astonishing subjectivism, this reduction of all experience within the chosen amatory field to the play of individual will and consciousness, that makes Donne an ancestor of the modern mind in a sense different from that employed by the new critics of the past. It may also be the reason for his continuing enjoyment by the surviving common reader, irrespective of all changes in critical fashion.

King's College, London University

———

Notes

1. *See* W. Milgate, "The Early References to John Donne," *Notes and Queries* 195 (1950): 229–31, 246–47, 290–92, 381–83; 198 (1953): 421–24. Helen Gardner, *Twentieth Century Views: John Donne* (Englewood Cliffs, N.J., 1962), pp. 1–12; Kathleen Tillotson, "Donne's Poetry in the Nineteenth Century," *Elizabethan and Jacobean Studies presented to Frank Percy Wilson* (Oxford, 1959), pp. 307–26. All quotations of Donne's poetry are from *The Poems of John Donne*, ed. H. J. C. Grierson, (Oxford, 1912).

2. *National Magazine and Monthly Critic* (April 1838), pp. 373–78, quoted by Kathleen Tillotson in "Donne's Poetry."

3. Arthur Symons, *The Symbolist Movement in Literature* (London, 1899).

4. A. J. Smith, "New Bearings in Donne: 'Air and Angels' " in *Twentieth Century Views: John Donne*, ed. Helen Gardner, pp. 171–9. Page numbers are indicated in subsequent quotations from Smith.

5. Walter Benjamin, *Illuminations: Essays and Reflections*, trans. Harry Zohn (New York, 1970), p. 164.

6. "There can be little doubt that so far Donne's marriage had been the deepest experience of his life" (R. C. Bald, *John Donne: A Life* [Oxford, 1970], p. 326).

7. R. C. Bald, *John Donne*, pp. 146–7.

8. *The Elegies and Songs and Sonnets*, ed. Helen Gardner (Oxford, 1965), pp. lxi–xii.

9. Leone Ebreo, *The Philosophy of Love* (*Dialoghu d'Amore*) trans. F. Friedeberg-Seeley and Jean H. Barnes (1937), pp. 296–97.

10. Leone Ebreo, *Philosophy of Love*, p. 345.

11. Cf. Aquinas, *Summa Theologica*, part I, question lxxv. article 6: "*generationes et corruptiones ex contrariis et in contraria sunt.*"

12. A Sermon of Commemoration of the Lady Danvers, Late Wife of Sir John Danvers (1627). *See Sermons*, ed. G. R. Potter and E. M. Simpson (Berkeley, 1953–62)

GEOFFREY BULLOUGH

❧

DONNE

THE MAN OF LAW

John Donne's close connection with the Inns of Court was twofold. After three years at Oxford and maybe three more at Cambridge he was admitted first to Thavies Inn in 1591 and then to
Lincoln's Inn on 6 May 1592 when he was twenty years old. He
studied there for about two and a half years (probably) before
going on his travels to Italy and Spain. Some twenty years later,
in the autumn of 1616, after taking Holy Orders, he was appointed Reader of Divinity to the Benchers of Lincoln's Inn,
where he preached about fifty sermons a year until he was made
dean of St. Paul's in 1621, after which he still kept his chamber
and occasionally preached in the chapel. So he resided in the
Inn both in what Walton called his "irregular youth" and in his
regenerate maturity.

That Donne loved Lincoln's Inn is clear from his own
words—and Walton's. His legal studies there and the atmosphere of the Inns of Court society strongly affected his writings.
He wrote to Sir Henry Goodyer in 1608 that he early realised
that he must "contribute something to the sustentation" of the
world: "This I made account that I begun early, when I understood the study of our laws: but was diverted by the worst voluptuousnes, which is an Hydroptique immoderate desire of

humane learning and languages: beautifull ornaments to great fortunes; but mine needed an occupation."[1] Nevertheless he did not forget his law, rather, as he developed his religious interests, he carried over into theological matters the legal turn of mind, and interest in various forms of law, and an ability to adapt rhetorical forms and habits to purposes other than those for which he had first used them during and soon after his first period at the Inn.

Although the effects of his university courses in classics, logic and rhetoric, dialectic, astronomy and cosmography, civil law (perhaps under Alberigo Gentile who arrived in Cambridge in 1587 and revived its study there) and the "Ecclesastical Law of our Realm" cannot be ignored, the training at the Inns was more intensive and personal, and the students attended the lawcourts nearby. They studied the lawyers' notes of cases, collected in year books since the time of Edward I (hence maybe Donne's delight in odd situations and strange dilemmas); the reports, the abridgements; the books about writs, procedure, and pleading; the writings of Bracton, Fitzherbert, Plowden, and Littleton. They studied the great forensic orators of the past, and they read historians, moralists and poets for analogies and illustrations of logical and emotional effects.

In the Lent and autumn terms there were readings by senior men in which new statutes were explained, the method being to raise all imaginable scruples and then to give a careful resolution of them. This method of elucidation by exposition, objection, and reply was habitual in legal training and was used in the moots in which barristers and jurors debated points of law and their application to particular cases. A good lawyer was expected to be able to make a case for or against any proposition, and at the Inns the declamatory exercises, customary in the universities until Milton's time, were directed for forensic purposes. Donne's skill at this sort of argument helped him to revolutionize English poetry, since it made possible the specious logic, the persuasive figures, and the witty eloquence of his erotic (and religious) verse.

Much more than the universities, the Inns of Court were a preparation for worldly life. They were less hidebound; they were in close touch with the monarch's court and their members participated in the full tide of London life. Not surprisingly, the Inns of Court produced many literary men with ready wits, widely read in classical and modern authors. Their delight in novelty both of matter and manner[2] produced a European rather than an insular outlook.

The Inns produced the first Senecan drama (Gorboduc); the best part of *The Mirror for Magistrates* (Sackville); Gasciogne's adventures in Italian tragedy and comedy, autobiographical fiction and satire; and a long series of literary experimenters including, in the eighties and nineties, Sir John Harington, Sir John Davies, Thomas Lodge, Marston, and Donne himself. The lively wit fostered by life at the Inns was lavishly displayed in the seasonal Revels for which entertainments, often attended by prominent courtiers, were specially written and produced. Donne played some part in the festivities of 1593 at his Inn and was elected steward of Christmas for 1594, but apparently "went down" early and was fined for not performing his duties. He cannot have seen the Gray's Inn entertainments of that season, published long afterwards as *Gesta Grayorum*, which have many important links with contemporary literature. The Inns' festivities also included the witty parody of law pursuits, a mock-trial, and the dubbing of Inner Temple guests as "Knights of the Helm" with amusing rules such as: "Every knight of this Order shall endeavor to add Conference and Experience by Reading . . . . . also frequent a Theatre and suchlike places of Experience, and resort to the better sort of Ordinaries for Conference, whereby they may not only become accomplished with Civil Conversations, and able to govern a Table with Discourse; but also sufficient, if need be, to make Epigrams, Emblems and other Devices appertaining to his Honour's learned Revels." This last injunction brings us to a consideration of some nondramatic verse forms, which included longer verse satires as well as paradoxes and problems, by which the Inns of Court men, especially Donne, influenced late Elizabethan and Jacobean literature.

Epigrams were not new. They had a vogue with More and John Heywood, but in the nineties, as cynicism and protest replaced idealism and Ovid's *Ars Amatoria* and *Amores* rivaled his *Metamorphoses* as popular models for erotic verse, the influence of Martial was overshadowed by that of longer Roman verse-satire. Inns of Court men probably began the fashion for epigram, satire, and other witty social criticism; at least they contributed a great deal to it. The two major epigrammatists of the time, Sir John Harington and Sir John Davies, were both Inns of Court men. Harington, eleven years older than Donne, had spent eighteen months at Lincoln's Inn but had "studied Littleton but to the title of discontinuance" (he declared) before he left to get married and go to court, where his witty sallies amused but scandalized the queen. He was the lifelong undergraduate in spirit, writing epigrams in Martial's manner, but less pungently. Sir John Davies, four years older than Donne, was less flighty than Harington who became a barrister in 1595, the year when his *Epigrams* were published along with Marlowe's version of Ovid's *Amores*, and eventually was appointed lord chief justice. Davies' volume probably encouraged Donne to write elegies as well as epigrams, although his epigrams are not as interesting as Sir John's, which are vignettes of shrewd observation of London life. Often longer than Martial's, they are amused rather than savage. Eleven out of Donne's nineteen epigrams, most attempting only a clever point, are a couplet long, as is one concerning "Pyramus and Thisbe" (*see John Donne, Poetry and Prose*, ed. Frank J. Warnke [New York, 1967] p. 101):

> *Two, by themselves, each other, love and feare*
> *Slaine, cruell friends, by parting have joyn'd here.*

The epigrammatic method is much more ably applied in
many of Donne's other poems, especially in his *Satyres*. Donne
indeed was an innovator in combining elements of Horace, Juve-
nal and Persius and in stringing together epigrammatic portraits with a strong quasi-dramatic or descriptive content. His
legalistic interests are most marked in *Satyres* II, IV, and V,
though in *Satyre* I he pretends to be a studious scholar of the
law dragged out of his tiny study ("standing chest")[3] by a "fondling motely humorist" and made to walk the town. *Satyre* II
seems to mock at the author of a sonnet-sequence, *Zepheria*
(1594) into which the anonymous author threw much legal
imagery. Maybe Donne guessed who this amorous lawyer was,
who "woos in language of the Pleas, and Bench." He gives a
snatch of his wooing in lawcourt terms:

> *"A motion, lady." "Speake Coscus." "I have beene*
> *In love ever since* tricesimo *of the Queene.*
> *Continuall claimes I have made, injunctions got*
> *To stay my rivals suit, that he should not*
> *Proceed." "Spare mee." "In Hillary term I went;*
> *You said, If I return's next 'size in Lent,*
> *I should be in remitter of your grace:*
> *In th' interim my letters should take place*
> *Of affidavits."*
>
> $(49-57)$[4]

Donne comments: "Words, words, which would teare / The
tender labyrinth of a soft maid's eare" (57–58).

The satire does not end there, for Coscus is a dishonest
pretentious lawyer. He always has a "bill" or brief in his hand

to show how busy he is; he tells lies to his suitors and to the judge; he battens on the prodigality of young heirs, geting possession of lands all over the country; when he sells land or makes out a conveyance he omits mention of the entail. In this piece Donne, who was never called to the bar, shows his inner knowledge of the legal profession.

In *Satyre* IV, probably written between his two sea-voyages with Essex, Donne introduced a host of topical allusions, including many to the law and its penalties, into his modernization of Horace's I. 9 about the bore. The bore, dressed in fusty black, is here a shifty out-at-heels hanger-on of the court,

> *One, whom the watch at noone lets scarce goe by,*
> *One, to whom, the examining Justice sure would cry,*
> *Sir, by your priesthood tell me what you are.*
>
> (27–29)

He "speaks no language"; he is the affected traveler, the news-monger and court gossip, maybe even an informer. When he begins to libel great men, to assert that offices are entail'd and officials are corrupt, Donne fears that by just listening to him he may fall prey to "One of our Giant Statutes" against sedition and rebellion. He gladly "pays a fine" to escape by lending the fellow a crown. After returning home the poet has a dream (like Dante's *Inferno*) in which he sees the queen's court very much as the gossip has described it. Much of the imagery springs from the suggestion that Donne has been in Hell or Purgatory, and that having confessed the truth, "Well; I may now receive [the Sacrament] and die" (1). References to relegous penalties abound; to Glaze who "did goe / To a Masse in jest" (8–9) and was heavily fined for so doing; to Jesuit priests caught skulking in disguise; to Jesuits as linguists. A fine young courtier paying court to a Lady

> *Protests, protests, protests,*
> *So much as at Rome would serve to have throwne*
> *Ten Cardinalls into the Inquisition;*
> *And whisper'd By Jesu, so often, that A*
> *Pursevant would have ravish'd him away*
> *For saying of our Ladies psalter.*
>
> (212–17)

Arrest for religious heresy may descend either on Catholic or Protestant in this world of harsh laws, spies, torture, fines, narrow escapes, persecution, which are Donne's deep preoccupations in this poem. Donne's brother Henry, jailed for sheltering a priest, had died of gaol-fever caught in 1593. Southwell, martyred in 1594, had been followed by others since. Donne has almost cast off his Romanism, but he is not yet an Anglican; his sympathy with victims of oppression extends to all.

Satyre III confirms that the poet had turned his back on Catholicism without giving himself to any other sect. Based on the distinction between human laws and the laws of God, the poem asks where true religion is to be found and rejects the absolute claims of all the quarreling sects:

> *Foole and wretch, wilt thou let they Soule by tyed*
> *To man lawes, by which she shall not be tryed*
> *At the last day? Oh, will it then boot thee*
> *To say a Philip, or a Gregory,*
> *A Harry, or a Martin taught thee this . . .*
> *That thou mayest rightly obey power, her bounds*
>   *know;*
> *Those past, her nature, and name is chang'd; to be*
> *Then humble to her is idolatrie.*
>
> (93–102)

For the first time Donne goes behind legalities and considers the foundations of faith, which are to be found only in God himself and (presumably) in His word "at the stream's calm head." The idea recurs often in his later work, even after Donne had come to accept the king as the head of the English church.

With *Satyre* V we are back in the world of human law and its manipulators. Donne was then secretary to Egerton, the lord keeper, who attempted between 1597 and 1603 to limit the extortionate fees charged by clerks of the Star Chamber. As in the previous satire he refuses merely to mock, for the issue is serious: "Officers rage and Suitors misery." Adapting the image of God as "the stream's calm head," he declares that the queen cannot know what goes on beneath her, but Egerton is beginning "To know and weed out this enormous sinne." Short, sharp epigrams pillory distortion, "demands, fees, and duties." Law is seen as a secondary power dealing out injustice:

> *If Law be the Judges heart, and hee*
> *Have no heart to resist letter, or fee,*
> *Where wilt thou appeale? powre of the Courts below*
> *Flow from the first maine head, and these can throw*
> *Thee, if they sucke thee in, to misery,*
> *To fetters, halters; . . .*
> > *Alas, thou go'st*
> *Against the stream, when upwards.*
> > (43–50)

Donne puns on the saying that "Judges are Gods," pointing out that God did not mean us to go to them by means of "Angels" or pay fees without prayers. He pictures a pursevant searching a house for a hidden priest or signs of a recent Mass, confiscating clothes, books and plate, pretending that they are Romish, then demanding a fee for so doing. Donne exclaims:

64

Oh, ne'r may
Faire lawes white reverend name be strumpeted
To warrant thefts: she is established
Recorded to Destiny . . .
(68–71)

He gives men their proper places in society:

She is all faire, but yet hath foule long nailes,
With which she scratcheth Suiters . . .
(74–75)

That is, minor officers of the law misbehave in carrying out
their functions, and redress for their actions is often made impossible. Such complaints were frequent in Jacobean satire, but
Donne's disgust and telling detail seem based on real knowledge. Doubtless his work for Egerton involved inquiry into the
machinery of the law and its working.

The "Emblems and other Devices" appertaining to his
honor's learned revels in *Gesta Grayorum* included imprese,
mottoes, posies, anagrams, and riddles, formal trifles which
Donne did not practice. His *Elegie* II was entitled *The Anagram*, not for any juggling with letters but because his mock
encomium represented Flavia as having her qualities grotesquely misplaced:

Though all her parts be not in th' usuall place,
She' hath yet an Anagram of a good face.
(15–16)

Years later in his *Catalogus Librorum Aulicorum*, a Rabelaisian
collection of satiric titles of fictitous books, Donne pleasantly
mocked Sir John Davies liking for such *jeux d' esprit*: "No. 16.

65

The Justice of England. Vacation exercises of John Davies on the Art of forming Anagrams approximately true, or Posies to engrave on Rings."[5]

For the paradoxes beloved of the Inns of Court men, Donne had much more sympathy. As late as 1618 the Gray's Inn Revels entertainment included "a mad fellow who . . . goes abroad by the name of Paradox" who calls himself "a meere Greek, a Sophister of Athens": "Know then, my name is Paradox, a strange name but purposed to my views; for, I blush not to tell you truth, I am a slip of darkness; my father a Jesuit, my mother an Anabaptist . . . And Methode breeds my name Paradox. I pray you, what is a Paradox? It is a *quodlibet*, or strain of wit and invention screwed above the vulgar conceit, to beget admiration."

The defence of paradoxes had always formed part of university and legal training. Socrates frequently used them; Cicero composed an exercise on six of the Stoic paradoxes; they were used seriously by scholastic philosophers and by alchemists. In the Renaissance the paradoxes of Ortensio Lando (1543) had a great vogue, and from their French translation by Charles Estienne (1553) they were Anglicized by A.M. (probably Anthony Munday) as *The Defense of Contraries: Paradoxes against common opinion, debated in the forme of declamations in place of publike censure: only to exercise yong wittes in difficult matters.*[6] Both translators followed Lando in asserting that "a good Lawyer . . . must adventure to defend such a case, as they that be most imployed refuse to maintaine," and that by disputing of paradoxes "opposed truth might appeare more cleere and apparent" (Munday).

Munday's translation caught, if it did not start, a fashion. Gabriel Harvey delighted in them; Donne's friend William Cornwallis wrote several. Donne himself composed a dozen or so, most of them no doubt before 1600 when he sent some to Henry Wotton at the latter's request, but apologetically, "for they carry with them a confession of their lightness . . . if they make you to find better reasons against them they do their office . . . they are rather alarums to truth to arme her then enemies . . . they are nothings" (*John Donne. Selected Prose*, ed. Evelyn Simpson [Oxford, 1967], p. 111). So most of them were. "A Defence of Women's Inconstancy" showed a young man's pleasure in defending the indefensible; "That Women Ought to Paint" states a case against virtue. "That Good Is More Common than Evil," "That Virginity is a Virtue," "That a Wise Man Is Known by Much Laughing" are not wholly flippant, while "That the Guifts of the Body are Better then Those of the Minde" at least shows the importance of the body to the mind (as he argued more seriously in *The Extasie*). In poetry at this time the paradox was one of the principal methods used to make a point, as the *Elegies* and erotic lyrics prove. The *Heroicall Epistle of Sapho to Philaenis* is a paradoxical monologue in praise of lesbianism. Later Donne was to expound the paradoxes of the Christian faith in the *Divine Poems* and *Sermons*. The paradox "That all things kill themselves" foreshadowed *Biathanatos* in its defence of suicide.[7]

Another of Donne's interests which probably came from his Inns of Court days and greatly affected his later writings was the problem. He wrote nineteen of these, in the form of brief essays explaining strange phenomena such as "Why Have Bastards the Best Fortune?", "Why Puritans Make Long Sermons?", "Why Did the Divell Reserve the Jesuites till the Latter Dayes?", "Why Hath the Common Opinion Afforded Women Soules?", "Why are new Officers Least Oppressing?" Problems form part of training in writing and declaiming speeches on difficult subjects. Quintilian classified them as either theses (abstract propositions such as "How can glory be attained?" without concrete examples) or hypotheses (difficult cases real or invented). Both theses and hypotheses abound in Renaissance literature. To the latter class belong the *Cent Histoires Tragi-*

ques of A. Van den Busche (Alexandre Sylvain), Paris, 1851, which Lazarus Piot translated as *The Orator: Handling a hundred severall Discourses, in forme of Declaration* (1596), asserting that they would be useful for students of law or divinity.

Each of Sylvain's declamations contains the summary of a moral or legal dilemma, a brief narrative outlining the situation around it, and (usually) two speeches presenting opposite views about it. No judgment is made between them. Many of the problems are taken from history, others from folklore or novelle, some are derived from Shakespeare, who probably knew Piot's version, which included the pound-of-flesh bond; the "terrible bargain" of *Measure for Measure*; the plight of a nun who, having saved her honor when immured in a brothel, is denied her place in the nunnery when she returns to it; "Of two maidens ravished by one man, for the which the one required his death, and the other desired him for her husband."

Donne's Problems are nearer to Quintilian's theses than to these modern hypotheses, but his mind turned naturally to specific cases for he delighted in the oddities of human nature and ironies of circumstance, anything paradoxical and outside the normal rules. When he examined Bellarmine (probably at Lincoln's Inn, 1593) and began to question the faith of his forebears, still more when he was working for Thomas Morton (1605–7), he was led to the Catholic "casuists" whose commentaries on "Cases of Conscience" were collected and distributed for the use of confessors.[8] *Biathanatos* and *Pseudo-Martyr* both show the effects of such reading, and contain references to several well-known modern casuists.

Biathanatos was a long defence of the paradox that suicide is not always against the laws of nature, reason and God. "The law of nature, of reason, and of God . . . are all one," but "many things which are of Naturall and Humane and Divine Law may be broken." Thus, "in a just warre a Parricide is not guilty . . . a sonne shall redeeme him selfe from banishment by killing his Father being also banished" (The Facsimile Text Society [New York, 1930], p. 35; subsequent quotations of *Biathanatos* are from this edition). Donne's marginal notes are sprinkled with paradoxes: "Nothing so evill, that is never good"; "No evill but disobedience"; "Lying naturally worse then Selfe-Homicide"; "Originall sin, cause of all sin, is from nature." Donne's main point in Part I is that any law may be broken if it conflicts with a higher law to which it is subordinate. Self-homicide is not against the law of nature, since "That cannot bee against the law of nature, which men have ever affected, if it be also (as this is) against sensitive nature, and so want the allurements which other sins have." He supports this argument with many instances of painful suicides, by swallowing one's breath, scalding or burning to death, swallowing burning coals. "Poore Terence because he lost his 108 translated Comedies, drown'd himselfe. And the Poet Labius, because his Satyricall Bookes were burned by Edict, burnt himselfe too . . . Hippionas the Poet rimed Bubalus the Painter to death with his Iambiques" (pp. 50–54).[9] Sir Thomas More, "a man of the most tender and delicate conscience" made his Priests and Magistrates in *Utopia* "exhort men afflicted with incurable diseases to kill themselves, and . . . they were obeyed as the interpreters of God's will."

Part II discusses the law of reason as applied in civil law and canon law, and finds nothing definitely against self-slaughter in them. Coming to the laws of particular nations he has to admit that the law of *felo de se* exists. Suicide is taken to be a crime because "The King hath lost a subject and his peace is broken." There are exceptions to every general rule; and here Donne waves away his opponents somewhat airily. Here again his illustrations are often piquant: for example, the friar "who being by his Abbat commanded to returne that the waters being risen, committed himselfe unto a raging torent, in such an obedience" (p. 139) and was drowned. Was this man blameworthy? From Aquinas comes the instance that "in a persecution, a private man, having food left sufficient only to sustaine one man, may give it to a publike person, and so perish. And only *Sotus* denyes, that in a shipwrack, if after wee have both beene in equally danger, I catch and possesse my selfe of any thing to sustaine me, I may give it to my Father, or to a Magistrate" (p. 128). Among other problems he faces that of the Virgin martyrs like Appollonia, "who, after the persecutors had beat out her teeth, and vexed her with many other tortures, when she was presented to the fire, being inflamed with a more then burning fire of the Holy Spirit, broke from the Officers' hands and leapt into the fire" (p. 191). Surely this was "a Noble and Christian act," Donne writes.

In Part III, "Of the Law of God," Donne accepts "Thou shalt not kill" as a general ordinance against self-murder, but he educes many exceptions. A man forced by a tyrant to commit idolatry might legitimately kill himself, if he knew that "his example would governe the people." Samson committed suicide (and some exegists had been shocked at this), yet because he did so for God's glory he is commended by the church. Origen suggests that even Judas's suicide was not held against him, for it was a sign of penitence (pp. 203–5).

The argument is ingenious, well-sustained, and serious. Donne did not publish it but liked it sufficiently to send a copy to his friend Sir Robert Ker when he himself was afraid he might not return from Germany in 1619. Anyone who read it must be told "that it is a Book written by *Jack Donne*, and not by *Dr. Donne*: Reserve it for me, if I live, and if I die, I only forbid it the Presse, and the Fire: publish it not, yet burn it not" (*Letters* [1651], p. 21).

Pseudo-Martyr (1610) concerned a special case of conscience, whether a Roman Catholic might properly take the Oath of Allegiance to King James despite the injunctions laid on them by the pope and his Jesuits not to do so.[10] Apparently the king, who knew that Donne had helped Morton in his controversial writings, discussed with the poet "many of the reasons which are usually urged against the taking of those Oaths" and was so struck by his acuteness that he bade him set down his arguments in a treatise. Donne, who was by this time an Anglican, called on Catholic recusants to stop being "Pseudo Martyrs" since there was no good reason why they should not take the oath and accept the rites of the Church of England. The main difference between him and his opponents is, he asserts, "whether a Subject may not obey his Prince, if the Turk or any other man forbid it." He himself has gone through the process he wants his readers to follow, for his upbringing as a Catholic delayed his full acceptance of the English church, although "this irresolution . . . retarded my fortune" and "endangered my spirituall reputation." His aim is "the unity and peace of His [Christ's] Church," and his tone is sweetly reasonable as he analyzes the legal and moral aspects of the Catholic dilemma, tracing the growth of the popes' claims to temporal jurisdiction, examining the "Missal Cases," the "Comique-Tragicall doctrine of Purgatory" (*Pseudo-Martyr* [London, 1610], p. 108; subsequent page numbers refer to this edition), "the deformity and corruption of the *Canons*" as these laws, "which contained the Decrees of certaine aunceint Councels as usually produced in after-Councels for their direction, and [were] by the intreaty of popes, admitted and incorporated into the body of the Romane and Imperiall Law" (p. 265). Decretals, Breves and Bulls are distinguished and controverted, and Donne's reading of them shows that the popes "have abstained . . . from giving any binding resolution on the question," "how farre the civill lawes of Princes doe binde the subjects conscience" (p. 323). Donne has no doubts about this: "Nothing in the world is more spirituall and delicate, and tender then the conscience of a man; yet by good consent of Divines, otherwise diversely perswaded in Religion . . . the civill lawes of Princes doe binde our consciences; and shall the persons of any men, or their temporall goods, be thought to be of so sublimed, and spirituall a nature, that the civill constitutions of Princes cannot worke upon them" (p. 30).

This is Donne's central contention, for obedience to the king is "imposed in generall by nature, and fastned with a new knot by an expresse law" (p. 326). The tortuous arguments are enlivened by witty sallies, and its learning supports Donne's claim to have "survayed and digested the whole body of Divinity, controverted between ours and the Romane Church" before becoming an Anglican. *Pseudo-Martyr* is concerned not with theology but with ecclesiastical law and the superstructure of doctrine. If it is impossible to read through today, that is because conditions and men's interests have changed. The prose works of Donne's middle years show that he was even more legalistically inclined than before. Whether for economic reasons or to satisfy his conscience, he had both intensified and broadened the scope of his legal studies by delving deep into the more arid regions of civil and Canon law and also by reflecting long and painfully on the relations between Divine and human law (as the *Essays in Divinity* reveal).

In 1607 Morton had tried to persuade Donne "to waive your court-hopes and enter into Holy Orders," but Donne refused, quoting "the best of Casuists: 'that God's Glory should be the first end, and a maintenance the second motive to embrace that calling.'" But by 1613 his financial straits, and "the inspirations (as I hope) of the Spirit of God" had decided him "to make my profession Divinity" (Letter to Somerset in Edward Le Comte, *Grace to a Witty Sinner* [New York, 1956], p. 141), but he did not take the decisive step until he knew of the king's desire "to prefer him that way." Meanwhile he wrote the *Essays in Divinity* out of his meditations. At one time during these last few years he had thought of taking up the law professionally, but he was too old to begin there, and his continual studies in civil and canon law were undoubtedly a symptom of the secret urgency driving him into the priesthood.[11] Ordained on 23 January 1614/15, "Now he had a new calling, new thoughts, and a new employment for his wit and eloquence" (Izaac Walton, *Life of Dr. Donne* [New York, 1907], p. 346).

Once he was ordained, Donne applied the methods of meditating and discoursing upon religious texts and topics that he had practised in the *Essays in Divinity*, more formally in public sermons before congregations, which often included important people. It is obvious that he took great care in preparing and memorizing his sermons. Although he spoke in church without written aids, he later would use his comprehensive notes in writing out or even expanding any sermon which he wished to preserve.[12]

Donne's powers and methods as a preacher[13] were enhanced by his choice of themes and his imagery, both obviously affected by his personal interests. In a beautiful sermon preached to Queen Anne on 14 December 1617, he pointed out that the writers of Scripture "do for the most part retain, and express in their writings some impressions, and some air of their former professions; . . . ever inserting into their writings some phrases, some metaphors, some allusions, taken from that profession which they had exercised before" (1: 236). Quite consciously Donne did the same, with images, allusions, memories from his former life and reading, and even before he returned to Lincoln's Inn his legal interests were in evidence. Thus, in his first sermon now extant, which was delivered on 30 April 1615 at Greenwich probably to businessmen and traders in the parish church, he plays upon their interest in money, referring to the several meanings of "Redemption," and to the legal results of declaring a man a prodigal, applying them to the condition of a man in sin: "He that is a Prodigall, in the Law, cannot dispose of his own Estate; whatsoever he gives, or sells, or leases, all is void, as of a mad-man, or of an Infant. . . . The Prodigall

73

person hath no power allowed him by the Law, to make a will, at his death: . . . He is presum'd to be disinherited by his father . . ." (1: 155). Having been spiritually prodigal all our lives we cannot achieve salvation on our death-beds. "The giving of all we have to the poor, at our death, will not do it; . . . we must be thrifty all our life, or we shall be too poor for that purchase" (1: 156). Referring to ancient Rome, he continues, "we think those Laws barbarous and inhumane, which permit the sale of men in debt, for the satisfaction of Creditors," and he mentions the folly of some Russians who "sell themselves, and their posterity, into everlasting bondage, for hot drink. . . . But we sell our selves, not for drink, but for thirst" (1: 157). He draws images from inventories and conveyances to teach the necessity and meaning of spiritual redemption and harps on finance to the end where he declares that Christ "redeemed us then without money; And as he bought so he sells: He paid no money, he asks no money . . . But you must come; and you must come to the market; to the Magazine of his graces, his Church" (1: 167).

Similarly, preaching before the court at Whitehall on 21 April 1616 about God's delayed sentences on guilty souls, Donne had many legal references. "A Law is not a Law without Execution" (1: 174), but there have been laws so grievous "that that Law might never come to execution," for example, the Roman law by which debtors might be cut in pieces and distributed among their creditors. Laws are sometimes made "without any purpose of ordinary execution," but the Prince "is made a Depository and a Feoffee in trust"; he uses them only in "emergent necessities." God's laws are not like that: with unexpected speed of execution the Lord of Hosts "can proceed by Martiall Law" (1: 176) upon sinners like Ananias and Sapphira, who would never have been condemned by an early court.

The legal analogies often go to show that men behave worse towards God than to their fellow-men. Thus at Whitehall on 2 November 1617, he asserts, "That which is not allowable in Courts of Justice, in criminal Causes, To hear Evidence against the King, we will admit against God . . . Nay, we suborn witnesses against God, and we make Philosophy and Reason speak against Religion, and against God . . . and we do more; we proceed by Recriminations, and a cross Bill, with a *Quia Deus*, because God does as he does, we may do as we do; Because God does not punish Sinners, we need not forbear Sins" (1: 225).

On 20 February 1617/18, four months after returning to Lincoln's Inn, Donne preached a Lent sermon before the court that contained an unusual amount of legal reference. When the converted thief on the cross says to his fellow-prisoner, "Fearest thou not God, being under the same condemnation" (Luke 23:40), Donne imagines him saying, in modern terms: "Though the Law have done the worst upon thee, Witnesses, Advocates, Judges, Executioners can put thee in no more fear; yet *Nonne times Deum?* Fearest thou not God? who hath another Tribunal, another execution for thee?" (1: 254). The condemned thief's conversation leads Donne to speak of the mystery of God's grace and to deplore such modern innovations in theology as discussions about "*Resistibility*, and *Irresistibility* of grace, which is every Artificers wearing now." This was "a stuff that our Fathers wore not, a language that pure antiquity spake not. They knew Gods ordinary proceeding. They knew his Common Law, and they knew his Chancery. They knew his chief Justice *Moses*, that denounced his Judgements upon transgressors of the Law: and they knew his Chancellor Christ Jesus, into whose hands he had put all Judgements, to mitigate the rigor and condemnation of the Law . . . But for Gods prerogative, what he could do of his absolute power, they knew Gods pleasure *Nolumus disputari*." (1: 255).

Donne was later to spin out many more similar extended analogies. His interest in legal history appears when he points out that vestal virgins at Rome "were buried within the city, because they dyed innocent"; so were executed criminals, "because they had satisfied the Law, and thereby seemed to be restored to their innocence" (1: 264). But God's judgment still remains for sinners after death. It was said of one of the Roman Emperors "That it was worse then the rack, to be examined by him." What then when "we come to stand naked before God?" (1: 265). We should beware of accusing others, since we may be guilty of the same crimes. We are all under the same condemnation (1: 267).

Donne's long friendship with Christopher Brooke and other lawyers bore fruit when in October 1616 he was appointed divinity reader of Lincoln's Inn, where he was to preach twice every Sunday during term and once on the Sabbath before and after each term as well as at other appointed times. He was given a chamber, and performed his duties (with a gap when he was abroad with Lord Doncaster between May 1619 and January 1619/20) until he resigned on 11 February 1621/22 to become dean of St. Paul's. He was very happy in his work and in the renewed companionship of his lawyer friends, who cannot for long have doubted the sincerity of this Saul of Tarsus remade, in Walton's words, "to become a Paul and preach salvation to his beloved brethren."

The twenty-five surviving sermons which we know or suppose were given at Lincoln's Inn show Donne's awareness of that particular congregation. His prodigal youth was well known there, so he occasionally refers to it, as when he declares that "their sin, that shall sinne by occasion of any wanton *writings* of mine, will be my sin, though they come after" (2: 88). Having lived through them he knows well the arrows of temptation at life's different ages: "An old man wonders then, how an arrow from an eye could wound him, when he was young, and how *love* could make him doe those things which hee did *then*: And an arrow from the tongue of inferiour people, that which we make shift to call honour, wounds him deeper now; and *ambition* makes him doe as strange things now, as *love* did then.

A fair day shoots arrows of *visits,* and *comedies,* and *conversation,* and so wee goe abroad: and a foul day shoots arrows of *gaming,* or *chambering,* and *wantonnesse,* and so we stay at home" (2: 61–62). On a hot afternoon he shortens his discourse and tells them "to walke with God in the cool of the Evening" (2: 132).

Sometimes he makes allusion to the shortcomings of students, telling them that study is a full-time occupation. Preaching on Trinity Sunday 1620 on the courtesy shown by Abraham to the three strangers who visited him before Sodom was destroyed, he points out that "even by the Saints of God, civill behaviour, and faire language, is conveniently exercised: A man does not therefore meane ill, because he speakes well: A man must not therefore be suspected to performe nothing, because he promises much . . . Harshnesse, and morosity in behaviour, rusticity, and coarseness of language, are no arguments in themselves, of a plaine and a direct meaning, and of a simple heart" (3: 136).

He has many humorous touches suited to his auditory. Discussing why Paul found fault "because you goe to Lawe with one another" (1 Cor. 6:7), he quotes Matt. 5:40, "If any man will sue thee at lawe for thy coate, Let him have thy cloake too," and adds, as if it were in the text, "for if thine adversary have it not, thine advocate will." He loves epigram and paradox: "Chastity is not chastity in an old man, but a disability to be unchast" (2: 244). . . . "Take heed . . . of being seduced to that church that is in one man . . . Christ loves not singularity: he called not one alone" (2: 280). . . . "An Hypocrite at Church, may doe more good, then a devout man in his Chamber at home, because the Hypocrites outward piety, though counterfeit, imprints a good example upon them, who doe not know it to bee counterfeit . . ." (2: 90)

Donne was always a methodical preacher, organizing his sermon in an orthodox way. In his Lincoln's Inn sermons he

seems to have been especially careful, and in the first few of
them which survive he calls particular attention to the skeletal
structure, as if to instruct the students (all practitioners in rhetoric) in technique. He summarizes the parts of his *Divisio*, then
discusses taking them up one by one (*see* vol. 2, Sermon 1) and
at the close he dismisses them "with such a re-collection, as you
may carry away with you" (2: 69). Often he keeps his auditory
abreast of his progress by recapitulation; or he will pass rapidly
over a section, "that we may husband our hour well, and reserve
as much as we can for our two last considerations . . ." (2: 319).
Indeed the self-conscious insistence on structure sometimes (*see*
vol. 2, Sermon 6, one of six sermons he preached on Psalm 38
in 1618) makes the address seem labored to a modern reader.
How well he knows the ways of worldly old men! As when,
drawing a parallel between the sick soul in us all with the behavior of wealthy curmudgeon: "The anguish of the disease,
nay, the officiousnesse of visitors, will not let him rest. Such send
to see him as would faine heare hee were dead, and such weep
about his sick-bed as would not weepe at his grave. . . . He shall
not onely not make a religious *restitution*, but he shall not make
a discreet *Will*. He shall suspect his wifes fidelity, and his chil-
drens frugality, and clogge them with Executors, and them with
Over-seers, and be, or be afraid hee shall bee over-seen in all"
(2: 83–84). Occasionally he will delight listeners with an extended metaphor drawn from their profession; in a sermon on
death and resurrection (1620) he says that we must all see death
and return to dust: *"Corruption on the Skin* says Job; In the
outward beauty, These be the Records of velim [vellum], these
be the parchmins, the endictments, and the evidences that shall
condemn many of us, at the last day, *our owne skins*; we have
the book of God, the Law, written in our own hearts; we have
the image of God imprinted in our own souls; wee have the
character, and seal of God stamped in us, in our baptism, and,
all this is bound up in this velim, in this parchmin, in this skin

of ours, and we neglect book, and image, and character, and seal, and all for the covering" (3: 103). Painting a gruesome picture of death and corruption, he says the law of nature calls for worms to destroy the body. "Thus farre all's Common Law, no Prerogative." It is God's prerogative which brings us to resurrection and rebirth.[14]

At a time when the law's delays were being much criticized, Donne made several references to them. One extended passage in a sermon preached in 1618 vividly illustrates the working of lawyer's minds and their temptations:

> Delayes in Courts of Princes, and in Courts of Justice, proceede out of this, that men are not Lords of their promises, masters of their words; *foris pugnae, intus timores*, may well be applyed here, there are afflictions within, and feares of offending without, Letters from above, kindred from within, money from both sides, which keepes them from beinge *Domini promissionis*, Lords of their promises, masters of their words; either they thinke that if they dispatch a suitor too soone, ther's an end of his observance, of his attendance, of his respect, he undervalewes the favor, if it be so soone shewed, and so ther's a delay out of state, to give a dignity a majesty to the busines; or else they see that when there is an end a dispatch of the cause, there is an end of the profitt too, that Mine is exhausted, that veine is dryed up, that Cow gives noe more milke, and therefore by references and conferences, they keepe open that which howsoever it be an udder to them, is a wound to them that beare it, and heer's a delay to keep a way open to extortion and bribery . . .
>
> (2:148)

As always, the preacher applies this illustration from a particular profession to the behavior of mankind in general, asserting God's knowledge of all our hidden motives. "All our actions are soe *in facie Judicis,* and there needs noe evidence, we are deprehended in the manner, in corners where nothing sees us, God sees us, and in hell where wee shall see nothinge, he shall see us too" (2: 150). Elsewhere (2: 117) he cites Seneca with approval, on the manifold sins of lawyers.

Two of Donne's Lincoln's Inn sermons were concerned with the building of a new chapel for the Inn. The first, preparing them to build their chapel, was probably preached early in 1619 before the corner-stone had been laid at a ceremony attended by Donne. Taking as his text Jacob's blessing of a stone at Bethel (Gen. 28:16–17) he makes an appeal for funds, referring to the discussion about the best site, and calling Jacob a "Surveyor" and a "Builder." Jacob's church needed "no contribution," but "such Churches as we now build doe" (2: 213), so Donne talks about charity in general, largely in financial terms, and particularly with regard to "the providing Christ a house, a dwelling" (2: 216). God does not need only to be worshipped in a church, yet churches are important. Donne alludes to their history and why they have the names of saints and martyrs. Although he calls the building of a church "an acceptable testimony of devotion," he insists that we must look on our own homes as the house of God, and ends with the agreeable thought that "there have been in this Kingdome, since the blessed reformation of Religion, more publick charitable works perform'd, more *Hospitals* and *Colleges* erected, and endowed, in threescore, then in some hundreds of years, of superstition before, so may God be pleased to adde one example more amongst us . . ." (2: 234).

Despite his ill health and his reluctance to leave his children (his wife had died in 1617), Donne went to the continent with Lord Doncaster's peace-mission to Germany soon after preaching this sermon. "I goe into the mouth of such adversaries as I cannot blame for hating me, the Jesuits, and yet I goe" (*Letters* [1651], p. 174). On April 18 he preached a farewell sermon to the benchers on the theme of remembrance (Eccles. 12:1), which culminated in a moving tribute to his lawyer friends: "And I shall remember your religious cheerfulness in hearing the word, and our christianly respect towards all them that bring that word unto you, and towards myself in particular far above my merit." They would meet each other in prayer and he hoped "that if I never meet you again till we have all passed the gate of death, yet in the gates of heaven, I may meet you all . . ." (2: 248).

When the new chapel was dedicated on Ascension day 1623 by the Bishop of London, Donne preached the sermon on John 10:22. His aim was twofold; to refute the Roman Catholic accusation that Anglicans neglected the ceremonies of the church by expounding the significance of holy days and feasts and to consider two aspects of dedication, the "Lay Dedication . . . the voluntary surrendring of this piece of ground, thus built, to God" (4: 371) and the "Ecclesiasticall Dedication." Here he traced the history of men's desire to offer God a place of worship, discussing the age of nature prior to Moses' law (Jacob at Bethel), the age under the law (Solomon's Temple), and the New Testament era.

Now dean of St. Paul's, Donne was concerned with improving the standard of behavior among its members. He gave a good part of this dedicatory address to advocating good order and courtesy in the chapel. He noted the irreverence of some worshippers and that some servants would put on their hats, in God's presence, before their masters. He comments: "Christ shall make *Master* and *Servant* equall; but not yet, not heere; nor ever equall to himselfe, how ever they become equall to one another. . . . God's house is no Ordinary" (4: 377–78).

He was sympathetic towards the weaknesses of infirm people who could not endure the rigours of a cold church, and the ailing should not feel that they must "always stand at the Gospell, or bow the knee at the name of Jesus." But with characteristic irony he hits at some of the courtiers present: "And yet Courts of Princes are strange *Bethesdaes*; how quickly they recover any man that is brought into that Poole? How much a little change of ayre does? and how well they can stand, and stand bare many houres, in the Privy Chamber, that would not melt and flowe out into Rhumes, and Catarrs, in a long *Gospell* heere?" (4: 377).

He praises the members of his Inn and their friends for giving freely towards the new chapel and rejoices to be with them "again in this laying of this first formall Stone, the Word and Sacrament, and shall ever desire to be so in the service of this place" (4: 371).

The sermons abound with allusions to all the many different kinds of law, divine and human. Donne's sense of a necessary order in the universe and in human life was not fundamentally shaken by his meditations on modern astronomy and contemporary social evils. Indeed he never really lost his sense that "all the world together, hath amazing greatness, and an amazing glory in it, for the order and harmony, and continuance of it" (3: 48).

He speaks often of "the natural Law" written in men's hearts, and of "the written Law" of Moses and the prophets (2: 195); he recognises that the churches do not always interpret aright the Law of the Gospel; as in earlier prose writings he criticises the canon law of the Roman Catholics, and he inveighs against the notion of "venial sins" which, based on an extravagant belief in God's charity, Romanists take so far "that, at the last, nothing shall be sin with them, except it kill God; that is, nothing." (2: 100). All sins are grievous and we cannot avoid responsibility for them; "We must not slip into sin because it is the way of our profession: No being a *Lawyer*, without serving the passion of the Client? No being a *Divine*, without sowing pillows under great men's elbows?" (2: 103–5). But Donne expected his lawyers to be interested in the operation of the ecclesiastical laws based on "The Apostles Canons" and "The Penitential Canons," which he described in a Trinity Sermon (1621) on 1 Cor. 16:22: "It is so in our Church still; Impugners of the Supremacy are excommunicated, and not restored but by the Archbishop: Impugners of the Common Prayer Booke excommunicated too, but may bee restored by the Bishop of the Place: Impugners of our Religion declared in the Articles, reserved to the Archbishop: Impugners of Ceremonies restored when they repent, and no Bishop named . . ." (3: 310).

Donne was an Erastian. He now accepted without question that the king was head of the Church, and he felt a proper awe towards the sovereign. Preaching at Whitehall on 16 February 1620/21 on mortification and humiliation he begins: "the experience of the present Place, where we now stand in Court, is, that the glory of the persons, in whose presence we stand, occasions Humility in us: the more glorious *they* are, the humbler *we* are" (3: 207), yet he was ever ready to counter "a mis-belief, a mis-concept, that all this religion is but a part of a civill government and order" (2: 189). Religion and civil government each had its own sphere and practitioners of the one should not interfere in the other. He was always against the intrusion of laymen, especially Puritans, into matters of doctrine. At the Hague (19 December 1619) he said, "It is well provided by your Lawes, that Divines and Ecclesiasticall persons may not take farmes, nor buy nor sell, for returne, in Markets. I would it were as well provided, that buyers and sellers, and farmers might not be Divines, nor censure them . . . I speake of censuring our Doctrines, and of appointing our doctrines . . . We have liberty enough by your Law, to hold enough for the maintenance of our bodies, and states; you have liberty enough by our Law, to know enough for the salvation of your soules" (2: 279).

Always careful not to dabble in politics, Donne made few direct preferences to affairs of state. His loyalty and detachment in the sermon preached at Lincoln's Inn in late November 1620 after the disastrous defeat of the Elector Palatine became known and many ardent Protestants in the city were agitating for the king to enter the war and save him. Donne condemns satires and libels on rulers "as a vexation of spirit in ourselves, and a defacing and a casting of dust in the face of God's image . . . of whom hee hath sayd, *They are Gods.*" We must not become disunited but trust our rulers to their best for us. He recognizes the growing opposition between two great political principles and avoids supporting either: "howsoever the affections of men, or the vicissitudes and changes of affairs may vary, or apply those two great axioms, and aphorisms of ancient Rome: *Salus populi suprema Lex esto,* The good of the people is above all Law, and then, *Quod Principi placet, lex esto,* The pleasure of the Prince is above all Law; howsoever I say, various occasions may vary their Laws, adhere to that Rule of the Law, which the Apostle prescribes that we always make *Finem precepti charitatem, The end of the Commandement Charity* . . ." (3: 185).

Donne's sermons on death and judgment form a notable group in which naturally references to law are frequent, for he was much preoccupied with the physical laws of growth, sickness and dissolution, as with the spiritual laws of penance, retribution and divine justice. One of his most sombre but magnificent addresses was given "to the Lords on Easter Day (1619) . . . the King being then dangerously sick at Newmarket." It begins with the assertion that we are all doomed, condemned to death from before our birth: "Wee are all conceived in close Prison; in our Mothers Wombes, we are close Prisoners all . . . and then all our life is but a going out to the place of Execution, to death. Now was ever any man seen to sleep in the Cart, between Newgate and Tyborne?" (2: 197). Yet we sleep; "from the womb to the grave we are never thoroughly awake." He runs through some of the ideas about modern man's degeneracy found in *The First Anniversary,* discusses what may happen to those found alive on earth when Christ comes again, and then comes to his hearers: "It is certain, a judgement thou must passe: If thy close and cautelous proceeding have saved thee from all informations in the Exchequer, thy clearnesse of thy title from all Courts at Common Law, thy moderation from the Chancery, and Star-Chamber, If heighth of thy place, and Authority, have saved thee, even from the tongues of men . . . All those judgements, and all the judgements of the world, are but interlocutory judgements; There is a finall judgement . . . against Prisoners and Judges too, where all shall be judged again" (2: 205–6). Christ will be that judge, who has himself known death. "He needed not have dyed by the rigor of any Law; all we must." Yet he died for us, and we may hope, through him, to accept our natural death, and to "finde out another death, *mortem raptus*, a death of rapture, of extasie, that death which S. Paul died more then once" (2: 210).

   At Lincoln's Inn on 30 January 1619/20, Donne preached a sermon on John 5:22 in which he discussed how God's judgement is committed to Christ. It is a schematic piece, summarised as follows: "Judgement is a proper and inseparable Character of God; that's first: the Father cannot devest himself of that; that's next. The third is that he hath committed it to another; And then the person that is his delegate, is his onely Sonne; and lastly his power is everlasting . . ." (2: 312).

   There are fewer bright flashes of imagination in this sermon than in a later one on Trinity Sunday, (probably 1621), where he speaks of the speed of Christ's judgment. On earth "when there is a long time to the Assizes, there may be some hope of taking off, or of smothering Evidence, or working upon the Judge, or preparing for a pardon." No such shifts are possible with Christ. "There shall be Information, Examination, Publication, Hearing, Judgement, and Execution, in a minute" (3: 290). These were of course stages in the development of any criminal case.

   Donne rarely chose for his main theme a text involving

a lengthy consideration of biblical legal questions; but two such sermons may be mentioned. In the sermon on Gen. 18:25, "Shall not the Judge of all the Earth do right?" concerning Abraham's plea to the visiting angels that God should not slay the just with the unjust inhabitants of the Cities of the Plain, Donne studies the question, "Could God make a wrong Judgement?" He concludes that whereas "an arbitrator or a Chancellor, that Judges by submission of parties, or according to the Dictates of his own understanding" might understandably err, "He did as his Conscience led him to. But shall not a *Judge* that hath certain Law to judge by, *do right*? Especially if he be such a Judge as is *Judge* of the whole earth?" (3: 147).

Donne refers to earthly safeguards against injustice such as "Certioraris from a higher Court, or an Appeal *to* a higher Court" and asserts that God would have been just whatever He did. "The just are as much punished here as the unjust" because their reward is hereafter. So God might have said: "I can destroy Sodome, and yet save the righteous; I can destroy the righteous, and yet make death an advantage to them; which soever way I take, I can do nothing unjustly." In fact God spared the wicked for the righteous, at Abraham's request, so much weight there was in the good man's "weak prayer" (3: 155).

Another sermon specifically on a legal problem was given at the Temple Church on Esther 4:16, concerning the predicament of Esther, who, despite her husband's order that nobody enter his presence unsummoned, did so in order to prevent Haman from destroying the children of Israel. Two breaches of law were involved here: the king's edict (and monarchs should be obeyed), and the general law of self-preservation which Esther flouted, saying, "If I perish, I perish." Here was one of those cases of conscience dear to Donne's heart. Some unjust laws which contravene divine and human justice must be broken, he explains, as when Darius the Persian ordered that no man for thirty days should ask anything of anybody save the king, and Daniel prayed to God, without subterfuge, by the open window of his chamber.

But what about the illegal secret conventicles of modern Puritans? They might perhaps be justified were religion not obtainable elsewhere, as a thief is not to be condemned if he steals food to avoid starvation. But the state provides religious food. The Puritans complain because "that meat which we may have, is not so dressed, so dished, so sauced, so served in, as [they] would have it." (5: 218) Such recusants are enemies of both Church and State: "When these men pray in their Conventicles, for the confusion, and rooting out of Idolatry and Antichrist, they intend by their Idolatry, a Cross in Baptism; and by their Antichrist, a man in a Surpless; and not only the persons, but the Authority that admits this Idolatry, and this Antichristianism. As vapors and winds shut up in Vaults, engender Earth-quakes; so these particular Spirits in their Vault-Prayers, and Cellar-Service, shake the Pillars of State and Church" (5: 219). Esther, however, Donne concludes after much argument, did well to risk both offending the king and also losing her own life in order to save the Jewish people, for "whensoever divers Laws concur and meet together, that Law which comes from the superior Magistrate, and is in the nature of the thing commanded, highest too, that Law must prevail . . . She was under two Laws, of which it was necessary to obey that which concerned the glory of God" (5: 225–27).

It was only rarely that Donne made so direct an onslaught on a contemporary group as that on the Puritans. There may be many topical references in the sermons, but they were usually oblique. One sermon, hitherto neglected, seems by its content and date to have unusual interest as touching on the fall of Lord Chancellor Bacon. Donne may have got to know Bacon quite early, for both were in the Essex circle; he must certainly have come across him when working for Egerton in connection with the latter's membership of a commission to inquire into abuses in the clerkship of the Star Chamber. Bacon held the reversion of that office and in 1597 had offered it to Egerton on the condition that Egerton would help him to become master of the rolls. After Bacon knew of Egerton's appointment he repeated his offer in a letter dated 12 November. Donne probably knew about this. He certainly did not forgive Bacon's forward part as queen's counsel in the trial of Essex for treason (the result of Essex's rising in February 1600/01), when Bacon did all he could to ensure his friend's conviction.

In his Rabelaisian *Catalogus Librorum Aulicorum* (c. 1608) in which he gave humorous or satiric titles of 34 fictitious books, he included three ascribed to Bacon: 27. *The Brazen Head of Francis Bacon: concerning Robert the First, King of England.* Here he gave to Bacon Edward Coke's saying that "he of his earldom should by Robert the last, that of a kingdom thought to be Robert the First." But Bacon had in fact written a paper defending his behavior by describing the treasons of "Robert, Earl of Essex." 28. *The Lawyer's Onion; or The Art of Lamenting in Courts of Law, by the Same* was a hit at Bacon's hypocrisy and oratorical power. *A Foreigner-and-a-half; or, Concerning the Half-and-half Jury* is obscure, but probably refers to Bacon's unsuccessful support of the king's wish in Parliament (February 1606/1607) and in the Exchequer in Calvin's Case (early 1608) to get all children born in England or Scotland after the Union of the Crowns regarded as naturalized in both countries. Was a Scotsman a foreigner? The question had great importance; it would affect the constitution of some juries, as special arrangements had to be made in cases involving foreigners. Maybe the title referred also to Bacon's ability to face both ways at once in his desire to please both parties.[15]

After Robert Cecil's death in 1612, Bacon's fortunes rose

steadily. He was made attorney-general in 1613, carried on a successful struggle with his rival Coke, became a privy councillor in 1616, and on 7 March 1616/17 succeeded Lord Ellesmere (Egerton) as lord keeper. A year later he became lord chancellor and Baron Verulum. He was now the principal spokesman for the royal policies in Parliament, and, though enemies such as Coke and Cranfield (master of the wards) were seeking occasions to attack him, he was riding high when on 27 January 1620/21 he was made Viscount St. Albans.

However, on 14 March 1620/21, a disappointed suitor, Christopher Aubrey, petitioned the Commons, alleging that the lord chancellor had received money from him to speed up his case. A similar complaint by one Edward Egerton soon followed, and on 17 March the Commons sent the complaints up to the Lords for investigation. Meanwhile Bacon had fallen ill and was unable to attend the inquiry when witnesses were heard. Charges were added, and although in no case could it be shown that his taking money had affected his judgment, yet he had done what he himself had said should never be done: he had taken presents before the finish of a suit. Bacon appealed to the king, for whom he had made some dubious judgments. The king did nothing, and on 26 March left the matter entirely to Parliament. For a fortnight Bacon's illness grew worse, and on 10 April he made his will. Then he got somewhat better and on 16 April saw the king and admitted that although he had never perverted justice he had taken presents both before and after cases had been decided. This latter time (after the verdict) he "conceived it to be no fault."

On 24 April an admission of his guilt was read to the Lords and the House was plainly moved: "No Lord spoke to it, after it was read, for a long time." The Great Seal was taken from him, and on 3 May he was fined 40,000 pounds, imprisoned in the Tower (for two days only), declared incapable of

any office, and banished forever from the court. When he re-
covered from his illness he retired to the country and gave himself up to writing and remorse, though he made several attempts
to obtain a pardon.

On 8 April 1621 Donne preached a sermon at Whitehall
on what Mrs. Simpson called "a curious text," from Prov. 26:16,
"Hast thou found honey? Eat so much as is sufficient for thee,
lest thou be filled therewith, and vomit it." "The sermon is not
particularly interesting," wrote Mrs. Simpson, "though it has
some shrewd passages on the insatiable nature of ambition and
covetousness. But the sermon is spoiled by Donne's too evident
desire to be learned and ingenious."[16]

Learned and ingenious the sermon is, with a mincing of
the text in the *Divisio* going back to Donne's earliest efforts. But
consider the circumstances: Donne was preaching while the
court was in a ferment, Bacon's case was still *sub judice* after
witnesses had been heard and believed, and the king had de-
clined to intervene, thus signifying his tacit acceptance that his
lord chancellor might be guilty. Bacon was sick and had entered
no defence. The moral result was certain, whatever the actual
verdict.

On 16 February in preaching before the king, Donne had
touched briefly on the slipperiness of court honours and titles
and had quoted from Prov. 25:27: "As it is not good for men to
eat much honey; so, for men to search their own glory, is not
glory." Probably in preparing the new sermon he saw the special relevance of the honey-image to the terrible scandal then
shaking the spheres of law and government. Bacon was sick; the
assiduous seeker after wealth and power might soon have to
vomit forth his sweet rewards. The text was peculiarly apt, and
Donne's learned wordplay may have been the result of haste,
or embarrassment. What else could he say under the appalling
circumstances, in a Court seething with rumour, malicious ex-

pectancy, and grievous shock. How to speak with some relevance to the situation insinuates personal application into general moralising, from the moment when he starts: "there is a
temporall unsatiableness of riches, and there is a spirituall unsatiableness of sin " (3: 225) Perhaps alluding to Bacon's scientific projects and his *New Atlantis* (written by 1617 but as yet
unpublished) he goes on: "as though this World were too little
to satisfie man, men are come to discover or imagine new worlds,
severall worlds in every Planet" (3: 225). There are other references to the danger of too much learning.

He discusses the ambiguities of men: "There hath al-
waies beene ambiguity and equivocation in words, but now in
actions, and almost every action will admit a diverse sense."
(How true of Bacon!) He quotes Origen: "For he whom the
Devill possesses is not *one*. . . . The same sinner is not the same
thing; . . . there he is an Eagle; and yet lies still grovelling, and
trodden upon at any greater mans threshold, there he is a
worme." When such a man falls, says Donne, "the same men
that have cryed *Hosanna,* are ready to cry *Crucifige*" (3: 228).

He discusses why men rise: "Greatness often comes by
Fortune," but Fortune can be God's instrument. "Thou wilt
not be drawne to confesse, that a Man hath an office, is presently
wiser then thou, or a man that is Knighted, presently valianter
then thou. Men have preferment for those parts, which other
men, equall to them in the same things, have not" (3: 230). And
he tells the courtiers "Make now thy selfe cheape, not vulgar,
have some respect to the selfe, to thine owne ingenuity, but
principally to the other, to thy great friend. . . . This is this
Hony, where thou hast accesse, yet does not push open every
doore, flinge up every hanging, but use thy favour modestly"
(3: 231). Of the modern tendency to "over-doe," to demand
more, he says: "An Office is but an Antipast, it gets them an
appetite to another Office; and a Title of Honour, but an Anti-

past, a new stomach to a new Title. The danger is, that we cannot goe upward directly; If wee have a staire, to goe any height, it must be a winding staire; It is a compassing, a circumventing, to rise . . . Though our meanes be direct in their owne nature, yet we put them upon crooked wayes . . . Have ye seene a glasse blowne to a handsome competancy, and with one breath more, broke?" (3: 234). "The world's a bubble" Bacon wrote in one of his few poems; he was now seen by a fellow Inns of Court man as a bubble of blown glass. Donne draws a parallel between vomiting and disgrace: "Rich men perish. . . . Their confidence in their riches provokes them to some unjustifiable actions, and their riches provoke others to a vehement persecution. And in this vomit of theirs, if we had time to doe so, we would consider first, The sordidnesse, and the contempt and scorne that this evacuated Man comes to in the world, when he hath had this vomit of all his Honey . . . So when such a person comes by justice, or malice to this vomit, every man becomes a Physitian, every man brings Inditements, and evidence against him, and can shew all his falshoods, and all his extortions in particular" (3: 237). The end is despair: "This man that vomits without, bleeds within; his fortune is broke, and his heart is broke, and he bleeds better blood than his owne, he bleeds out the blood of Christ Jesus himselfe . . . (and) when that is lost by this vomit, he mournes for all, in a sad and everlasting mourning, in such a disconsolate dejection of spirit as ends either in an utter inconsideration of God, or in a desperation of his mercies" (3: 238).

All of this was of course not intended to apply to Lord Bacon, but I find it hard to believe that none of it was, or that Donne's congregation would not think of the lord chancellor as he preached, making them realize not only the sins of the fallen man but the mixed motives of many of those who helped to pull him down; above all, the spiritual agony suffered by the sinner in such a case. This was the verdict of a preacher-poet who had himself sought offices and had "an hydroptic thirst for human learning" but had (with difficulty) turned from them to the service of God, pronounced upon a great man who, besides setting the laws of nature and reason above the divine, had betrayed the human justice he had so long studied and invoked.

Edinburgh

———

Notes

1. John Donne, *Letters to Severall Persons of Honour* (London, 1651), p. 51.

2. From the Inner Temple came Sackville and Norton, William Browne, Sir John Davies, and Donne's Oxford friends, Henry Wotton and John Hoskyns; from Gray's Inn came Edward Hall the chronicler, G. Gascoigne, Francis Davison, Francis Bacon and Thomas Campion; from Lincoln's Inn came Sir Thomas More, Thomas Lodge, Sir John Harington, John Donne, Francis Quarles, Edmund Waller. In addition Thomas Watson, W. Warner, G. Whetstone, John Marston, R. Fanshawe, H. Vaughan, spent some time at the Inns of Court.

3. Donne shared a "chamber" with his Oxford friend Christopher Brooke.

4. Unless otherwise noted, all quotations of Donne's poetry are from *The Poems of John Donne*, ed. H. J. C. Grierson (Oxford, 1912).

5. *The Courtier's Library*, ed. E. M. Simpson, (Oxford, 1930).

6. *The Defence of Contraries* (London, 1593). Cf. A. E. Malloch, "The Techniques and Function of the Renaissance Paradox," *SP*, 53 (1956), 191–203; M. McCaules, "Paradox in Donne," *SR*, 13 (1966), 266–87; H. K. Miller, "The Paradoxical Encomium," *MP*, 53 (1956), 145–78; B. Vickers, "King Lear and the Renaissance Paradoxes," *MLR*, 63 (1968), 305–14.

7. Cf. *Juvenilia, or Certain Paradoxes and Problems by John Donne*, ed. R. E. Bennett, (Facsimile Text Society, New York, 1936); E. M. Simpson, "Donnes Paradoxes and Problems," in *A Garland for John Donne*, ed. T. Spencer, (Cambridge, Mass. 1931), pp. 23–49.

8. A. E. Malloch 'John Donne and the Casuists', *SEL*, II (1962), 57–76, writes that some 600 appeared between 1564 and 1660. Donne himself made a "little book of Cases" which he sent to Goodyer in 1621, and Walton

says that after his death they found "copies of divers Letters and Cases of Conscience that had concerned his friends, with his observations and solutions of them."

9. This seems more like a horrible murder than suicide; but Donne liked a joke.

10. Cf. E. M. Simpson, *A Study of the Prose Works of John Donne,* (Oxford, 1924), Ch. 8.

11. The manysidedness of Donne's interest in law may be suggested by listing the kinds of law treated by Richard Hooker and by William Fulbeck. Hooker was Master of the Temple (1585–91) and the first four books of his *Ecclesiastical Polity* appeared while Donne was a student at Lincoln's Inn. Book I, defining Divine and Human Law, specified: (i) the laws of the divine Being itself which governs all things: (ii) natural law, working through the unconscious, unthinking operations of the lesser creatures, and the "intellectual natures of voluntary agents such as men"; (iii) "a law celestial and heavily . . . which Angels do clearly hehold"; (iv) "a law of Reason, that which bindeth creatures reasonable in the world"; (v) "that which . . . is not known but by special revelation from God, Divine Law"; (vi) "Human law, that which out of the law either of reason or of God, men probably gathering to be expedient, they make it a law." As Dame Helen Gardner points out, "Donne's debt to Hooker is not a verbal one: but his treatment of law, for instance, in *Pseudo-Martyr,* constantly recalls Hooker" (*Divine Poems,* ed. Helen Gardner [Oxford, 1952], p. xxl). In the *Sermons* too, one might add.

Fulbeck, a Gray's Inn man (1584–1600) wrote *A Direction or Preparative to the Study of the Law* in which he distinguished eight branches of law accepted in the English courts: (i) laws of nature; (ii) laws of nations; (iii) civil law; (iv) common law; (v) statute law; (vi) customary law; (vii) *jus merum*; (viii) *jus aequum et bonum.* (Cf. Ives, "The Law and the Lawyers" in *Shakespeare Survey* 17, [1964]: 73–86.) To them must be added canon law. All of these kinds of law were well known to Donne.

12. Cf. *Sermons,* ed. G. R. Potter and E. M. Simpson, 10 vols. (Berkeley, 1953–62) vol. 2, Sermon 7, preached at Whitehall, Feb. 12, 1618/19 at the beginning of Lent, has much on his ideas of preaching, and whimsically lists the stages of *hearing* a sermon as Expectation, Acceptation, Acclamation, Congratulation, Remuneration (2: 175). Subsequent quotations from the *Sermons* are from this edition.

13. *See* W. R. Mueller, *John Donne, Preacher,* 1962. J. Webber *Contrary Music,* (Madison, Wisconsin, 1963).

14. This image of common law and prerogative recurs frequently in Donne's *Essays in Divinity,* ed. Evelyn Simpson (Oxford, 1967).

15. Cf. *The Courtier's Library,* ed. E. M. Simpson (Oxford, 1930).

16. *Sermons,* 3: 19.

WILLIAM EMPSON

✺

RESCUING DONNE

In the twenties, when my eyes were opening, it was usual for
critics to consider that Donne in his earlier poetry held broad
and enlightened views on church and state, that he was influenced by the recent great scientific discoveries, and that he used
the theme of freedom in love partly as a vehicle for these ideas
to show what the ideological and sociological effects of Paracelsus and Copernicus would turn out to be. A critic of the time
wrote: "he stands almost on a level with H. G. Wells for pierc-
ing insight." I was imitating this Donne, the poet as so conceived, in my own verse at the time with love and wonder, and
I have never in later years come across any good reason for the
universal change of opinion about him at the start of the thir-
ties. I am anxious not to give too feeble an impression of the
loathing with which I regard the present image of him. The
habitual mean-mindedness of modern academic criticism, its
moral emptiness combined with incessant moral nagging, and its
scrubbed prison-like isolation are particularly misleading in the
case of Donne; in fact, we are the ones who need rescuing, not
the poet. But the text of the love poems does literally need rescuing, at a small number of crucial points, from the recent edition edited by Professor Helen Gardner (*The Elegies and the
Songs and Sonnets* [Oxford, 1965]). I am of course glad to accept
the main results of the massive work which has been put into
the manuscripts, but I am chiefly concerned with the interpre-

tation of them. The problem of the manuscripts is still very puzzling, and the simple theory which I propose would at least clear up one of the major difficulties.

It was not until my "Donne the Spaceman" appeared in *The Kenyon Review* (Summer 1957) that I first realized that my colleagues and I disagreed so vehemently on this matter. My "Donne in the New Edition" (*The Critical Quarterly* [Autumn 1966]) was a reaction to the first shock of reading Professor Gardner, who apparently had felt that she was bringing to ripeness the accepted scholarly conclusions on the subject, and could hardly believe that anyone disagreed with them. Part of my case has been presented in my previous articles, which are concerned mainly with the intellectual interests of the young Donne; here I have focused on the text.

The chief event in the textual field since the Gardner edition of the love poems has been the companion edition of the *Satires* and *Verse Letters* by Wesley Milgate. It has helped my case a good deal, especially by clearing up the subject of manuscript W. Donne became famous during his lifetime for poems which he refused to print, so that they gradually got into circulation in a variety of manuscripts. Even as a young man, wanting to become a civil servant and politician (before he was converted and became a parson), he feared that the love poems would stand in his way, and tried to keep them out of manuscript circulation. But the satires could be shown round; they had claims to be grave and moral, and anyway writing satires was considered a respectable pastime. However, manuscripts that provide an early form of the text show that manuscript W is not the original version. In Satire 4, line 48, Donne spoiled one of his own jokes out of professional caution. The real text, after remarking that all men are liars but the biggest liars are ecclesiastical historians, instanced one papist and one Protestant historian; but nearly all the surviving manuscripts give two papists. This had already been pointed out by Grierson in his magnificent edition of 1912; Mr. Milgate presents additional proof that the change was made in 1598 when Donne had just been made secretary to Egerton, for whom he was actually writing another satire to help forward some legal reform. Egerton would need to be assured that Donne was now a staunch Protestant. Mr. Milgate's further evidence (p. lviii) is rather hard to summarize but it is strong. Thus I can accept it as an admission by my opponents, since Mr. Milgate writes as a loyal disciple of Professor Gardner. For the *Satires*, in this clear case and a number of minor ones, manuscript W gives the doctored text. The first part of W is held to be not later than 1598, so the date established by Mr. Milgate is crucial; and the poet would have the same reason for a little doctoring of both satires and elegies. Even if lawyer Egerton wanted only satires, Donne would meet a number of important gentlemen with whom he needed to make friends, and many of them would be agog for the elegies. This group of poems, on the whole set pieces written to a dramatic theme, appears to have got into a very limited circulation before he became cautious about showing poems, so that they would be known and asked for; whereas those of the songs and sonnets which were already written were kept secret. He would mull over the elegies, after he had consented to read a few poems after dinner, considering which would do, and occasionally writing a less upsetting word or phrase above the line. Fun with sex would not upset that audience, but a suspicion of heresy (about sex or anything else) would. I cannot say whether the young ladies of Egerton's household were present or not; probably it would not make much difference. Donne would write out and present to Egerton a doctored text of the satires, but need not have written out the doctored elegies at all; in any case, as writing paper was expensive, he kept the old sheets on which he had written corrections, with the first draft plainly visible below. This became the basic source for the manuscripts.

There is only one major crux in the *Elegies*: "To His Mistris Going to Bed" presents the poet as coaxing a richly dressed lady, the wife of a city businessman, to undress for him. (I agree here with Professor Gardner's note and its cross-reference to "Loves Usury.") He makes a series of encouraging comparisons, designed to prove that this is the right thing to do, which amount to erecting personal love into a rival to Christianity. She is America, where one is out of reach of both the queen and the pope, and the first hint comes of making her a habitable planet, presumably requiring a unique relation to the Redeemer. Calvin had ruled that men can only be admitted to heaven by a whim of God, because all men are infinitely unworthy of it; Donne is thus immensely reverential to the lady when he says (using the technical term) that he is one of those allowed by "imputed grace" to see her revealed. It is all a kind of joke, sure enough, but it tries out a position which might become very serious; so there is no change of tone when he arrives at the tremendous penultimate couplet: "cast all, yea, this white lynnen hence, / There is no pennance due to innocence." To call an act of illicit sex "innocent" might well strike a listener as heretical and might excite embarrassing discussion, so he drew a line through *due to* on his manuscript and wrote *much less* above it, thus ending the poem with an orthodox but ugly sneer. Donne's loyal friend Woodward gladly accepted the improvement, but he could not have put *Here* for *There*, because that helpful accommodation was invented by editorial coypists a long while after. What else, after all, could have happened? The only alternative theory yet proposed is that the line got torn, or smudged, and the copier invented *due to* as a stopgap. But how could this botcher write so much better than the poet had done, in the characteristic manner of the poet? Since

Donne's tone was not characteristically sneering, there is very little temptation to assume that he is sneering at this point.

However, to show that the origins of W are late enough to have been bowdlerized is only half the requirement; the origins of the manuscripts which vote against W cannot possibly be *early* enough since there is a gap of a generation and more. The Group V manuscripts appeared to give the text as it was before Donne altered it; this seemed plain in the initial case of *due to* and I began to realize that they did it habitually. In fact, many students of the subject have had this idea before me, some of them earnestly wishing it could be true, but have retired baffled by sheer historical impossibility. Obviously, these critics felt that the Group V manuscripts have no such long pedigree.

Of the five groups, Group I is held to date from 1614; Donne was told by his criminal patron Somerset to print his poems before taking orders (on a promise of immediate preferment from Somerset), as we know because a surviving letter from the poet asks a friend to return some texts. He was much upset by the insolent ruling and was probably tempted to bowdlerize for the occasion, but apparently did not. Somehow he was spared from having to print the poems, but the incident, as well as fathering one of the groups of manuscripts, would leave him a collected and prepared set of his poems, which no doubt he retained after he had taken orders. Grierson wrote indignantly that Donne cannot be supposed to have held on to the early poems even in his last fierce asceticism, but his mind was always complex and statesmanlike. Maybe he genuinely wished he could destroy the early poems, but he knew that other people held copies that they could publish after his death and that they might add worse things than he had written. Furthermore, he spent whole days writing out sermons so his children could publish them, should they need money after his death. He regularly presented himself in sermons as a sinner when young; he might have relished the exposure as a further penance. Besides, I doubt that he always hated the prospect of eternal fame. I am in agreement with Professor Gardner here; she proposed in her edition of the *Divine Poems* that "some time after 1625 Donne must have allowed a copy of the poems in his possession to be taken," and that this copy became the basis of Group II. But some Group II manuscripts had other poems not in Donne's own collection added afterwards, and some of their texts may have recorded early uncorrected versions. Group IV was copied from Donne's own handwriting by his old friend Woodward. The four manuscripts of Group III are also held to derive from one source, but they are very late, two of them were incomplete after the death of the poet, and other manuscripts were collated in preparation for the posthumous edition. It seems obvious that *what* was collated was the Group V manuscripts, or their sources, but this is never said; very little can be summarized about Group V from the discussion of Professor Gardner. There are ten manuscripts, with a leader and three groups of three. They are not considered to derive from one source, and their sources are not believed to be early. They are slovenly and untrustworthy. But they often offer a better alternative, and sometimes they vote all together with a decisive answer to a problem. One finds in examining the detail of Professor Gardner's editing that she pays them a remarkable amount of attention, far more than would be gathered from her introduction. It is an impressive record of good sense retained under the distraction of a wrong theory, and the times when she is being wrenched in this way make the most interesting parts of her paradoxical edition, which still leaves the problem of the Group V manuscripts crying out for a simple factual explanation.

As I combed through the text for evidence that might help to solve the problem, I took for granted that Group V copiers, for whom I at once felt a natural sympathy, had done what I would have done in their situation; it took a great deal of bumbling about before I realized that my assumptions (and I even thought that Professor Gardner had made the same assumptions) amounted to a new theory. It is likely that the dean finally allowed his poems to be copied, on one occasion for Group II. Therefore he would be likely to allow it again, though only for some special friend, as a great favor, once every few years. A man who was granted this honor would be urged by his more knowing friends to put a copyist to work at once. He would be strictly instructed to ignore the later corrections because the literary world had taken into its head that the heretical ecstacies of young Jack could be retained in this way, whereas the semi-official copies had been gelded by the dean. Perhaps this friend, who would have been put up at the deanery, would beg leave to take the precious documents to his bedroom and mull over them during the night, and then hand them out the window to his accomplice on the stairs. In any case, surely I cannot be wrong in assuming that interest and suspicion would be very keen about these texts; imagine if W. H. Auden had refused to publish during his lifetime, and was definitely known in at least one case to have sabotaged the great poetry he had written. This sentiment was still strong a generation later, when the Restoration made possible an unhampered edition (the seventh). Although every scrap of fun with sex was dug up from the manuscripts, Group V readings were often adhered to even when (as usual) they gave the duller version of the two. The second edition of Donne's poems, only two years after the first, was already thoroughly infected with Group V readings. I do not know how this was done, but the Group V man would need to have some convincing story. The speed and thoroughness of the movement on the one hand, and its lasting so long on the other, give a very different impression from the flabby incompetence that Professor Gardner describes. In fact, almost certainly one man was at work, not three ancestral copyists; his proof was the corroborating documents. But I still think it likely that other men had done the same job, and their results agreed simply because they had worked on the same principle.

Professor Gardner was very unlikely to have taken this point of view. We must respect her for her endurance, in checking through all those documents, which seemed to her so sordidly unscholarly, and no wonder she regards the writers of them with contempt. Dirty, lazy and ignorant she expects them to be; but actually plotting against authority among themselves she would regard as inconceivable. I was misled by her note on "The Good-Morrow," one of the two poems which the poet admittedly altered. One might suppose, she says, if the author did not write out a fair copy, that: "The ancestor of L74, Group II, etc, would then be a copy of the original poem; the ancestor of Group III a copy of the corrected version which incorporated most but not all of the corrections; and the ancestor of H40 and Group I would be a copy that included all the second thoughts. Or it might be held that there were three stages . . ." She winces at the thought of an independent-minded copyist, but even in considering the possibility she has only envisaged him as an aesthete, choosing the variant he preferred. I think this process did occur, and may well have occurred in Group II, where I do not understand the voting; Group II never seems to provide an interesting reading, anyway. The voting of the manuscripts over whether to read *grow* or *groan* in "Twicknam Garden" is I think partly of this aesthetic kind, though we can deduce a change by the author in 1614. Lady Bedford had only taken the house in Twickenham a few years before, so the poem was fresh in his mind. He refuses to leave the garden, and pretends to be despairingly in love with the lady—she was sickly, and of inflexible virtue, and appears to have looked rather like a spider, so we may presume that Donne was drawing upon other experiences, though real ones, for his splendid compliment (unless otherwise noted, quotations of poetry are from *The Poems of John Donne*, ed. H. J. C. Grierson [Oxford, 1912]):

> *. . . Love let mee*
> *Some senslesse peece of this place bee;*
> *Make me a mandrake, that I may groane here,*
> *Or a stone fountaine weeping out my yeare.*

Professor Gardner prints *grow* and comments: " 'Groane,' the reading of Groups I and II, could have arisen independently from the strong association of mandrakes with groans. But the mandrake was not held up to groan when *in situ*, it only groaned when it was torn up; see Browne . . ."

She does not actually deny that the poet made the correction himself in 1614, despite her theory of the Groups, so I think she must be breaking one of the rules of scholarly editors —the final text authorized by a poet must be printed, even if he changed the original draft under threat of torture. Evidently Donne had appreciated the professor's objection, and had selected *grow* because it sounds like *groan* but would not be grumbled at (hearing the poem sung, it would be hard to tell which text was used); but then, when it came to print, he permitted himself to write what he had always wanted. Everybody knew that the mandrake was only a kind of emblem, so that what you said about it did not matter, and some of the Group I manuscripts agree with HK2 here. (Professor Gardner's note admits that she is siding with HK2.) I think that Grierson was plainly right, as usual, to print *groan*; it is a glowingly romantic poem, not at all hurt by a little frank absurdity. But the Group V manuscripts are not arty at all; they are vowed to copy the text as it was before it was mucked up, however seductive the alterations may appear.

Professor Gardner has a major objection to treating the

Group V manuscripts as a serious source of evidence, to which I must give full weight: they are slovenly, and full of trivial slips. Surely, the reason is that they were made by amateurs; they set out to be unofficial versions, giving the lowdown. It strikes me that the disciplinary attitude of Professor Gardner makes her confuse two different matters here. If I had to do this copying, I too would do it messily; but I would not write down bland tidy nonsense, like the professional scribes of Groups I and II. When Professor Gardner chooses to destroy a poem, remarking with buttoned lips that the authority against Grierson and the first edition (for some killing variant) is overwhelming, I feel I am in the hands of a nurse who says: "I will not believe you when you tell me the house is burning down, because you have dribbled on your bib."

This confusion does something to explain a long and earnest section of her introduction (p. lxxv–ix) which claims to refute any such deduction as I am making from her apparatus. The first four of the ten Group V manuscripts, she says, may sometimes report "an alternative version," but only if it is also found in, and derived from, L74, a manuscript almost in Group II but partly independent, which may tap early sources: "In the twenty-three lyrics common to HK2 and L74, it is plain that HK2 contains an inferior version of the text in L74. It shares its rare errors and adds to them errors and distinctive readings of its own. . . . In any of the Songs and Sonnets where there are a sufficient number of significant variants to allow the construction of a stemma, Cy, O and P will always be found below HK2, and in the remainder it is nearly always clear that their text is a corruption of the text of HK2. Their readings are, therefore, valueless in any attempt to construct the original text." Professor Gardner has objected earnestly that her apparatus, being highly selective, cannot be used backwards as a means of testing her assertions; but surely what it has selected are precisely the errors which are meaningful, as apart from the trivial and careless ones. I have no doubt that her assertions here are based on a careful statistical analysis of the errors, but then the trivial ones are bound to predominate. I still say that her assertions are plainly untrue of the meaningful variants recorded in her apparatus. The sequence L74, Cy, O, P does sometimes occur in full, but HK2 behaves much the same way whether L74 is present or not, so do Cy, O and P whether HK2 is present or not; and nearly always, when you get the full sequence, the rest of Group V also behaves consistently. Surely she does not claim that they all derive from L74. The fact is, this whole line of argument collapses as soon as you envisage copyists who refused to accept the alterations written above the line. The only reason for needing a "pedigree" to prove that a variant is early is the presumption that, because a copyist cannot think, he must have been set to copy a page on which the later version had not been written.

There is one case, "The Curse," which seems refreshingly clear; all agree that the poet thought of a better joke, three lines long, and wrote it onto the manuscript to replace his previous joke. The poem was considered almost a satire and allowed entry into Q, the early manuscript of the satires that gave Mr. Milgate the undoctored text. Professor Gardner's notes give a really impressive proof that Donne thought of the new joke in 1598. Sure enough, L74, HK2 and P stick to the old version. But so do all the rest of Group V (except B, and Cy which omits). And so do all of Group II, though their ancestor must have had Donne's own text available to him because the poem is in Group I. I have just been trying to speak up for the copyists, but do not know what motive I can ascribe to this Group II man; perhaps he thought that the duller joke was the more decorous one. The ancestors of Group V, of course, were acting on their rule.

Coming at last to some examples, I must first try to win a little respect for Group V. In the elegy "Love's Progress," Donne is explaining that if you want to get to the center of a woman it is more practical to start caressing her feet:

> *How much they erre that set out at the face!*
> *The hair a Forest is of Ambushes,*
> *Of springes, snares, fetters and manacles:*

All manuscripts of Groups I and II write *springs* instead of *springes*, nonsense which does not even scan, and in Group III only manuscript O'F, the last stage of the editing process, gets round to the right word; whereas *every one* of the Group V manuscripts, however slovenly and dirty-minded they may be, gets it right. It comes as rather a jolt, after you have learned from Professor Gardner's "Textual Introduction" that these manuscripts are "valueless in any attempt to construct the original text," to find that she accepts their ruling without comment, without any note on the passage. It is comforting to find that there was some use, after all, in her labor of collating them.

We find a similar case on the first page of the *Songs and Sonnets*, as she arranges them, and here a note by the professor, with her immense calming dignity, is felt to be needed to put the matter in its right light.

> *If thou beest borne to strange sights,*
> > *Things invisible to see,*
> *Ride ten thousand daies and nights*
> > *Till age snow white haires on thee, . . .*

All manuscripts of Groups I and II omit *to* in the second line, making nonsense which does not even scan, and two of Group III (including the final O'F) are still following them, but the other two supply *go*. S agrees with this, but all other Group V manuscripts, except B before correction, supply our familiar *to*, thus agreeing with the first and all subsequent editions. A block decision of this kind is like a high wind; it sweeps away any discussion of whether we have here one of the "distinctive readings" of HK2, and whether all distinctive readings are bad ones. Professor Gardner offers a bold distraction: "*1633* appears to have made an obvious correction of the defective line in Groups I and II. The true reading has possibly been preserved in Group III (*Dob, S96*) which reads 'goe see,' giving an imperative to balance 'Ride': 'If you are already gifted with the power to see marvels, go and see the invisible.' The manuscripts that agree with *1633* may do so accidentally through having made the same correction in the defective line in Group II with which they are all textually connected." Surely, Professor Gardner must know why this imperative is not a better reading, because otherwise she would print it. The song is a tease for the ladies, pretending to make accusations against them even while sung in their very boudoirs. Hence it requires to be light, and the thudding insistence of two imperatives is not a balance at all; *what* would it balance? I am sure, if I were set to emend that truncated line, I would come up with *go* or some worse verb; I did not appreciate the grace of the construction with *to*, implying somehow that the well-born soul does not need to struggle, till I realized how hard it would be to reinvent. The effect of praising the clumsy wrong invention here is to distract attention from the small triumph of Group V.

Most readers of the edition, indeed, can have no idea of what is going on; it has cost me many a tumble to acquire my uneasy mastery of this tricky technique. After a square bracket, the apparatus does not list the manuscripts which agree with the editor, but only gives a list of variant readings, each followed by its supporting manuscripts (out of a selected list of manuscripts given at the start). It is lucky for her not to have to tell the reader here that only the Group V manuscripts agree with her. As to her last sentence, you must remove S and B from the ten, and K omits the poem, and she has maintained that the sequence HK2, Cy, O and P are all derived from L74, which is a special Group II manuscript. The apparatus omits D17, which is anyway classed with A25 and JC, and these two, the only ones left, are actually said in the "Textual Introduction" (pp. lxxviii–ix) to agree frequently with HK2. Professor Gardner's statement is therefore properly covered. But what use is there in saying that the bad manuscripts sound less disgraceful if they have respectable connections when they are right and their decent connections wrong? I am drawing attention to a high piece of literary artistry in this note, far more tense and absorbed than anything in the careless song upon which it is supposed to comment.

In both these examples, the handwriting must have made the needed extra letters rather hard to read, though not too hard for each of the Group V ancestor copiers to catch them. They would naturally be more interested and alerted than the professional copiers. There is no question of a change by the author. But evidence is needed for the assumption that the Group V manuscripts often report the text of Donne as it was before correction. The garbling of a copier may be exactly like the first clumsy effort of an author. It might even be doubted whether Donne corrected his poems at all since he liked to speak casually about them; but he often worked over them a great deal. Mr. Milgate has shown that the passage in Satire 3 about seeking truth "On a huge hill," which is famous for making the sound fit the sense, was not in its present form until Donne presented his satires to Lady Bedford in 1608, about fourteen years after first writing it. However, there are also cases where a poet changes a word almost at once, as his plan develops, during the original act of writing; and this is likely to give the best evidence, because the poem itself as it goes on makes the rejected word irrelevant; or anyway, one can see that the poet needed to change it. Thus we are told in "Loves Progress" that Cupid lived underground, like Pluto: "Men to such Gods, their sacrificing Coals / Did not in Altars lay, but pits and holes." One manuscript out of each of the three sets of Group V reads "on Alters." Clearly, Donne was thinking of altars and forgetting the other half of the antithesis, so he first wrote *on*, but then, when he read the passage over, or maybe at once, saw that he needed another word to cover the case of *holes*. The copyists were not under the same need for invention, and would not think of the mistake three times independently. Then, a lot of the minor variants record doubts whether to use the subjunctive after *if*, and whether to use *which* of a person; the final decision is sometimes more "correct" and sometimes less, so it is not a matter of a pedantic scribe correcting a careless poet. It may seem a bit surprizing that he first wrote in "Loves Growth": "Love's not so pure *an* abstract, as they use / To say, who have no Mistresse but their Muse" (my italics). This phrase, which states that love is not a refined platonic abstraction, is more philosophic than the final version because Donne came to feel that he needed to sound more straightforward here, so the phrase became "pure, *and* abstract, as they use / To say, which . . ." This, by the way, is a good case to test the "connection" of Group V with Group II through L74 and HK2. Both those manuscripts omit the poem, but Cy and P bear their witness as usual, and are supported by Group V manuscripts from both other sets—by all of Group V, apart from another omission. The end of "The Apparition" gives a striking example:

109

> *... and since my love is spent,*
> *I' had rather thou shouldst painfully repent,*
> *Than by my threatenings rest still innocent.*

I had thought of this as emerging white hot from the anvil, already needing a heavy stress on *thou*, implying "as I do now," with two great pauses to mark the increasing hammer-blows of "*rest ... still ... inn—.*" But a first draft "keep thee innocent" is attested by Cy, P, A25, JC (and again omit L74, HK2). I suppose that too could be pronounced with a heavy irony on *innocent*, and maybe it is a comfort to find that the poet could only slowly cook up the pretence of being so cross. It is fairly strong evidence of revision; here again, one might say that the copyist merely garbled, but two independent sets of Group V would have to garble the same way.

As a rule, Donne's corrections were improvements, and he made extremely few changes for religious, political or sexual security; so most of his changes tell us little. One sometimes finds him misled by a current fashion. Thus, towards the end of that determinedly good-humored poem about loss of money, "The Bracelet," the curse on the imaginary finder rises for a moment to real solemnity:

> *... love; marriage*
> *Afflict thee, and, at thy lives last moment,*
> *May thy swolne sinnes themselves to thee present.*
> *But, I forgive; Repent thou honest man:*
> *Gold is restorative, restore it then ...*

Last is attested by A25, Cy, P, B—all three sets of Group V; and accepted by Grierson and the first edition which prints the poem. But Professor Gardner prints *latest*, following all the reputable manuscripts. Very likely Donne made the change in 1614, when he had often been accused of "deserving hanging for not keeping accent." In an effort to appear more decorous, he adopted what we now think very ugly, a "Simpsonian rhyme." This means rhyming an unstressed syllable with a stressed syllable, as happens without effort if you put *latest*; but the ear of Donne had been much better employed in the first version, where awe and solemn delay turn *moment* into a spondee. However, maybe neither version is very good, and the reader of Professor Gardner is more likely to be shocked at the start of "The Legacie":

> *When I dyed last, and, Deare, I dye*
> *As often as from thee I goe,*
> *Though it be but an hour agoe,*
> *And Lovers hours be full eternity,*
> *I can remember yet, that I . . .*

Professor Gardner omits *but*, with strong authority from Groups I and II, saying that to add this word "gives eight syllables at the cost of sense. The point is that even though it was as long as an hour ago he can still remember." This capacity for chop-logic in Professor Gardner's work seemed to me at first to make her peculiarly unable to interpret the poems of Donne. "The point is" that our minds are endowed with several different ways of experiencing or estimating time, immensely out of step with one another, so that logic would be equally satisfied by "as long as" (I can yet remember) and "as short as" (I am already in despair). To convey this idea of the double time scale decisively, at the start of a lyric, it is essential to have an apparent illogic, to have the paradox of *but*. No wonder that the first edition and Grierson retain *but*, and it is attested by HK4 (the other Group V manuscripts seem to fall down here, but HK4 is the chief of them). However, after giving full weight to this, one must still agree with Professor Gardner that Donne himself cut out *but* in 1614, presumably for the very reason she has

111

given. I now think that she is in close touch with a part of his mind, but one that his editors have been quite right in rejecting, and should continue to reject, because it harms, rather than improves, his poems.

The songs, and as she remarks this poem is "near to song," make a separate problem because Donne was evidently trying to help the composer, and perhaps coax a particular composer. In "The Prohibition," I thought at first that Professor Gardner was being merely malignant when she printed for the last lines: "Then, least thy love, hate and mee thou undoe, / O let mee live, yet love and hate mee too." Grierson and the first edition, with sturdy Group V support (HK2, P, B), give an ending which (instead of these hideous gasps) can be read with calm pleasure as completing a demonstration: "Lest thou thy love and hate and mee undoe, / To let mee live, O love and hate mee too." Surely this is what should be printed, but she is probably right in estimating that her version is the final draft that Donne had written on the page. He was envisaging a very operatic performance by a singer; but did composers in the 1590s write in that way? I wish I were less ignorant about this interesting case. No contemporary setting has survived.

The best of the songs, and the first to appear in a song-book, is the "The Expiration," and here it is illuminating to have available the first stage in the writing, probably altered almost at once, when he added the final couplet of the verse. What it shows is that the poetry depended on a story, which the hearer of the song must guess at, and Donne altered the words to fit when he invented a bit more story:

> *So, so, leave off this last lamenting kisse,*
> *Which sucks two soules, and vapors Both away,*
> *Turn thou ghost that way, and let mee turn this,*
> *And let our souls benight our happy day.*

I give the first draft, as recorded by Groups III and V, hoping the reader may thus appreciate how strong and consistent it is so far. The legend that a devil sucked out a soul in a kiss gets extended to the idea that each lover is a devil to the other, and the souls thus extracted make a fog, darkening a day previously sunlit. So far they are merely lovers with feelings that drag them into conflict; but then he began inventing a larger and more Byronic story, which starts with the couplet added to the first quatrain. They have run away together, and already on the first day they are both ruined by their mutual love, they find they hate each other; or rather, they find that life has become unendurable, either together or apart. The previous picture or conceit needs now to be blurred or enlarged; it is their wilfulness or their inherent characters, their *selves* and not any trivial superstition, which spoil what ought to be the *happiest* day of their lives.

To finish this brief survey of the songs, I need to give a clear example of the moral strength of the editor in "The Message":

> *Send home my harmlesse heart againe,*
> *Which no unworthy thought should staine,*
> *But if it be taught by thine*
> > *To make jestings*
> > *Of protestings . . .*

Easy grace takes a lot of struggle, and Donne had evidently (when you see all the trivial variants in the apparatus) worked hard, scribbling above the lines, before he felt content; then he wrote out the verse separately. This in itself would create a puzzle for a commited Group V copier. Feeling now at ease, the poet himself made a slip more usual among copiers; he wrote *which* instead of *but* at the start of the third line, "catching it up" from the line before. Little did he know that he would encounter the serious side of Professor Gardner: "It is impossible, having regard to the agreement of I, II, *Dob*, S96, to regard 'But' as anything but an emendation in *Lut* to avoid the repetition that Grierson disliked. The remaining manuscripts rewrite the line to make it conform to 1. 3, HK2 and A25 showing a first stage in a process completed in P, B, JC." No literary considerations, none of that chop-logic that is her softer side, are interposed here; it is a straight kill. And yet what really happened must be perfectly well known to Professor Gardner; she hardly pretends otherwise. If a copyist had made this mistake, she would have thrown it out at once, feeling that she was putting the man in his place; but when the author does it, she insists that he must abide by it. It is interesting to find here that she regards the Group V manuscripts as making contacts across their sets; but perhaps one or two of the ancestors of Group V, when confronted with this difficult case, wrote down one or two alternatives.

Keynes' account of induction says that a theory becomes more probable each time it is verified, but only by a process of multiplication, so that if the probability was zero to start with it remains zero after however many times. Of course I think that my theory has a positive initial probability, but I can hardly hope that these minor examples would ever convince a settled opponent. The following case appears decisive to me because no tolerable alternative theory can be proposed. In "The Dreame" the poet apologizes to the lady for mistaking her for God (as Petrarchan poets do) because he realizes now that, since she is better than God, she was insulted by the comparison. All Group V report him saying: "I do confess, I could not choose but be / Profane, to think thee anything but thee." and when, in all manuscripts except the Group V ones, he is made to say "*it* could not choose . . . / *Profaneness* . . . ," it is plain that the poet himself got cold feet, and inserted a useless precaution. No one else would have thought that this tiny indirection would be enough to make him safe; and therefore the Group V manuscripts must be reporting his first version.

Another decisive case is found in the elegy "Natures Lay Ideot," which presents the poet as scolding a girl whom he taught how to make love, with the result that she married a wealthy husband. The husband is jealous and tries to seclude her, but the poet suspects that she has a platoon of lovers, and why is he, the very source of all this busy happiness, not among them? The indignant tutor claims that he has

> *with amorous delicacies*
> *Refin'd thee into a blisful Paradise.*
> *Thy graces and good words my creatures be; . . .*

Then Donne waited for a moment, to decide how to finish the couplet. That he has established her in a paradise is the starting point, so she is Eve, and has acquired risky but important knowledge; he is the creator of the woman she has now become —hence the word *creatures*. There is an ambiguity about *paradise*; she has herself become a paradise for men, but also she is enjoying unwonted luxury; he has both changed her into a paradise and led her into one. And so far as he can remember, he selected this dull girl by a pure whim. In fact, he behaved like the God of Calvin, deciding at random which men to send to heaven and which to hell. The crucial debate about whether men are saved by grace or by works would thus come to his mind; and, come to think of it, he has a fair claim to be the serpent as well. He drew a line through *words,* writing *works* above it, and could now lay down the clincher: "I planted knowledge and life's tree in thee." In this case, what the page retained was evidence not of a later improvement but of the actual process of composition.

It is pathetic to see in the apparatus how all the prosy

manuscripts of Groups I and II give the sexy variant *works,*
whereas all the Group V manuscripts give the dull variant
words. Professor Gardner, to do her justice, can spot which is
the dull one, and she is determined to print that, though it is
embarrassing to have to agree with Group V. The Restoration
editor could also see the point, so he broke with Group V here,
thus continuing to disagree with Professor Gardner. Her note
says: " 'Works' would appear to have arisen independently in
Group I, TCC, and *Dob,* owing to the influence of 'graces.' The
editor of 1633 presumably corrected his Group I manuscript
by recourse to his Group II manuscript which read with TCD.
'Good words' takes us back to 1. 13. Taught by him she can
now both flatter and praise." Undoubtedly it takes us back,
but a phrase in a poem sometimes needs to take us forward as
well as back; and, even if we only look back, the poem insists
that her callow flattery would never have caught her this rich
husband. Her good works are something she has learned
through the implanting of life's tree, and one is tempted to
think they are a skill at pleasing men in bed; that indeed is
the joke, but the meaning needs to be something larger as well
—it was not in bed, presumably, that she first charmed the pro-
spective husband. I daresay the witty repartee of the traditional
barmaid had more to do with it than flattery, and this would
allow Donne, when he initially wrote *good words,* to intend a
contrast with line 13 (which says: "Remember since all thy
words us'd to bee/ To every suitor; *I, 'if my friends agree.*")

It is wildly improbable that Groups I, II, and III all
independently made the same mistake, as Professor Gardner
supposes. No doubt one often heard about grace and works in
sermons, but here the "graces" of a young woman are in question, a sufficiently positive idea; the mind would not habitually
leap away from that to a highly technical use of the word in the
singular. Admittedly, the mind of Donne did it once; but he
had a very special reason for such a leap—it felt deliciously

absurd to make his own love as capricious as the love of the God of Calvin. Having once thought of the joke, he repeated it; in the first line of the elegy "Change," where he is saying that he does not expect his mistress to be faithful: "Although thy hand and faith, and good workes too, / Have seal'd thy love which nothing should undoe . . ." It has become a boring joke, which he throws away. According to Professor Gardner, Donne could not have thought of this joke, but three copiers, none of them thinking it a joke, wrote it down by a verbal association with a pair of words often heard in church. It may be answered that my view also entails improbability, because at least one of the Group II copiers, with *workes* before him, has to reinvent *words*. But he might well do this to avoid the suggestion of blasphemy, so he need not be supposed to do it by a meaningless verbal association.

Many people, I should say, have at the back of their minds a real moral objection to the earlier Donne love poems because they regard the poet as a cad who boasts of getting girls into trouble, as in "Love's Alchymie," a particularly boyish poem: "I have lov'd, and got, and told . . ." So far from that, "Nature's Lay Ideot" shows him feeling confident, in a rough brotherly way, that he is giving the girls a leg up in the world, or doing them good, anyhow. I had felt that the distaste of Professor Gardner for the poet deserved respect if it had this kind of ground, but then I was taken aback by her introductory note to "Love's Lay Ideot": "This Elegy may owe something to Tibullus, I.vi.5–14, though it is more innocent. Only 'Jealousy' among Donne's *Elegies* is concerned with adultery." Both Grierson and Leishmann, whose advice she generally considers, would have told her that the girl is now married. It might be argued that the girl has merely found a rich keeper; but this would only remove the point of the homely story. When Donne first met her she was using charms to learn her future husband's name and negotiating with suitors; now Donne says

"Thou art not by so many duties his" (the man who is trying to keep her in purdah) "as mine" (because the poet enabled her to achieve her present status). Surely the duties to a husband need to be the other half of the paradox, or it has no bite. Besides, she has enough security of tenure to risk having lovers on the side, and the poet boasts that he brought her to this strong position. Tibullus, I find, writes about one adulterer supplanting another; in the iron marriage market of the grandees of imperial Rome, a girl would not catch a rich husband merely by her charms. Nor would she among Elizabethan grandees, but city life had more room for exceptions. I expect that this girl, as she was living respectably and had advisers, though separated from her family, would be working in a shop. The world described by Donne really is more innocent, though that would hardly be what Professor Gardner meant. Maybe she just thinks that the poet had a lustful daydream after one of his Latin lessons, and never met a girl at all. But the poem breathes a rather comfortable air, belonging to the time when he was spending his inheritance, so we should try to clear our minds of bitter irony. He really did consider that a girl was engaged in good works when she learned how to give men pleasure.

Grierson considered that the first edition was likely to be right, and that corrections from the manuscripts should be made only when a poem required them to restore its beauty. It was essential for Professor Gardner to reduce the authority of this edition, or she could not introduce so many novelties (and, if they are all ugly ones, it is fair to remember that Grierson had first pick). She maintains firmly that the author had no voice in the edition. Obviously Donne should have put his affairs in the hands of a good lawyer, but he was restrained by a mixture of motives, some devotional, some worldly, and probably some just superstitious; so that it is rather hard to guess how he would behave. He was very accustomed to negotiating fine points of conscience, weighing up the opposing claims of immensely diverse influences. Several people, we know, were preparing a text for publication as soon as he died; and they would think this a reason, not for hiding from him, but for obtaining an audience so as to coax him. It would be easy to place their requests on high grounds. The divine poems were of course to be included; and while he was choosing one of his poems to be sung at his funeral, did he consider himself forbidden to get its text right? While he was posing in his coffin for the sculptor, would Donne tell the editor that he was too busy about the Lord's work for earthly vanities? A good deal of elegant affectation of that sort would no doubt be expected and allowed for, but he could probably be coaxed into giving a certain amount of help. Professor Gardner says "there is no sign" of it, but signs of it would be just what he took care to avoid. Probably an old friend would be primed with a list of specific questions about doubtful passages; it would be easy to compile. Donne, after all, might reasonably have become offended if he had not been approached in this way. But one may suspect that, after cooperating the first time, he refused when a second batch of questions were brought the following week. The editor himself then made some bold decisions, though without this encouragement and annoyance he would not have presumed. We get some bad bold decisions, as Professor Gardner says, but also some good ones; and if we get any good ones we may reasonably expect they come from the author.

The reading *contract,* instead of *extract* at the end of "The Canonization" seems to me a clear case. After defending his runaway marriage, Donne claims that he and his wife will

119

eventually become saints and apostles of the religion of true love (implying that the pretentions of Christianity to be a religion of love have been exposed, but the dean could simply ignore that part); people will invoke them saying:

> *You, to whom love was peace, that now is rage;*
> *Who did the worlds whole soule contract, and drove*
> > *Into the glasses of your eyes,*
> > *(So made such mirrors, and such spies,*
> *That they did all to you epitomize,)*
> > *Countries, Towns, Courts: Beg from above*
> > *A patterne of your love!*

There is a second change, of *your* to *our* in the last line, but this is also found in two Group I manuscripts. Donne might well have felt in 1614 that this made the covert meaning a bit more tolerable, after wondering perhaps whether he ought to suppress the poem altogether; it says "Ask God to teach us the kind of love we all need to learn" rather than "Ask God to teach us to love like you." So probably this is also a change by the author, though it makes little difference. Professor Gardner's note says that the reading *contract* "destroys the alchemical metaphor and with it the pun on glasses and makes the verb 'drove' unintelligible. . . . The 'soul' of the world is extracted and driven into their eyes . . . by sublimation and distillation, driving it through the pipes of the still into the 'glasses,' or vessels, in which it is stored. These 'glasses' then become mirrors." Also she refers us to her introduction (p. lxxxvi) where she says that the alchemical metaphor "is reduced to the apparently more obvious notion of 'contracting' the soul of the 'whole world' into the small space of the lovers' eyes. But, on reflection, it can be seen that it is absurd to apply spatial notions to the soul, and that this idea of much in little weakly anticipates the next thought: that the eyes, by the infusion of the *anima mundi*, are made mirrors and spies to epitomize all . . ." Just so, I expect, would the young man have defended his text, but I still think that the old one was right to change it. What does the thought gain by dragging in the chemistry on top of the optics? They are both only illustrations of the thought of the microcosm, and there is no room for both in one sentence. The "glasses" have to be grotesquely transformed from containers to lenses the very instant after they have been mentioned ("glasses *of* your eyes"); the young man would say that this insists upon the full complexity of the thought, and illustrates the compression described, but the old man would call this "showing off." The limbeck and the telescope habitually came into the poet's mind together, meaning the same kind of thing, and here they are crudely jammed on top of one another. It is not even as if he used the world-soul when he has got it; the prayer goes "above," presumably to heaven. To say that the simplification *contract* "weakly anticipates the next thought" presumes that there is a progress or at least a succession of thoughts, but they are jumbled together within one sentence, one breath. And it is not true that the correction makes the verb *drove* unintelligible; writers on optics habitually say that the lenses *direct* the rays of light, and Donne himself says it in the "Refusal to Woodward": "for as / Men force the sunne with much more force to passe, / By gathering his beames with a cristall glasse, / So wee . . ." (had better only read our own poems). The view of Professor Gardner that light is not spiritual enough to describe the soul, which needs instead a strong brew of organic matter, may be very sound; but surely she would not claim to rewrite every text in which the metaphor occurs. However, I am not sure that these considerations would be the decisive ones. The old Donne had had experience of doctors, and the distilled medicines of Paracelsus were re-

121

markably kill-or-cure; maybe he now realized that pumping stuff like that into lovers' eyes would not convey the detached but universally healing balm that he had intended. I can understand a reader preferring the manuscript version, but surely it is hard to deny that the change for the edition was made by the author.

The variant in "A Valediction: Of the Booke" can also be defended; poems exalting his marriage would no doubt strike the old man as high-minded enough to deserve his attention. Anne's collection of their hasty notes of assignation will become a sacred book, the gospel of the religion of true love, powerful enough to build another civilization after a new Dark Age. Everything can be extracted from it; statesmen, for instance (says the poem), will understand their occupation from ours, because both love and statescraft are spoiled if they are analyzed:

> *In both they doe excell*
> *Who the present governe well,*
> *Whose weaknesse none doth, or dares tell;*
> *In this thy booke, such will their something see*
> *As in the Bible some can find Alchimy.*

The first edition has *something*, but all manuscripts (except two) have *nothing*. Professor Gardner remarks in her note: "I regard the agreement of O and P with 1633 in reading 'there something' as coincidental. It is an obvious sophistication of an at first sight difficult reading." In her introduction (p. lxxxvii), she adds: "Here we have not only a weak anticipation of the following lines, but also a redundant 'there'. In this case the edition has the support of two degenerate manuscripts, O and P, agreeing accidentally with one of their characteristic corruptions." The verse begins "Here Statesmen (or of them, they which can reade)"; after that, even for a copier, it cannot be very difficult to think of their art as "nothing"; one might instead call this fun rather cheap, though fair enough from a poet who has just daffed the world aside. Professor Gardner's complaint about "weak anticipation" of the next line (not *lines*, as it is the last one of the verse) is puzzling because any comparison (introduced with "As") must be anticipated by the thing it is compared to; how is this different if you read "nothing"? I suspect she just means that the word *some* occurs twice with different meanings, but Donne was too concentrated upon the meaning to be distracted by such an echo. Professor Gardner's accusation of redundance is justified if you attach importance to the misspelling of *their*; but surely there must be a lot of other misspellings not recorded in the apparatus. Queried passages were read aloud to Donne, who did not mull over the text, so misspellings probably were often overlooked. Furthermore, Grierson, who was experienced in these spellings, treats this as insignificant.

In this poem, Donne is not mainly concerned with distributing contempt. Every skill nurtured within a civilized society has some kind of merit, he is saying, even if a very paltry one, and that merit, even if not derived from, is irradiated by the central belief on which the whole society is constructed. In the new society, when the crucial belief is in sexual love as exemplified by Donne and his wife, the politicians will be bound to understand their odd duties much more clearly; if Donne had gone into the matter further, we might find that some of the worst faults of the profession, if not justified, were at least made to appear in a better light. Speaking in his rough manly way, even while in this mood of charitable casuistry, he might describe the tiny merit of their trade as practically nothing. But he would not agree with the explanatory note of Professor Gardner: "Statesmen will find their own 'nothing' in the 'nothing' of the lovers in the same way as Alchemists find support for their doctrines in the Bible." This is neo-Christian cynicism run mad. Donne really does intend to boast about his marriage; you can impute bad motives to him, or lies, and you are within the field of human probability, but if you say he insinuated a bitter irony into the middle of this fighting and defiant praise of the most decisive action of his life you are mistaking him for some other author. The glittering praises of ambition, such as law and politics have to offer, are sure to corrupt, but he drives this home chiefly to heighten the contrast with his own incorruptible love. When Professor Gardner prints with quote-marks "the 'nothing' of the lovers" she implies that Donne himself calls his love nothing; and he does not in this poem, at any rate. He might perhaps imply a defiant recognition that it is nothing in the eyes of the world, but even that would be quite secondary. Does she suppose that he calls the Bible nothing, too?

All the same, it evidently did cross his mind, at some later stage, that the whole passage, beginning with the humorous admission of the mystery of love, might be misunderstood in the way his editor now does; that was why he changed *nothing* to *something*. Also the old man would reflect that he had had a certain amount to do with political decisions, and that the jealous impatience of the young man had rather spoiled the logic of the passage by calling all such work "nothing." The change is much more likely to be made by the author, at any rate, than by a printer so innocent that he never heard of jeering at politicians. This much seems clear, and I am rather sorry to risk confusing it by a conjecture; but the testimony of O and P might be true as well. When Donne was first thrown out of the world, because of his marriage, he was defiant but not sour about the world—he expected to make a come-back. It was only gradually that he lost hope of gaining civil employment by recommending himself to politicians; so he might have written in "nothing" one later day to express his irritation. But then, "they which can read" at the beginning of the verse has already a good deal of this cheerful contempt. I only feel that, as Professor Gardner makes unduly heavy demands upon coincidence, they had better be reduced where possible.

I am also emboldened to plead for another case: the beauty of a line in the *Divine Poems* (ed. Helen Gardner [Oxford, 1952])—the only case in that earlier edition where she could be accused of spoiling a line. Following all manuscripts, and rejecting all editions, she printed a line in *Holy Sonnets added in 1635*, number 3 as: "Because I did suffer I must suffer pain." Her note added, as additional reason for rejecting *'Cause*, that "There is no other example in the *Concordance* of Donne's using this abbreviation." It was a splendid defiance or declaration of a program and the only trouble was that she then explained, to comfort us, how the line should be read aloud. Stresses are on *cause, did, suff, must suff, pain*, making six not five but, as I understand, rightly treating *must suff* as a spondee, or a jammed stress. Now, this reading is far too awful: it is the voice of a determinedly cheerful teacher drumming the point into the heads of some hideously thick-witted class. Donne is regarding himself as a predestined victim and speaking with a kind of awe; we do not easily like him for it, but we should allow him to say: "all those girls gave me hell, now God will give me hell because I tried to please all those girls." It needs to be read as if liturgically, with almost the same stresses all along—the victim is in a trance. (There are some who maintain that he is lying to God here, just as earlier he lied to his smart young friends, because he never really had any mistresses at all. If this were the case, I myself would think that the pronunciation of the poems hardly mattered.) During his lifetime, Donne was often accused of being metrically rough, but he probably did not intend to be, except in the *Satires*; he just relied on the reader to give the lines the intonation demanded by the meaning, which in itself was often strained. No doubt he was accustomed to make this answer, in a general way; so the questioner would be likely to have such a case on his list. Donne would readily pronounce the line so that the "be" of *because* though present did not spoil the rhythm, and would be told: "Yes, but unless you alter it they will go on pronouncing it like this": he would then be made to hear the Gardner intonation and would agree at once even to printing the "poetical" form *'Cause*, which he would naturally dislike. He assumed that this sacrifice would be enough, and so it was for three centuries, but Professor Gardner got him in the end. The purpose of imagining this little scene is to test whether it feels possible, and it feels to me positively likely. Surely one ought to be very chary of rejecting a variant in the first edition for which such an intelligible motive can be found.

One or two other remarks about rhythm may be fitted in here as general support. Professor Gardner is often wrong when she gives the scansion; for example, in "A Valediction: of Weeping," "Weep me not dead, in thine arms, but forbear" is given stresses on *weep, me, dead, thine, arms, bear.* I thought at first the extra stress on *me* was one of the misprints, but she adds: "The line depends on our giving the metrical stress, which as often in Donne falls on pronouns, sufficient weight." A stress on *thine* is wanted, I agree, to imply "It is odd to be in danger when in the arms of any woman, but in yours above all," but what can be the implications of the stress on *me?* "Weep yourself dead in mine, you pig," or more elaborately: "I suppose you have a queue of men coming to do this. Well, I'm the one that's going to get away." Of course she did not intend this, but she does seem to mean by it that the poet was egotistical. The third line of "The Flea" says "It suck'd me first, and now sucks thee," thus giving a firm foundation for the metaphysical arguments that follow. Professor Gardner prints "Me it suck'd," with the note: "The inversion throws the stress where it is needed, on the two personal pronouns." But there is no such need; he intends to sound cool here, before he starts to drive home his argument. And Professor Gardner is following L74, HK2, Cy, P. The main body of Group I is against her, so she must attach some importance to the choice. However, Group II agrees with her, and indeed the line-up of the manuscripts is rather eccentric; it was his best-known poem, and at such a point a scribe might often ignore the text he was copying. I expect her theory is right here, only she did not draw the conclusion. Her introduction allowed some respect for the combination L74, HK2 (unlike any of the rest of Group V) as perhaps sometimes reporting an earlier version, later corrected by the poet himself. She was right about the detail "Me it suck'd"; Donne first wrote in a blaze of comic argument, and later (perhaps as late as 1614) realized that a cooler lead-in gave a better effect. By the rules, surely, Professor Gardner is not allowed to print the author's first thoughts. I think they often ought to be printed, but in this case Donne, by smoothing the dramatic effect, made an actual tiny improvement, which ought to be preserved.

The reputation of Donne as metrically uncivilized still hangs about, and I think nowadays chiefly from the one line, introducing a splendidly bland and smooth romantic poem: "Blasted with sighs, and surrounded with teares." *Surround* is from *superundare,* and the *Oxford English Dictionary* (1961) tells us that it was sometimes spelt "sur-und" even into the eighteenth century. Editors would be well advised to print "sur-unded" here, to make plain that the word was pronounced like "sur-tax." I find that this discovery was anticipated by John Crowe Ransom in *The New Criticism* (Norfolk, Conn., 1941) and by others; Professor Gardner need not have been reduced to blaming the line for "a lack of metrical tact." On another occasion she does envisage an archaic stress, but needlessly, I think, in "A Feaver":

> *And yet she cannot wast by this*
> > *Nor long beare this torturing wrong,*
> *For much corruption needful is*
> > *To fuell such a feaver long.*

Tormenting instead of *torturing* is read by HK2, JC, S (that is, one from each set of Group V), and in Group III O'F corrects *torturing* to *tormenting*. Professor Gardner's note says: "If the French or Latin stress is given the line runs smoothly . . . With the usual stress the line is harsh and the reading 'tormenting', found in some manuscripts of weak authority, is an obvious attempt to smooth it and avoid two successive inverted stresses." As I understand, a stress on *ure* in *torture* would have been likely a generation or two earlier, but Donne was determinedly not an archaist, and would pronounce the word as Shakespeare or Jonson expected actors to do on stage. (J. A. Bartlett's *Shakespeare Concordance* [London, 1906] is decisive for the modern intonation.) Donne first wrote what Group V reports, *tormenting*, and because *long* and *ment* stand out this feels like a smooth line. Too smooth for the meaning, the poet decided when looking it over (but whether a few minutes later or ten years later I cannot tell), so he wrote *torturing* above the line (not later than 1614) for the purpose of making the scansion more strained. There now has to be a jammed stress or spondee; the stresses are *nor, long bear, tort,* and *wrong,* making the whole verse very graceful and expressive. O'F made the change back to *tormenting* because O'F (here and elsewhere) was becoming increasingly inclined to think that the bold policy of the Group V copyists had been the correct one.

The dating of the poems is an important part of rescuing Donne, because it is capable of having great effect on judgment of the poet's character. I should however testify at once that to have the *Songs and Sonnets* put in an order which can be more or less remembered is an immense convenience; going back to the Grierson edition, after using the Gardner, is like having the lights go out.

The "Refusal to Woodward," as it needs to be called, a verse letter beginning "Like one who'in her third widowhood," is crucial here and Mr. Milgate's edition has been a great help about it. He agrees with Professor Gardner that it was written in 1597–98, whereas I stick to Grierson's dating of 1603–4, not long after Donne's marriage. It seems to me that my opponents fail to imagine the letter as a real one, conveying a real snub, and therefore do not grasp how damaging to Donne's character their date would be. In 1597, after bringing himself into favorable notice by volunteering for the Islands voyage, and making friends on it with a number of well-placed young men, he and Wotton (as Mr. Milgate remarks) "were securing positions at Court"; and early next year Donne became secretary to the lord keeper. We have two verse letters to Wotton at this time, which were handed to Woodward for his collection, and they do, I grant, speak with lordly contempt for the great world which he is observing, but they make no bones about his desire to succeed in it. The letter to Woodward, on the other hand, might be from a yogi in a cave, fed by the local peasants; it recommends complete retirement and self-concentration, so that, if a man is still a poet (as Donne is not), he should read only his own poems and not those of his friends. It is a noble poem, fierce and bare, but it is perhaps a bit presuming even when Donne has been thrown out of his worldly job, and would be gross impudence if written when he was just seeking one or settling into one. In the later part of 1597, Donne had sent Woodward a verse letter praising him for having achieved philosophic retirement, and then another (if Mr. Milgate puts them in order of composition) thanking him extravagantly for sending a poem which had brought Donne back to life. Woodward must be supposed to ask him for poems in return, and receives this astonishing snub. To strengthen his date, Mr. Milgate even accepts a note of manuscript K, saying that the poem was written at court. That would make it farcically hypocritical, fit for Dickens. Mr. Milgate himself speaks of manuscript K with severe contempt, and would certainly not use it for any less desired conclusion (poor K was merely remembering one of the letters to Wotton, which says it was written from court). Maybe critics assume that bad taste must be expected in the metaphysical style, so that it can be ignored; but, in any style, *manure thyselfe then* is a great snub: it has to mean "Roll in your own dung; do not come nosing round after mine." Surely it is likely to mark a real break, with a cause for it, and we know that Woodward was never able to copy out the songs and sonnets. But he was allowed to copy out the two letters to Wotton, probably later that year, and the altered text of the satires the year after.

The main argument of Professor Gardner for this date is that all the poems in the first section of W are not later than 1598, "with one explicable exception." This is a sonnet to an earl, introducing a series of holy sonnets, which after being presented to the earl somehow became available for Woodward to copy, and for no other copyist. He put the introductory sonnet among his verse letters, which had had no addition for a long time. Yes, but this explanation, showing that any verse letter could be added to the list, applies just as well to the snub from Donne. It is a classic example of the "proof" which is a total illusion; but somehow the phrase "with one explicable exception," perhaps because it is hard to pronounce, freezes all objection upon the lips of the common reader; it is the voice of science in person. Next we have a real argument, though a slight one; that most of the manuscripts agree in putting the "Refusal" near to the "Storm" and the first two letters to Wotton. But Woodward's collection was necessarily the only source for the "Refusal," and probably for the two letters to Wotton; the copiers did not want any of the rest of Woodward's collection, the trivial letters of the youthful Donne to his friends, so these were written out together. I grant that, on my view, Woodward made a slight break in the order of time, putting the "Refusal" before the two Wotton letters, but he was not committed to any order; he might put this final letter to himself at the end of the letters to early friends, before starting on letters to impressive social figures. Or he may have wanted the refusal to look less like a snub, but quite possibly he never knew he had been snubbed; in its incidentals, the "Refusal" is almost unctuously affectionate, as if Donne felt determined to choke off the demand but without making an enemy. It was rather a disagreeable job, so he might not have wanted to keep a copy of the poem, not being at all a spiteful man. I have last to consider Mr. Milgate's argument from the style. The poet would feel socially embarrassed, and it is natural that he began in the formless unbuttoned style of his letters when younger; but he soon managed to ride away grandly on his moral high horse, in a uniquely grand use of his later style. This did not have to be written at a date in between them. After the initial verses, both the style and the exalted stoicism, as Grierson remarks, are nearest to a letter written to Goodyer from Mitcham, where Donne went to a cottage with his family in 1605.

Around 1603–4, after a mood of defiant exaltation over

his marriage which produced a few poems, Donne had settled into a mood from which the "Refusal" could be written sincerely. Also Woodward was preparing to go to Venice on the embassy of Wotton, and might well ask for a text of the *Songs and Sonnets,* which would help him to make grand friends. These are strong reasons, but I think more is needed to explain the fierceness of the reply. I think Donne was advised, probably by Wotton who was now in a position to hear such things, that Woodward had shown round his collection of Donne's verse letters too freely, and that this had been bad for Donne's prospects of renewal official employment. He recently had had to defend his marriage, we should remember, by an official assurance that he had not been a seducer of young ladies; no doubt he told his friends (like Byron) that he had been more raped than anybody since the Trojan War, but it would leave his nerves a bit raw. Mr. Milgate gives very helpful background notes on the early letters. It turns out that when Donne was twenty he wrote several of them to Woodward's younger brother Tom, aged eighteen, threatening to die for love of him and suchlike; the collection included an answer from Tom. This poem is very plucky and admiring, and much more like real poetry than what Donne had written to him (it is in Grierson as well as Milgate, tucked away in the notes). It would leave a scandalmonger in no doubt that the two lads had been up to something together, and also it insinuated that the wit of Donne's poetry or the interest of his conversation perhaps derived from secret heretical opinions: "The nimble fyre which in thy braynes doth dwell, / It is the fyre of Heaven or that of hell?" Indeed, several of the witty comparisons in the surviving letters to young friends would have been considered blasphemous, as we know (Mr. Milgate points out) because all of the copyists who accepted these letters omitted the comparisons. One way or another, Donne would find this a peculiarly exasperating corpse to emerge from the glacier just at that time. Maybe the sheer success of Tom's poem was an extra irritant; O and P both copy it out on two separate occasions, and though they of course were written much later, that in itself might be regarded as evidence for a prolonged vogue. So poor Donne need hardly be blamed for his rudeness to Woodward, who may, in any case, have remained confident that the poems were to the credit of all concerned.

Grierson in the apparatus to his text gives some interesting variants in the "Refusal," mainly from the Group V manuscripts Cy and P; the Group III manuscripts S96 and O'F sometimes agree with them. Most of these variants seem plainly wrong, and the first edition right; but the second, and later editions, even until 1669, tend to adopt them; this poem is a particularly striking example of a general trend. This pro-Group V faction at least shows that the problems of text were getting attention. Mr. Milgate's apparatus tells us nothing about such matters, as he is a disciple of Professor Gardner. She herself records the Group V variants very fully, as she has sometimes a use for them; but she tells us earnestly that they are valueless. He believes what she says, so he thinks recording them must be a waste of time. As a minor example, consider:

> *You know, Physitians, when they would infuse*
> *Into any' oyle, the Soules of Simples, use*
> *Places, where they may lie still warme, to chuse.*

Mr. Milgate prints "Soule," and his apparatus says: "Soule MSS: Soules 1633." It is literally correct, because he only undertakes to record the variants from a few manuscripts, listed separately for each poem, and habitually excluding Group V. But it is the wrong reading, and the entry is part of a cumulative smear against the first edition. The plural *soules* is needed because different essences or medicines were distilled from different herbs, but this might be "understood"; also, as Mr.

Milgate himself makes clear in his note, it was the distilled essences, not the untreated herbs, which were kept warm—*they* has to refer to *soules*. Grierson's apparatus has "Soules 1633–69, Cy, P"; it is the one occasion in the poem where the first edition anticipates the swing-over to Group V readings among the six later editions. But some of the Group V readings here are certainly wrong; as when at the beginning of the fourth verse ("For, though to use it seem") has *use* by influence from the beginning of the third ("Though to use, and love poetry"), which weakens the sentence but happens not to make nonsense; this typical copyist's error cannot be Donne's first draft. Nor should we expect that, because the poem could not be taken from one. It appears among the Group I manuscripts, deriving from 1614, whereas the other distinctive verse letters of Woodward do not. One letter to young Tom gets in, perhaps the dullest of them, and a Group I manuscript heads it "An old letter." Evidently it had just happened to be kept among Donne's papers. Woodward had got hold of one of the *Songs and Sonnets*, "A Jet Ring Set," and this did not appear in Group I either. So we may be sure that Donne had still not forgiven him in 1614. His fault had been to put unpermitted material into circulation, and he firmly did the same to the poem which snubbed him for it; so Donne could get a copy of his poem in 1614, but not in his own handwriting. He corrected its errors from memory and the resulting document joined his collection, for the use of all subsequent copiers; but here only a fanatical Group V ancestor would reject the corrections, as they were the only part in Donne's handwriting; they were only rejected by the ancestor of Cy and P. This actual plural was probably not erased by Donne, but merely rather hard to read. We of course have manuscript W, copied in old age from the original letter by the man who had received it, but he makes at least one error (line four has to read *too* not *so*), and Donne might be slightly wrong about what he had written ten years

134

before. Still, the survival of W is enough to make sure that Donne did not say his Muse was as a chaste *holiness,* which would have been bad taste. I think my theory stands up well to this unusual case.

There is good reason to suppose that the break with Woodward occurred before 1605, when he is known to have been in Venice on Wotton's staff, also that Wotton was concerned in the break, because Woodward was never allowed to copy Donne's verse letter of congratulation to Wotton on becoming ambassador. It is extremely innocuous, so that there could have been no intention of secrecy, or feeling of intimacy in showing it to a subordinate; indeed, it only survives because it was copied in Wotton's Commonplace Book by one of his secretaries. Surely it is remarkable that Woodward could not get a copy, even when on the staff. Elizabethans of course had a keen sense of class, but many habitually crossed class lines. To gratify a cultured inferior by letting him study a piece of one's own grand equipment in public so as to raise him above his colleagues, but playfully as if humouring a foible was the kind of thing Izaak Walton admired Wotton for knowing just how to do. He would not have missed the opportunity if he had not turned against Woodward shortly after the appointment of this subordinate. Indeed, one might suspect that making Woodward act as courier and spy, a job he does not seem to have been especially good at (he got caught), was a means of getting him out of earshot. He was home again in two years, much battered.

One might suppose that he was eventually allowed to copy the *Songs and Sonnets,* and they just got removed from manuscript W, during its centuries in the earl's library, as the most interesting part. But Grierson remarks that the manuscript is still "bound in its original vellum," so that if there had been any excisions, they would have been visible. However, he did again become an intimate friend of Donne when they were quite old, because he alone was given four *Holy Sonnets,* first published by Grierson, which were to be hidden from the world though they seem harmless now. Perhaps by that time he was no longer keen to copy out the *Songs and Sonnets.*

The dating of this minor poem throws a considerable spanner into the theory of Professor Gardner; Donne is found writing that his muse is in a chaste fallowness just when she has him in full production for half the *Songs and Sonnets.* He was not at leisure, she thinks, to read neo-platonic authors till he married for ambition and failed to get the money; the resulting mortification turned his mind to higher things, and though he never experienced fulfillment in love he had a lot of daydreams about it, recorded in poems which appear to be about adultery but are merely the results of sulking to spite his wife. Of course, this habit of reflection upon spiritual matters was gradually leading him towards the church . . . I find almost every aspect of the theory detestable, but I feel now that my *Critical Quarterly* article, though mostly right, was wrong in assuming that Donne could not be neo-platonic, an assumption based on the fact that when he started writing, he revolted against the outlook of Spenser, so he would not have discovered neo-platonism when unemployed. But Plato was widely diffused, and Donne might well go on encountering more of him. A medical man of the time, as C. S. Lewis pointed out, would take *platonic* to mean the belief in middle spirits of earth, air, fire, and water; and it does seem plain that Donne was influenced by Paracelsus, though this has not yet been fully investigated. And then there were the Radical Reformers. The chief support for my position about Donne that has appeared since my "Donne the Spaceman" is to be found in *The Pursuit of the Millenium* (London, 1957), by Norman Cohn and *The Everlasting Gospel* (London, 1958) by A. L. Morton, which dug up evidence about the fanatics of Donne's time. Recent critics have tended to despise poems which recommend freedom of love, calling them soft and sentimental (this has been the "tough" reason for rejecting "There is no pennance due to innocence"); but when Donne said such things they would sound defiant—that was why he was so keen to restrict the circulation of the songs and sonnets. He is recalling the fanatic position, surely, when he writes: "as infinite as it" in "Love's Progress" (l. 38); "all love is wonder" in "Anagram" (l. 25); "all divinity / Is love or wonder" in "Valediction: of the Book" (l. 25). Professor Gardner in her notes generously tells us she cannot trace these to their sources. Donne of course was not himself a Radical Reformer; in a way, he was the opposite, and may have felt that to recall them helped to make an ex-Catholic more acceptable, but anyhow he was alert to the whole theological field. The Reformers were notorious for their sexual as well as their political freedom, and were being stamped out in blood and fire. Though everyone remarked on the ignorance of these low-class fanatics, howling outside in the street, they habitually claimed to have derived their doctrines from Plato.

From the twelfth century onwards, there was a left wing of Christianity in Europe, half quietist and half revolutionary, which maintained that every man may become Christ, may become an avatar of the Logos, as Jesus did. It is the same doctrine as the Hindu "That art Thou"—"At bottom, the soul of each man is the soul of the world." Thus a seventeenth-century writer reports that Harry Nicholas (Morton, *Everlasting Gospel*, p. 39): "maketh every one of his Family of Love to be Christ; yea, and God, and himself God, and Christ in a more excellent manner." At the end of *The Alchemist* one of the disappointed sectarians (Ananias) is jeered off the stage by being called a Harry Nicholas, and Jonson would not have done this unless the sect was familiar to his audience; indeed, Morton assures us that it was well established in England by

1600 (p. 40). Cohn (*Pursuit of Millenium*, p. 304) after full documentation for medieval Europe, gives quotations proving that the doctrine was still firmly held in Cromwell's England: "I do not apprehend that God was only manifest in the flesh of Christ, or the man called Christ; but that he really and substantially dwells in the flesh of other men and Creatures, as in the man Christ." Donne in the love poems often presents himself as a Christ of True Love, founding a colony or teaching a school to promulgate his new doctrine; when you realize this, you are no longer tempted to deny the obvious meaning of the lines in "The Relic": "Thou shalt be a Mary Magdalene, and I / A something else thereby." One might almost say, it is inherent in the idea of the microcosm that each man can represent the whole world; and yet it was enough to turn the commonplace into a dangerous idea, liable to persecution. Then again, we can hardly help feeling in "The Dreame" that Donne is being intellectually facetious, or pointlessly flippant, when he says that his mistress is so much better than God that to mistake her for God would be profane, but some of the adepts of the free spirit, Mr. Cohn tells us, really did entertain this idea, as a result of expecting such a radical improvement (p. 185): "Once the absolute stillness of the divine Oneness has been reached, neither knowledge nor praise nor even the love of God exist any more. 'At the highest point of being, God himself is abandoned by himself in himself'; meaning that the God of Christianity is left behind, in favour of the God of pantheist ecstasy." The authors do not give an actual source for "all divinity is love or wonder," but to find oneself turning into God must excite such feelings as the phrase recalls. This is clear in the Ranter Jacob Bottomley, who while serving in Cromwell's army wrote *The Light and Dark Sides of God* (Cohn, *Pursuit of Millenium*, p. 303): "if I say I see thee, it is nothing but thy seeing of thyself; for there is nothing in me capable of seeing thee but thyself." At any rate, religion was certainly not keeping commandments or performing rituals.

"Infinite as it" would be merely a sex joke, and probably a jeer, if it were not such good poetry. The vagina is as infinite as the soul, and the soul has just been compared to the starry heavens (from "Love's Progress," a rich and mysterious piece of fun). Cupid, we have been told, is an earth-god:

> *Men to such Gods, their sacrificing Coles*
> *Did not in Altars lay, but pits and holes.*
> *Although we see Celestial bodies move*
> *Above the earth, the earth we Till and love:*
> *So we her ayres contemplate, words and heart,*
> *And virtues; but we love the Centrique part.*
>   *Nor is the soul more worthy, or more fit*
> *For love than this, as infinite as it.*
> *But in attaining this desired place*
> *How much they erre; that set out at the face? . . .*

A conscientious historian might feel that we ought not to read back the sentiments of D. H. Lawrence into these obscure oppositions; but they were already familiar. Coppe was a boisterous Cromwellian Ranter who from early youth had been tormented by a craving to swear, and for him the greatest relief of becoming illuminated was that he might now swear even in his sermons (Morton, *Everlasting Gospel*, p. 51): "I had rather hear a mighty Angel (in man) swearing a full-mouthed Oath . . . than hear a zealous Presbyterian, Independent or Spiritual Notionist pray, preach or exercise." "Spiritual Notionist" is a phrase that Lawrence would have enjoyed, and it makes just his usual appeal to class sentiment; the white-collar men, Coppe implies, will spoil everything unless they are prevented from doing so. Norman Cohn regards his Millenarians with cold horror, and indeed many of the medieval continental messiahs ended in a ghastly betrayal of their own ideals; but A. L. Mortin approves of his Ranters, feeling that they foreshadow the Labour party as well as William Blake. They do often strike a note of sturdy innocence, for example the Ranter who "hoped to see the poor Devil cleared of a great many slanders, which had been cast upon him" (p. 45). Donne of course was always aristocratic in attitude, but he could not use this tone of popular good humor. In any case, it was not at all new to say that the individual soul was as huge as the night sky; Cohn has his mystics saying (p. 173): "The soul is so vast that all the saints and angels would not fill it, so beautiful that the beauty of the saints and angels cannot approach it. It fills all things." Also they would earnestly regard a sexual ecstasy as a divine one, to a purified soul. They considered that the third age was dawning, and for its illuminati all laws were abrogated by Jesus. Nakedness and adultery were symbols of the achieved freedom, and "Some adepts attributed a transcendental quasi-mystical value to the sexual act itself, when it was performed by such as they. . . . The leader of the *Homines intelligentiae* claimed to have a special way of performing the sexual act which was that practiced by Adam and Eve in the Garden of Eden" (Cohn, *Pursuit of Millenium,* p. 180). He would of course teach it to favoured disciples, just as there is a grave third figure beside each of the couples in Bosch's Garden of Delights; or as a pupil watches the lovers in "The Ecstasy." Coppe, says Anthony Wood, "was accustomed to preach stark naked . . . and in the night be drunk and lie with a wench that had also been his hearer stark naked" (Morton, *Everlasting Gospel,* p. 52. Coppe denied this, but some naked preaching seems well attested). The Ranter Clarkson, in his tract *A Single Eye all Light, no Darkness* (1650) actually uses the word *centre* as Donne does (Cohn, *Pursuit of Millenium,* p. 315): ". . . thy body consisting of flesh and bone, is made of the dust of the earth, therefore when thy body is reduced to its centre, then (and not till then) is thy body alive, perfected in its happiness." In his autobiography, he says he had believed when a Ranter said that "no man could attain perfection but by this way." Of course, these figures come later than Donne, but they echo the medieval mystics very closely, and the only reason why we have no such writing from the time of Donne's youth is that it was firmly suppressed. His love poetry has much more solidity if you assume him to have heard of the Family of Love.

If I may turn back now to the theory that Donne never experienced love, but only engaged in daydreams about it after his marriage, so as to sulk and insult his wife. This fancy is not merely an invention of Professor Gardner. She regarded it as an established result of scholarship, and it is indeed typical of modern English literature. It seems to have been invented by J. B. Leishmann in *The Monarch of Wit* (London, 1959), and he is much more disagreeable about it than Professor Gardner. The leering worldliness with which he assures the children that grown-ups only have daydreams seems to me a prime example of: "Any lie whatsoever so long as it discourages the young people from going to bed together." He draws his main evidence from "The Dreame," Donne's confession to have dreamed about making love, and the critic can suppose that this means a voluntary daydream not a true dream, and thence that all the poems are only about daydreams. Professor Gardner echoes this with rather too much confidence, during some cosy praise of the poet in her Introduction (p. xxi). She is remarking that he often takes a stock theme but at once transforms it; for example, poems about dreaming of love had long been familiar, but Donne added "the brilliant stroke of bringing the lady herself into the room just as the dream reaches its climax of joy; and for the sadness of waking there is substituted disappointment in actuality and a return to the pleasure of dreaming." This is grossly false, and I had better quote the whole verse to leave no doubt:

> *Comming and staying show'd thee, thee,*
> *But rising makes me doubt, that now*
> > *Thou art not thou.*
> *That love is weake, where feare's as strong as hee;*
> *'Tis not all spirit, pure and brave,*
> *If mixture it of* Feare, Shame, Honor *have.*
> *Perchance as torches which must ready bee,*
> *Men light and put out, so thou deal'st with mee,*
> *Thou cam'st to kindle, goest to come; Then I*
> *Will dreame that hope againe, but else would die.*

Comming to his bed at just the right moment showed her to be omniscient, like God, and *staying* was another action worthy of her divine nature; *rising* explains that while staying she got into bed. There is no hint of disappointment so far; it only appears when she goes away again, out of fear that they may be discovered. (Probably she visits him in the morning, shortly before the servants begin coming to the bedrooms; maybe they are both guests at a country house, or perhaps they are in the palace of the keeper of the great seal). This caution is not ideally heroic of her, but he can praise her whole action if it has a practical aim, of getting him ready to start the work of love at once on the next brief opportunity. If so, he will consent to dream of her again, but only as "dreaming of hope," preparing for the actuality. Rather than accept a life of mere fantasy, he would kill himself. He seems anxious, one might say pedantically anxious if his precautions had not proved inadequate, to leave no loophole for the misreading of Mr. Leishmann and Professor Gardner.

She draws attention to a similar movement of thought,

and applies to it the same false logic, in a poem she calls "Image and Dream." I agree (on second thoughts) that he had probably been reading Ebreo, or some other expert on visionary love (a thing he might do at any date), because otherwise it seems gratuitous to threaten to return her miniature portrait in order to have daydreams about her more comfortably; but this does not prove he is converted to the doctrine. The poem gives a cosy recommendation to the safe and convenient practice of fantasy, but the poem's last six lines amount to a convulsive rejection of dreams. He will keep her picture, he decides at the end, to secure him against this escapism: "Fill'd with her love, may I be rather grown / Mad with much *heart,* than *ideott* with none." I don't quite agree with Donne here; in the educational field, at any rate, I would not prevent the children from daydreaming at the cost of their sanity. Nevertheless the scholarly misrepresentation here of what he meant to say is startling.

Having both the Milgate and Gardner editions available also facilitates a convenient statistical check on Professor Gardner's dating of the poems. I think that about a dozen of the poems in her *Songs and Sonnets II* ought to be put back into *I,* the group written before marriage, to avoid maligning the poet and allow an intelligible development of his character. There is practically no evidence either way; she relies on a principle that the poems using "philosophical" ideas about love (some of them very boyish and raw) belong to his later life, when he is beginning to be thoughtful (anglican); whereas in fact all these ideas, not treated so gravely but treated as familiar, appear in the *Satires, Verse Letters,* and *Elegies,* admittedly written some time before his marriage. *Songs and Sonnets I* does succeed in giving a picture of a rather empty-headed young man, but it is incredible that he should always refrain from using these ideas, which are particularly suitable to the themes of the love-poems, if he is already using them elsewhere.

The word *king*, though not very philosophical, helps to show how artificial the arrangement is. Two of Donne's poems, which mention a king, have been triumphantly dated as written under James, and I agree that they were written after Donne's marriage, though maybe before Elizabeth died. *Songs and Sonnets I* have been selected so that the word *king* never appears at all. But consider Satire 4, where he describes himself visiting Elizabeth's court; *king* is incessantly repeated, as if he dislikes to admit that he is being ruled by a queen.

Donne, like Dylan Thomas, has only a few philosophical ideas in his poetry, though they are important ones. The microcosm, the new medicine, the new astronomy are about enough. Now, the limbeck of Paracelsus comes into "The Comparison," an elegy which may be as early as 1594 (Professor Gardner prints it second); and Donne is already feeling wonder at it, even though he is only praising his own mistress as part of a tiresome joke argument:

> *Then like the Chymicks masculine equall fire,*
> *Which in the Lymbecks warme wombe doth inspire*
> *Into th' earths worthlesse durt a soul of Gold,*
> *Such cherishing heat her best lov'd part doth hold*

He already assumes that the technique of distillation extracts a soul or essence, and therefore yields profound analogies with human affairs. In Satire 4 (l. 95) we gather he has watched the machine working "as a Still, which staies / A Sembrief, 'twixt each drop." There are references to astronomy in "Loves Progress, which Professor Gardner puts at about the middle of the

Elegies, dating them 1593–96. You should start toward the center of a woman by caressing her feet, not her face, and the celestial spheres can advise us about that, though Cupid is infernal and lives underground:

> *For as free Spheres move faster far than can*
> *Birds, whom the air resists, so may that man*
> *Which goes this empty and Ætherial way*
> *Than if at beauties elements he stay.*

On any theory, the heavenly bodies have to move at speeds unknown in common life; the air cannot extend up to the moon, or the moon would slow down. Donne cannot mention the subject, even for this farcical purpose, without showing that he knows the basic problems about it. With "The Autumnal" (about 1600), we get him using a technical term "lation" which staggered the more intelligent coypists; he must have read a good deal in the subject by the time he did that. The thought of space travel, taking us to other habitable planets, is first hinted at in "Love's War," which Professor Gardner dates back to 1594. The strife of love, says the poet, is better than fighting for one's country, and why? Because patriotic fighting, whether in Ireland, Spain or Flanders, always means getting into a *boat*:

> *And ships are carts for executions.*
> *Yea they are Deaths; Is it not all one to flye*
> *Into another World, as t'is to dye?*

"Another world" might be the New World of America, as it was already called, but a voyage that means death is bound to suggest going to heaven, where the planets are. Of course this is not part of the joke argument, but the poetry often comes from the play of mind all around that. The first idea of a loved

woman as a planet comes I think in the elegy "To His Mistris
Going to Bed" (1596 perhaps), but he only recognizes it in
passing as a theme to be developed later: "Off with that girdle,
like heavens zone glittering, / But a far fairer world incompass-
ing." The Milky Way was quite prominent in the sixteenth-
century mind; the voyage to India around the cape had found
that it really does encircle the heavens, as the ancients had
assumed it would. Professor Gardner's note says that this
"zone" is *either* the girdle of Orion *or* the whole orb of the
fixed stars; but Orion's girdle does not encompass any world,
and a complete sphere is not usually said to be a zone. Here
as so often she has no contact with the poet's interests. The
merit of the Milky Way here is that it would girdle any planet,
even of another solar system perhaps; the lady may be far
grander than our earthly world, and yet have the same zone.
Donne notices, almost in passing, that a firm hold of the old
cliché could lead one into an entirely new country.

I had expected the microcosm to have been familiar to
Donne in the schoolroom, but there seem to be only two early
references, and Mr. Milgate dates them unexpectedly late. The
letter to Rowland Woodward beginning "If, as mine is, thy
life . . ." was probably written in August 1579, he decides,
while waiting at Plymouth as part of the Islands Voyage:

> *If men be worlds, there is in every one*
> *Some thing to answere in some proportion*
> *All the worlds riches; And in good men,*
>   *this,*
> *Virtue, our formes forme and our soules*
>   *soule, is.*

Maybe he was already getting rather tired of keeping up a high
enough moral tone to gratify Woodward; just as, in the other
example, he felt he was doing hackwork when he wrote Satire 5

to please his new employer, Egerton, early in 1798. Donne is labouring to support some proposed change of law, and displays philosophic breadth near the start by saying: "If all things be in all" (as they must because they are made of the same elements), then each thing "implies or represents" each other thing—"then each man is a world." But at once the law courts are compared to a landscape, so that the world is a man, and the moral is (very truly no doubt) that you will be ruined if you go to law. This is sad stuff, and one might think (as I had assumed) that he regarded the idea as commonplace; but he actually does not seem to have mentioned it before. It is tiresome not to be sure whether he had just returned from extensive travel. However, these prosy references are enough to prove that he did not acquire the idea of the microcosm during the retirement after his marriage.

Professor Gardner does not use the term *microcosm* in her edition, thinking perhaps that too much fuss has been made about it, and also not caring to join in the exaltation of the isolated human couple. However, a particularly grand use of that trope is found in "A Valediction: Of the Booke." As I remarked earlier, Donne is boasting that the scribbled notes which passed between himself and Anne during the hectic time before their runaway marriage, if digested into a treatise, could survive the next Dark Age and become the gospel of the next Renaissance. It would be the root from which an entire new civilization could grow, this time genuinely based upon the religion of love:

> *When this booke is made thus,*
> *Should againe the ravenous*
> *Vandals and Goths inundate us,*
> *Learning were safe; in this our Universe*
> *Schooles might learne Sciences, Spheares Musick,*
> *Angels Verse.*

147

Professor Gardner remarks: "Since 'university' was frequently used for 'universe' at this period, I assume that Donne regards the words as interchangeable." Only at Oxford would a don take for granted that the university teaches the angels how to sing before God. So far from intending this cosy picture, the poet must be supposed to presume that the ruins of Oxford are only being inhabited by a few roving predators. A Dark Age is to be expected because the present representatives of a religion of love are busy burning each other alive, and persecuting any genuine lovers they may encounter. The eventual new civilization will find very little use in their relics and must extract all learning from the one book which has life in it; inventing a new heaven will be quite incidental. Such an outlook is by no means sceptical; it really does believe in the religion of love. But it cannot believe in the uniqueness of the historical Jesus, since any man (or married couple) aware of the truth may be called on to act as messiah, as in America or on the planet Mars, and may do it well enough. Belief in immortality also must become rather dubious, because this particular heaven will be a function of the doctrines worked out by the society from its basic text; but maybe all such societies have a sufficient likeness to give a kind of permanence.

Controversy often strikes the observer as tedious, but the participant feels he is learning all the time. I now realize that I never really appreciated the poems until it became necessary to defend them. What other seventeenth-century author had such a grasp of the historical process that he could envisage, if only for a defiant joke, the invention of a new heaven after a renewed Dark Age? It was not absurd of the twenties, I still think, to compare him to H. G. Wells.

The University of Sheffield

WESLEY MILGATE

✦

"AIRE AND ANGELS" AND THE DISCRIMINATION OF EXPERIENCE

Among the many kinds of poems, and the several kinds of lyric, written by Donne, the group most widely discussed is that consisting of poems which everyone agrees in calling "metaphysical"; and in this group "Aire and Angels" is central, as an example both of his finest lyrical work in this mode and of the treatment of one of his most characteristic lyrical themes. Though the meaning and even the ultimate success of the poem are still in some respects in dispute, the many discussions it has provoked have established a reasonable consensus; and it is possible to hold the opinion (all the more confidently because the opinion is impossible to refute) that we are now capable of a greater understanding and appreciation of the poem than readers have shown at any time in the past, even in Donne's own lifetime. His contemporaries, indeed, were not well placed to make certain distinctions that we now think it helpful to make: as, for instance, that the substance and "wit" of "Aire and Angels" are "metaphysical," and those of, say, "The Message" or "Loves Diet," in any precise sense, are not. The whole meaning and the imaginative process of "Aire and Angels" depend on ideas about the relation of the material and physical world with things and forces beyond the physical: necessarily so, since man is both matter and spirit, body and soul, and the nature of his finest and most powerful experiences, such as a perfect love between man and woman, can be interpreted only by meditating on the whole nature of things, material and immaterial. In some of Donne's lyrics the nature of the universal order is not seriously involved; but in "Aire and Angels" a subtle and deeply imaginative "wit" is engaged throughout with profound metaphysical speculation—not ponderously, but with glancing brilliance and humour, and not abstractly, since the preoccupation of the poem is the discrimination of what in the realms of theory answers to what is valid and truly human in love as it is experienced in a whole and perfect relationship.

It may therefore be helpful to recall briefly the metaphysics upon which the imaginative fabric of the poem is built, familiar as the "world-picture" it assumes might be to many modern readers. When nowadays we consider the nature of the universe or the nature of man, we think in terms of process, development and evolution. Donne and his contemporaries did not do this; to explain the nature of things was, for them, to find out as clearly as possible of what things were composed or "elemented"—the nature of their substance, not the processes that brought them into being. Even a subject like that of love was treated in this way: just what does love consist of in material and spiritual substance? The distinction between matter and spirit was not, however, absolute. The universe was thought of as a continuous hierarchy or scale or ladder of being, in which gross material things shaded off in their increasing, and thus rising, purity through what Donne calls, in *The First Anniversary* (l. 247), "the worlds subtilst immateriall parts" into the hierarchy of heavenly beings, crowned by the pure spirit of the Godhead. "Aire and Angels," among its other purposes, tries to "place" the love of men and women, which has both physical and spiritual elements, properly in this hierarchy of being, to "locate" it by finding out its true substance. Parts of the total hierarchy, moreover, could be thought of separately, each having its own ascending order: the heavenly world, the world of pure spirit, the world of social and political organization, the state; the world of man as an individual, the microcosm; the worlds of beasts, of fish, of plants, and of metals. It was thought illuminating to be able to find in anything you wanted to characterize an analogy or correspondence with some other part of the universe, for this served to "place" it and define its substance and nature more clearly. The central problem of "Aire and Angels" is to define how perfect love, which is in large part spiritual, can manifest itself and be active in the physical world to which man also belongs; and this definition is to be attained by finding a proper analogy on another plane of being, the means by which an angel—a spirit—can appear and be operative in the material world. The attempt to find correspondences between parts of the universe is the source of most, perhaps of all, "metaphysical conceits"; we cannot confidently say of many metaphors and similes in seventeenth-century poetry whether they were thought of primarily as poetic images, or as philosophical statements or scientific concepts. That they were, in any case, "metaphysical" is usually clear enough; for most such correspondences and analogies are used to relate the physical to the spiritual, the world beyond the physical. This theory assumed the universe to be static; it had been created complete, and the discovery of truth consisted in noticing new links in the chain of being, or correspondences between one part of it and another; in this was the wit of men, including poets, most obviously shown.

151

Donne's view of human life, however, was not only in this sense philosophical, but it was also dramatic. Like the contemporary dramatists, he was intensely aware that human experience is not static, but contains large dynamic elements of change and conflict. Much of the richness of his best lyrics is due to the tension and interaction between a view of the universal frame of things as static and a view of human experience as dynamic. This tension in particular determines the structure of "Aire and Angels," for the poem has a double force and, indeed, a double sense of time. It purports to define and place in a static order of things what true love is between men and women, as the lovers in the poem may experience it now and lastingly—as it "will ever bee"—and also to show that love between men and women develops and grows and is *achieved*; that each stage of its growth is rich and complex; but that its final perfection depends on a discrimination of what is valid and lasting in each stage of its growth and of the proper emphases and priorities that will ensure its perfection and continuance. The poem is both an account of what the perfect love of these two people is, or might be now, and also (in the past tense) a narration of how it has developed in the speaker's experience. It is on the one hand a meditative recalling of the speaker's growth into perfect love, and on the other an address to the woman whom he loves, though her response to his address is left in doubt. While the poem is not dramatic in the sense that it shows us persons confronted in conflict or dialogue, its narrative does give a sense of dramatic progression as the speaker vividly recalls and assesses the movements of complex experience to the present, or desired state of mutual adjustment of which he now speaks to his lady. Love is shown, as always in Donne's poetry, as a relation, or rather, as he presents it here, as an adjustment of relations, between human personalities; and it is further shown as a lasting and perennially comprehensible experience. The poem also, however, shows that this perfect relationship is not realized at once; the psychological progress of love at first involves other attitudes to the beloved, each natural and inevitable, but in itself unable to provide the basis of a lasting mutual love. The speaker defines what true love is, as he feels it now and as it will ever be, but also by the use of "double time" the poem shows how it grew in the past. In this way Donne is able to achieve the immediacy and (it is made to seem) the "personal" quality of the lyrical mode while preserving the dynamic progress of a changing situation. If, however, the lover is right in thinking that his relationship with his lady is now (at least in the degree to which she will share it) indeed perfect, there must be a parallel in the static universal scheme of things, a resemblance that confirms and illuminates the experience of the lover. The discovery of this parallel, the knowing of what true love is now, as the speaker talks to his beloved, is the confirmation and proof that his love is indeed soundly based.

The common idea through which the definition of perfect love is found, as we have seen, is that something impalpable and spiritual must find an appropriate embodiment before it can manifest itself and be operative in human affairs; and the final satisfactory description of love as a lasting human relationship is to be made in terms of angels in relation to air. The orthodox belief of the Church was that in appearing to men, as Aquinas puts it, "the angels assume bodies of air, condensing it by Divine power in so far as is needful for forming the assumed body." This is the doctrine with which Donne tries to square the definition of the relationship of true lovers; the orthodox opinion is treated as unquestionable; to this body of thought and to none less orthodox or less precise must the proper "conceit" or concept of love be related. The church fathers and theologians were, however, by no means in agreement about this matter of the bodies of angels; for instance, there will be found in such a work as Ludovico Molina's *Com-*

mentary on Aquinas (1592) over 350 closely-packed folio columns recording the different conceptions of the nature and
appearances of angels held since the early days of the church.
It was orthodox opinion by Donne's time (though there was
still dispute about the matter) that angels were by nature incorporeal; but when they appeared to men and spoke to them
they must clearly have had bodies of some kind. The psalmist
had said (Ps. 104:4) that God "maketh his angels spirits; his
ministers a flaming fire"; others, however, had objected with
Aquinas that if the angels had fiery bodies they would burn up
anyone they approached. Many therefore believed that an
angel's assumed body was aethereal, made of the incorruptible
and subtle air above the moon, where, as Milton puts it at the
beginning of *Comus,*

> . . . *those immortal shapes*
> *Of bright aëreal Spirits live insphear'd*
> *In Regions milde of calm and serene Ayr.*

Certainly, by the time Donne's poem was written, the idea that
angels appeared in bodies of fire, or as "a shapelesse flame,"
was unorthodox; and for Donne unorthodox ideas had a fascination, a romantic charm, akin to that possessed by discoveries
in new-found lands. In the beginning of the poem the experience of falling in love is like seeing the vision of an angel—an
unsteady, formless, wavering, brief but lovely and glorious
light—and hearing its voice. So Eliphaz, in the Book of Job
(4: 15–16), tells how "a spirit passed before my face. . . . It stood
still, but I could not discern the form thereof; an image was
before mine eyes, there was silence, and I heard a voice." "Aire
and Angels" begins in a rapt and melodious style that embodies
the romantic ardour of the speaker (all quotations of Donne's
poetry are from *The Elegies and the Songs and the Sonnets,* ed.
Helen Gardner [Oxford, 1965]):

Twice or thrice had I lov'd thee,
Before I knew thy face or name;
So in a voice, so in a shapelesse flame,
Angells *affect us oft, and worship'd bee;*
Still when, to where thou wert, I came,
Some lovely glorious nothing I did see.

If the opening is sensuous and passionate, however, it is anything but uncomplicated in mood. "Twice or thrice," "oft": the attitude is tender, but a trifle off-hand, whimsical and nonchalant. The speaker is at once within the experience and yet, in the later and mature state of love which he has achieved, outside it. He recalls the ardour of the first coming of his love, but speaks from the vantage-point of the fully developed and comprehended feeling he now experiences; and the first lines of the poem suggest the elements of adoration, patronage, tenderness and amusement that have lasted into, and are part of, his love as he now enjoys and understands it. Donne elsewhere uses deprecatory qualifications or half-wistful, half-humorous modifiers in this way:

Or chide my palsie, or my gout,
My five *gray haires, or ruin'd fortune flout*
("The Canonization")

All women shall adore us, and some *men*
("The Relique")

Whoever comes to shroud me, do not harme
Nor question much
That subtile wreath of haire which crowns mine arme
("The Funerall")

155

The effect is a disarming mixture of intimacy and assurance. Indeed, it is part of the effectiveness of "Aire and Angels" that Donne's most seductive style should be employed in what Walter de la Mare called the "wonderful onset" of the poem. While the opening lines have rich implications about the quality of the speaker's present, as well as of his first, love for his lady, they also make a direct assertion. The speaker says that he had had a romantic passion for several women in the past, but this feeling had in fact been directed at the partial manifestation in them of an ideal mistress, who became fully actual only when he saw his true beloved. His love for her was first felt as a generalized romantic passion focused upon an ideal; the first act in the progress of his love was the blinding recognition that, when at last he really confronted her in this glorious vision, the ideal had been fully realized. At this stage he could have said, like the speaker in "The Good-morrow,"

> *If ever any beauty I did see,*
> *Which I desir'd, and got, 'twas but a dreame*
> *of thee.*

This conception of love, expressed with exquisite control of sound and rhythm, in a striking and beautiful image, and in a tone of tender, intimate adoration, might have deluded a contemporary reader into thinking that he was in for yet another Neo-Platonic rhapsody on the subject. He might have been struck, as we are, by the masterly poetic shorthand by which Donne conveys the essence of a way of describing love indulged in at vaster length by Italian Neo-Platonic theorists, and also by the fact that what they speculated about abstractly is here presented as a living and dynamic experience. Commentators on Donne's poem have adduced passages from Italian treatises on love—by Ficino, Sperone, Guinizelli, and Bembo—that parallel the idea of the opening lines, and it would not be difficult to multiply such similarities. Some words of Ficino, however, will suffice: the lover, he says, "desires the splendor of the divine light shining through bodies, and is amazed and awed by it. For this reason lovers never know what it is they desire or seek, for they do not know God Himself . . . certainly we do not know what we desire and what we suffer. Hence also it always happens that lovers somehow both worship and fear the sight of the beloved." It must be noted, however, that this experience and this conception of love seemed convincing before the lover knew the "face and name" of his lady; for later he wants to know "what thou wert, and who"—what it is that he desires and seeks. As in others of his lyrics, Donne offers at first an imaginative conception which is later surprisingly and even paradoxically transformed, subtly modified, or rejected altogether. That the first ardent emotion of the lover in "Aire and Angels," and the conception of love it implies, must in large degree be rejected soon becomes clear; but for the moment the onset of love left the lover in his unknowing Neo-Platonic state of worship and awe. This state is presented in the poem for all it is worth as a valid and recognizably authentic kind of human experience.

With characteristic perceptiveness and imaginative daring, Donne proceeds to show that the exalted conception of spiritual love on the exposition of which the Neo-Platonists labored with such ingenious care is only a stage in the development of true love. It is not the steady basis of a lasting mutual relationship, though it has valid elements which, properly discriminated from the false or extravagant, do form a part of the full and perfect experience of love. That the conception of love expressed in the opening lines must be rejected is shown in various ways that explain why Donne was recognized, as Thomas Carew said of him, as the ruler of the monarchy of wit. One way is the use of the notion that angels appeared in bodies of fire, which was unorthodox—that is, simply untrue. The refine-

ment of "wit" which Donne displays here is to image a wrong
conception of true and lasting love in a way which, though al-
luring, involved a theory of the nature of angelic appearances
that was, in fact, false. Angels, the lover says further, "affect us";
and they do so in both senses of the word: they affect or "love
us mortal wretches with a zealous pity," as St. Augustine puts
it. By appearing and speaking to men they can affect our
thoughts in a very limited way—according to Dionysius the
Areopagite, by stimulating and assisting us to thoughts and
purposes in the direction in which our desire is already tending.
When angels do appear, men are moved to worship them; Josh-
ua, for example (5:14), "fell on his face to the earth, and did
worship" an angel. It might seem that Donne is making the
lover use the word "worship" in a loose colloquial way, as in
trite amorous talk ("I worship you"); but another refinement of
wit that shows this first experience of love to be invalid and
wrongly conceived involves a precise theological point: it is
wrong to worship angels. In Revelation 22:8–9 we read: "And
I John saw these things, and heard them. And when I had
heard and seen, I fell down to worship before the feet of the
angel which showed me these things. Then saith he unto me,
See thou do it not: for I am thy fellowservant . . . : worship
God." Again, therefore, Donne indicates, by the choice of the
word "worship," which describes a thoroughly unsatisfactory
relation between angels and men the fact that, in this opening
idea of what true love is like, the relationship between the lovers is also thoroughly unsatisfactory. The point is clinched more
obviously in the word "nothing"; the lady was lovely and
glorious, but her part in a love thus idealistically conceived was
that of a "nothing." Thus the falseness, instability and inadequacy of this conception of love are shown even as it is being
most alluringly described for us; and it is characteristic of the
profound imaginative wit of the poem that the etherealized

notions of the opening lines are shown to be inadequate, with psychological as well as imaginative truth, in the terms of this philosophy of love itself. The poem also skilfully suggests that the wonder and adoration which the speaker first felt is still a valid element in his present, more soundly based love.

The first onset of the lover's passion was not in itself the discovery of the fulness of love primarily because one must know who it is that fills one with wonder and adoration. Indeed, Castiglione in *The Courtier* (which we know Donne had read), although generally Neo-Platonic in his theory of love, differs from Ficino in asserting, as orthodox scholastic philosophy also asserted, that we cannot love until we know what it is we love.

> *But since my soule, whose child love is,*
> *Takes limmes of flesh, and else could nothing doe,*
> *More subtile then the parent is,*
> *Love must not be, but take a body too,*
> *And therefore what thou wert, and who,*
> *I bid Love aske, and now*
> *That it assume the body, I allow,*
> *And fixe it selfe in thy lip, eye, and brow.*

The Neo-Platonists were right in saying that love is the child of, or produced by, the soul; and the lover now realizes that his love must therefore be bound by the same laws as the human soul, which can, as all philosophers agreed, do nothing without the body. Again the underlying notion is that a spiritual and incorporeal being (an angel, the human soul, or love itself) is powerless to act in human experience without a material embodiment. The soul, which in the individual (the microcosm) corresponds to the king in the state, needs the emotions and powers of the body in order to function in human life; as Donne puts it in "The Extasie":

159

> *So must pure lovers soules descend*
> *T'affections, and to faculties,*
> *That sense may reach and apprehend,*
> *Else a great Prince in prison lies.*

The speaker's love in "Aire and Angels" can be no more subtle than its parent, the soul; and by "subtile" Donne might mean either "fastidious," "discriminating," or "attenuated," "spiritualized," or both. His love must have a body through which to act, just as its parent must; so he attempts to "fixe" his love in his lady's physical charms, having identified her as an individual now that the romantic haze of his first emotions has been penetrated.

That love could be "fixed" in the body, or that it was always so based, was a contention of other Italian writers, who did not follow Neo-Platonic theory. In the second movement of the poem Donne represents this attitude to love as he had represented the Neo-Platonic, by a masterly poetic summary of the attitude itself, and by a lively representation of what it corresponds to in the authentic movements of human experience; and this attitude too is eventually shown to be an inadequate basis for a perfect and lasting relationship. Love of this "physical" kind can take two main forms. It can idealize the lady's beauties in the manner of many Elizabethan sonnets, exhibiting

> *the blazon of sweet beauty's best,*
> *Of hand, of foot, of lip, of eye, of brow*

(Shakespeare, Sonnet 106)

in the familiar comparisons of the lady's teeth to pearls, her lips to cherries, her eyes to jewels, her hair to sunbeams or to golden wires. Such idealizing Donne expresses in poetic shorthand in the brilliant phrase that comes later: "things / Extreme and scatt'ring bright," which carries on the imagery of light from "shapelesse flame" and keeps alive in the lover's emotions the wonder and admiration of the first stage of his love. The tone of high compliment to the lady herself is also maintained. Love based on the physical charms of the lady can, however, take another form, that of lust, poetically represented by the bawdy suggestions that some readers have found to hover over this part of the poem. In the word "pinnace," which was a slang term for a loose woman, in "overfraught," and in the line "Ev'ry thy haire for love to worke upon," one can find *doubles entendres* according to one's own capacities in this line. Such suggestions do not seem to work very centrally in the development of the poem, but to the extent that they occur to the reader's mind, they are functional in pointing to an element which persists even in the perfect love to which the speaker is progressing. The overtones of lustful desire are kept in check by further suggestions in the language, for the idea of love working upon "ev'ry hair" recalls the revelation by Christ of the all-embracing particular care of God's providence: "the very hairs of your head are all numbered" (Matt. 10:30; Luke 12:7). Donne keeps this reminiscence at a beautifully judged distance, avoiding gratuitous profanity, and, rather in George Herbert's manner, exposing with humorous irony the folly of the lover's attempt to "fixe" his love entirely on the body. A sonneteer who celebrates his mistress' hair as golden wires or sunbeams is well on the way to absurdity; the lover's concern for his lady's every single hair is poetically emblematic of his even greater foolishness (emphasized by the Latin turn of the phrase "Ev'ry thy haire") in centering his love on the bewildering particularities of her physical beauty. The lover himself realizes that these are "much too much" for him, not only because she has too many to attend to at once, but also because love is itself threatened by being absorbed in the physical. The ironic Biblical overtone, however, suggests (like the word "worship" earlier, but in a somewhat different way) the essential falseness and inadequacy

161

of a love "fixed" in the body. It is not only hopeless and absurd to attempt to love the body with a whole and minutely scattered love as only God can, but it is also wrong and undiscriminating since God cares for the soul of man as much, or more. Nevertheless, the suggestion of an absorbed, tender care for his lady's person continues to be felt as a valid element in the true love to which the lover progresses. Thus, although the speaker recalls a stage in his love's growth in which he felt some loss of control, the language Donne puts into his mouth is beautifully controlled so that any suggestion (this side of unreason) that it brings to the reader's mind works to delineate the full range, idealizing or fleshly, of the physical desires of the lover. It may have been the exigencies of rhyming that led to a change of tense in "bid," "now . . . allow"; in the interests of the narrative we might read the passage as in the "historic present"; but also, as in the double use of "is" as a rhyme-word, the present tenses convey to us that in the lover's last psychological progress there were impulses that, in properly discriminated proportion, are still part (but only part) of the complex experience of true love to which he is moving, based on an adequate conception of love and, of course, on a more worthy and lasting attitude toward his beloved.

It is clear that to try to "fixe" love on the plane of the physical is to court disaster. To such a conception of love one might apply the word "sinke" in two senses, which carry a double disparagement of love as the lover felt and understood it at this stage of its development: love centered on the physical is "sunk," drowned, overwhelmed, destroyed by the physical. Desire for physical gratification is destroyed by its own surfeit, and the "admiration" that is part of a true and lasting love is "sunk" or debased by a concentration of love on the charms of the body. It is clear that in such a perfect love the element of "admiration"—that is, of wonder and respectful awe—must not be "sunk," but must be kept alive. Indeed, a common opinion was that "admiration" was the first step towards truth; the idea is found in Plato's *Theaetetus,* and Donne quotes it with approval in one of his sermons, in the phrasing of Clement of Alexandria: *Principium veritatis est res admirari.* The wonder of the first impact of his love prompted the lover to enquire further after the truth about the object of his love. His notion, in the second movement of the poem, that this object might be the physical beauty of his mistress was almost calamitous in the result:

> *Whilst thus to ballast love, I thought,*
> *And so more steddily to have gone,*
> *With wares which would sinke admiration,*
> *I saw, I had loves pinnace overfraught,*
> *Ev'ry thy haire for love to worke upon*
> *Is much too much, some fitter must be sought;*
> *For, nor in nothing, nor in things*
> *Extreme, and scatt'ring bright, can love inhere . . .*

His love for a "shapelesse flame" at the beginning was unsteady, because it was wrongly conceived, and directed at a "nothing." Seeking a more steady love, he tried to give his ardor weight and substance by directing it upon the lady's tangible physical charms. The main image now employed is that of love as a pinnace, a small scouting ship used for such purposes as exploring the coast of a new-found land before it was possessed. In seeking out his lady's identity he thought that his passion might be steadied by the "ballast" of her beauties, whether they were enjoyed in their ideal splendor or in lustful desire, but the wares he found in this new land were too much for his love to dwell upon. If at first his nebulous romantic passion was too insubstantial, and love's pinnace was in danger of capsizing, now the danger is that the wonder and adoration which was, and must continue to be, a genuine part of his love will be destroyed, and love's pinnace will be overweighted and sunk. Whereas at first the lover's devotion was set upon a nothing, a defective object, now in his mistress's body it is set upon too much, something excessive; but love, as the word "ballast" implies, must be embodied in something which, like virtue in Aristotle's theory, is a mean between defect and excess, between the capsizing and sinking of love, between a beautiful nothing and a scattered profusion of extremely bright and physically titillating beauties.

Meantime a little drama pertaining to the poem's main problem of defining love itself has been developing among four words that apply to the relationship of a spiritual being to that in which it can be embodied. These words are "assume," "fixe," "inhere," and "weare." The fact is that, despite the appearance of necessary logic and inevitable sequence in the phrases *"So* in a voice, *so* . . ."; *"But since"*; "and *therefore"*; "I saw"; *"For*; nor in nothing . . ."; "Then *as* . . . *So* thy love"; *"Just such"*; and despite the undeniable sense of dramatic progress and onward movement that the phrases create, there is a good deal of illogic and sleight of hand going on in the language. Two of the four words that concern the main "conceit" of the poem, "assume" and "weare," refer to an impermanent relation; the other two, "fixe" and "inhere," refer to a permanent relation. Donne wishes to use as the perfect analogy of lasting love the adoption of a body of air by an angel operating in the world of human experience, but the words that accurately describe this relationship are "assume" and "weare." So Aquinas says that "angels assume bodies of air . . . in so far as is needful" —that is, without defect or excess—"for forming the assumed body"; and when the angel is finished with its air-body it discards it, as a man wears and takes off clothes—it is not a permanent relationship. Donne deals deftly with the word "assume." When the lover allows his love to "assume" the lady's body, in one quick stroke the association of an angel with the lady, made at the beginning of the poem, is changed, and it is now man's love that is compared to an angel seeking an embodiment. Further, in countenancing the word "assume" at this stage, the lover is unknowingly admitting that the attempt to embody his love permanently in the physical beauties of his lady is delusive; "assume" is a word which argues against the validity of the conception of perfect love which the lover is at this stage too undiscriminatingly acting upon. Then with equal skill, Donne neutralizes the technical word for the angel's use of its air-body, "assume," stifling it with the word "fixe," which implies a steady and lasting relationship. But the lover's use of the word "fixe" (as he now realizes, though he did not do so at the time) was equally a delusion. The idea that love can be "fixed" in the physical, whether by idealizing the lady's bodily beauty or by indulging fleshly desire, must be rejected as surely as the idea that it can be fixed in the worship of an idealized nothing. The proper technical term that Donne needs to describe lasting union between lovers is "inhere," for only things of like substance can inhere permanently in each other; love can inhere, not in nothings or in physical things, but only in love.

There is, in fact, a serious contradiction in Donne's basic conceit, in that, whereas angels only "weare" their bodies, lasting love "inheres" in its body. If we read the poem, properly, as an unfolding narrative sequence, a progressive revelation and discrimination of what is valid and lasting in the development of true love, and if we do not expect from it the consistency of a logical demonstration or that of a symbolist poem in which all the parts support one another and contribute simultaneously to the whole effect, we shall find convincing both Donne's deployment of the "argument" of the poem and also his control of the flow of the meaning throughout most of its length. We shall also salute the skill with which he postpones until the last four lines, and in large measure averts, the po-

tential disaster latent in the deficiency of the basic conceit. Part
of the reason for our not noticing this deficiency is the disarming off-hand, intimate tone which we noticed in the opening
phrase, "Twice or thrice," which is continued in the half-
humorous idea of the lover's giving permission to Love to
assume the lady's bodily charms, in the bawdy suggestions, in
the sly mockery of the lover's hopeless emulation of providen-
tial care, and in the frank admission that "some fitter must be
sought." The last statement is wittily ambiguous: the lover has
reached the stage at which a more fit conception of what love
really means is needed; and Donne the poet needs a fitter simile
in which to image and define true love. Further, until four lines
from the end we are fully beguiled into accepting the fiction of
the poem that the lover is faithfully recounting the stages by
which he arrived at a true conception of perfect mutual love;
and his muddled thinking (revealed in his use of such words as
"worship'd," "assume," and "fixe") and his pseudo-logic are
perfectly natural and convincing because they arise from, and
reflect, a muddled and insufficiently discriminating experience
and consideration of love. Only gradually, step by step, does
the lover sort out what is lasting in his developing passion, and
we are disposed to take the last step with him, and to accept the
"fitter" conception to which he has now attained:

> *Then as an Angell, face, and wings*
> *Or aire, not pure as it, yet pure doth weare,*
> *So thy love may be my loves spheare;*
> *Just such disparitie*
> *As is twixt Aire and Angells puritie,*
> *'Twixt womens love, and mens will ever bee.*

The embodiment of his love, child of his soul, is like the body
of an angel, something between the purely spiritual nothing
he first thought it was and the physicality of the lady's bodily

charms he next thought it was. His love in relation to the lady's love for him is like the angel in relation to the air-body it assumes. But other ideas are also needed to define more accurately what the lover feels his true love really is: the idea of "purity," for there is a "disparitie" between man's love and woman's, though both are "pure," and the ideas contained in the word "spheare."

The notion that there is a disparity between men's love and women's, and that women's is in some way inferior to men's, have disturbed some critics in their remarks upon the poem. They have used phrases such as these: "the quiet insult at the end"; Donne brushes the conception of love he has established in the poem "aside with a witticism"; "lofty speculation" changes to a "cheap gibe"; the close of the poem is "touched with cynical humor," or manifests a "blandly insolent matter-of-factness." Yet that men's love is superior to women's was to the theologians, the scholastics, and the Neo-Platonists alike—to everyone, indeed—literally matter of fact. This was orthodox opinion, and like the proper theory of the substance of an angel's body and the wrongness of men's worship of angels, it was a fact with which a conception of the substance of true love must be squared. Even so genial a writer as Thomas Fuller (characterizing "The Good Husband" in *The Holy State*) remarks as an obvious fact that "the soul of a man is planted so high, that he overshoots such low matters as lie levell to a womans eye"; and the love of women was generally supposed to reflect their naturally less constant and forceful cast of mind and, as Orsino puts it in *Twelfth Night*, to "lack retention." Far from being cynical, insulting, gibing or insolent, the lover in Donne's poem is straining every ounce of his being to take account of this fact about women's love in relation to men's in the most complimentary, and indeed most truly loving way possible.

The love of both men and women is said to be "pure."

Basically a pure substance was a simple substance, unmixed, unadulterated; and in the continuum or hierarchy of the universe, as between material and spiritual things, purity was also a measure of relative approach to the spiritual. The air of which an angel makes its body is a physical substance nearest in purity, stability, and (since the element of fire was "quite put out") in actual position in the universe, to the spiritual—the "calm and serene Ayr" of the regions in which "bright aëreal Spirits live insphear'd." If this kind of air is the nearest thing to spirit, an angel is the nearest good thing in the spiritual hierarchy to the material; and man was made only a little lower than the angels. Clearly the lover is trying to make the recognized disparity between men's love and women's as little as possible; the phrase "Just such" is not a gloat ("There's at least as much") but a loving compliment ("There's only so much, and so little, difference between our loves"). It would be unusual, however, if Donne's use of these metaphysical speculations remained detached from an awareness of the palpable flesh-and-blood experience out of which they ultimately arose. It has been suggested, with truth, that it is not absurd to believe that women's love is not as "pure" as men's, and that it is "mixed" usually with other elements, anxieties and insecurities, to which men are less sensitive. The lover in Donne's lyric "The Dreame," at any rate, seems in the end to feel that his lady's love is made weak by the "mixture" of other elements:

> *That love is weake, where feare's as strong as*
> *hee;*
> *'Tis not all spirit, pure, and brave,*
> *If mixture it of* Feare, Shame, Honor, *have.*

This is consistent with the idea that man's love is the stronger, and that in a relationship of perfect love man is the dominant partner.

To make this clear, a further analogy is put forward in the poem, that the woman's love is the "spheare" of the man's love for her. An angel or intelligence, a "bright aëreal Spirit," controls each of the heavenly spheres in which the planets and stars revolve, and it was believed that the intelligence loves its sphere and controls it with care to fit its motion to the heavenly order and harmony. The relations of an angelic intelligence to its sphere and of an angel to its assumed body are described in scholastic commentaries (as in that of Molina mentioned earlier) in identical terms—as that of the "mover" to the "thing moved." The difference is that, while the angel assumes its air-body temporarily, the angelic intelligence is always at its station; and Donne introduces the word "spheare" primarily to suggest this essential element of permanence in the constitution of perfect love, an idea missing from his basic analogy of the angel and its body. The further analogy between the man's love and the angelic intelligence also makes it clear that in mutual love it is the man who makes the dominant and controlling contribution. There is a further sense of the word "spheare" which is relevant here, as in the phrase used by Donne in one of his sermons, "sphaera activitatis," a sphere of operation. Love without a body can "nothing doe"; but, embodied in the woman's love for him, the man's love can fully exist and be operative.

It is, no doubt, the assumption at the end of the poem that in perfect love the man plays the dominant role that has caused some readers to feel that here Donne displays a bland insolence. Yet he is always aware of and respects the simple, instinctive currents of feeling and attitudes that seem natural to the bulk of mankind. Thus it still seems to be generally felt that there is something less than perfect in a love relationship in which the woman has to make the advances and take the initiative, despite Bernard Shaw's contention that, as it were, woman proposes and woman also disposes. It still seems part

169

of the natural idea of love that the man proposes, and the woman responds. Donne speaks of this elsewhere in terms of "active" and "passive"—the active male principle and the complementary female principle—as in "Loves Deitie," where the god of love's office was

> *indulgently to fit*
> *Actives to passives: Correspondencie*
> *Only his subject was. It cannot bee*
> *Love, till I love her, that loves mee.*

This "fitting" of man's active love to woman's responsive love is the conception to which the lover in "Aire and Angels" attains. The only proper body for the love of a man is the love of a woman; in this only can his love be "active"; indeed, it cannot *be* love till the woman responds with love. The main point of the poem, in fact, is a refined statement of what is still a popular truism—that love can exist only as it is returned. I do not think that a woman would be insulted or would feel it to be a cheap jibe if her lover said this to her. However this may be, the "fitter" analogy for, and conception of, the love felt at the last by the speaker in "Aire and Angels" amounts to this: though love passes through the stages of wonder and worship, and various kinds of physical attraction and desire, love can find its only appropriate fulfillment when it relates itself to the love that the woman gives in return, not to the woman herself.

In a full discussion of the poem it is perhaps unfortunate that the greater part must concern the ideas and the nuances of expression connected with the narrative, meditative and "defining" elements in its working. The fact that there is little, if any, sense of dramatic confrontation, and that we have no indication of the woman's feelings as the lover speaks to her, makes it easy to overlook the element of appeal and wooing which can be found in the language, and which is obviously implied by the very conception of perfect love which the poem puts forward. In the fourth line from the end, the phrase "may be" is on the one hand used in the mode of philosophical demonstration ("Thus it may be seen"); but on the other hand it is a conditional, as it concerns the present relationship of the lovers ("If you respond, your love may be the sphere of mine"). The man in the poem is "active," he is the "mover," the proposer; his wooing is suggested by such words as "came," "aske," "sought," as well as by the lively attitudes he shows towards his lady, by his need to know what he loves, by the changing and yet constant nature of what he desires in and from her, even by the overtones of questing in the image of the pinnace, and the urgency of finding that in her which his love can "worke upon." Essentially, what he *must* find is her responding love. It seems impossible from the poem itself to determine whether the wooing lover is asking for a return of his love which the lady has never yet given, or whether, knowing that she is already giving him her love, he is asking for its constant renewal and continuance. We are uncertain whether his passion has been fully comprehended and "placed" because she has shown him, by giving her love, in what true love consists; whether comprehension and "definition" have limped after passionate experience; or whether the mind has outstripped the emotions, and the lover knows what true love must be, but awaits her responding love before his passion can be fully operative. This uncertainty is not, I think, disruptive to, but rather an enrichment of the poem. As we turn it over in our minds, we might at one time think that the poem shows reason and understanding outstripping the full exercise of passions already understood, at another that the mind is struggling to encompass and "place" passions already fully experienced; and it is perhaps not too fanciful to see the poem in this respect as a vivid rendering of the complex movements of understanding and passion in authentic human experience. The uncertain state of the lady's feelings in the poem does not disturb, but is thoroughly consistent with the main implication of its "thesis": that man's love is really at the mercy of his beloved, and that it waits upon her first giving of love in return and upon her continual response thereafter. For these lovers and for all others, this is how true love "will ever bee."

The interpretation of "Aire and Angels" here put forward has not included detailed arguments about points still in dispute, for other interpretations seem to me to do violence to Donne's poetic method and to his characteristic thought. For instance, the phrase "not pure as it" seems obviously to mean "not pure as the angel itself." The pronoun "it" (not "he" or "she") is appropriate, since angels, being pure spirit, have no "difference of sex" (as Donne makes clear in "The Relique"), and in heaven there is neither marriage nor giving in marriage. Thus Spenser writes in his *Hymn of Beauty*: "so every spirit, as it is most pure." But others have proposed that "it" means "air," or refers to "thy (the woman's) love," which is like pure air, while the man's is like the less pure air of angelic bodies. It is possible in this way to torture meanings from the poem which make nonsense of it. One of Donne's most striking qualities as a poet is that his use of English is direct and central; and, like Shakespeare, he has a marvelous sense of what English idiom, the central nerve of the language, can do. In this respect also, Donne has his simplicities. It is an error to assume that he exemplifies in his use of language the tortuous ingenuity that sometimes characterizes the use of ideas in his poetry. "Aire and Angels" is typical of Donne's poetic writing in other respects—not only in its diction, but also in the command of the intonation and rhythms of the speaking voice, in the sense of a man speaking out of a passionate experience which engages the speculations of the mind as well as the imagination and the emotions. The poem also

172

typically shows Donne's ability to treat serious and profound subjects with deft wit and humor and without portentous solemnity. In "Aire and Angels" this lightness of touch actually helps to create the sense of assurance in the true love that the speaker has now attained, that is so profoundly felt that he can be detached, self-critical and even playful as well as passionately loving. The activity of the lover's mind is in a special way characteristic of Donne's love lyrics, in that the fervent intellectual life in the poem is both a kind of metaphor, and also a guarantee of the depth of the emotional experience being presented.

Even in the falling off of the poem at the end, "Aire and Angels" is less fortunately typical; for it cannot be denied that the sense of disappointment with its close felt by most readers has justification. The partial failure at the end is not properly to be accounted for, I think, by the ideas expressed about the relative places of man's and woman's love in the whole relationship. It is due rather to the basic inadequacy of the final, supposedly clinching, analogy by which this relationship is to be defined and imaged. In believing that the angel's relation to its air-body is a parallel to the relation of a man's love to a woman's, the lover is, to put it bluntly, almost as muddled as he showed himself to be in the earlier stages of his love. Because his analogy is put forward as "fitter," however (and the whole movement of the poem leads us to believe that it is in fact the fittest and most precise analogy), his muddleheadedness cannot be treated with irony and detachment, as it was earlier in the poem. Instead, Donne tries hard to plug the hole in the crucial "conceit" about the proper embodiment of love. It is in the word "spheare" that the trouble begins and the basic weakness in the "fit" analogy becomes a poetic embarrassment. To add the idea of permanence (an element missing from the angel's connection with its air-body) and to suggest more precisely the controlling force of the man's love in the mutual relationship (when achieved), Donne places an immense burden of purely intellectual meaning upon "spheare." It is too much to expect that in addition the word could continue the imagery of brightness so beautifully exploited earlier in the phrases "shapelesse flame" and "Extreme, and scatt'ring bright"; and the angel itself appears now more as the symbol of an abstract idea than as a "bright aëreal Spirit." With the virtual disappearance of rich figurative expression from the closing lines inevitably goes also the ardent passion that the imagery embodied. In general the last four lines are thin in poetic texture and almost bereft of the emotional warmth that is realized in, and that vivifies, the rest of the poem; the true love at the end, as the poetry reveals it, is less, and not more, rich and compelling than the falsely based love which the speaker claims to have transcended. Unsupported by passion, the nonchalance and humor lose their dimension of tender assurance and can no longer reinforce the sense of security in a love soundly based and comprehended, and there is a partial failure in tone, so that the last lines tend to sound merely jaunty. We feel too much that the outcome of the poem is a triumph, not of perfect love, but of intellectual play. In this lyric, moreover (as in many of his others), Donne sets himself a formal problem, and a challenge. The first stanza is beautifully wrought as an embodiment of thought and feeling (it has been recognized as being based on the sonnet, with the sestet preceding the octave); the challenge was then to write a matching stanza. For all his virtuosity in stanza-construction, however, and for all a poet's (and an Elizabethan's) delight in intricate craftsmanship, in "Aire and Angels" he simply has not room in the second stanza to do all that the poem requires him to do; too many ideas crowd into the last six lines to be properly displayed in climactic imaginative richness; and the rhyme-scheme compels him to give equal emphasis to the rhyme-words "weare" (to which he would not wish to give prominence) and "inhere" (which makes a vital point about the embodiment of true love). Thus, if we judge (I think, rightly) that by its own high standards "Aire and Angels" falls off poetically at the end, it seems that the defects of the poem can be accounted for in purely literary terms. Although the inadequacy of the "fit" conceit lies ultimately behind the relative failure of the last few lines, the success or failure of "Aire and Angels" as a poem is not finally to be measured by the "truth" of the conceit, or even by the validity (in its philosophical context) of the "fit" analogy put forward by the lover. Like the apparent logic in his account of his love's progress ("But since," "and therefore," and so on), the analogy of his love to the angel in its air-body is not to be judged by the canons of abstract reasoning. Both "logic" and "conceit" are vehicles of the real subject of the poem—the mutual love of man and woman in its growth and perfecting; and of this subject "Aire and Angels" offers an astonishingly rich and subtle treatment.

Despite blemishes, therefore, it is a fine "metaphysical" lyric. It studies its subject in large perspectives of time, showing how a passionate experience arises out of the past and opens upon a never-ending future. It is more especially "metaphysical" because it presents and defines the contours of human experience in relation to the spiritual substance of the universe itself. The use of the metaphysical dimension is a means by which the idealizing imagination and the desires of the flesh, reason and passion, can be assigned their proper place and proportion in the complicated texture of experience. It is perhaps more noticeable in Donne than in other "metaphysical" poets that an experience is felt to be valid only in proportion as it is understood and as the mind can discriminate the relative importance of its components. Whether in Donne's poetry or in that of others, however, metaphysical poetry is one of the kinds of poetry that show mortal experience in perspectives of the spiritual and the eternal. It is one of the modes in which the poet can both raise a mortal to the skies and draw an angel down.

The Australian National University

DAVID DAICHES

❦

A READING OF
THE "GOOD-MORROW"

In the course of its three stanzas this poem moves from simple question to a complex "metaphysical" argument. This kind of progression is not uncommon in Donne's love poetry, which often starts with a seemingly spontaneous exclamation ("Busie old foole, unruly Sunne / Why dost thou thus, / Through windowes and through curtaines call on us?"; "For Godsake hold your tongue, and let me love"; "If yet I have not all thy love, Deare, I shall never have it all") and only becomes more ratiocinative in texture after the opening stanza has set the emotional key (all quotations of poetry are from *The Poems of John Donne*, ed. H. J. C. Grierson [Oxford, 1912]). In fact, the often admired combination of passion and reason in Donne is rarely something which we find evenly distributed throughout a given poem. The shape of the stanza as well as the mood of the poem is defined initially by a stanza which is quite often a simple, passionate utterance, and later stanzas that seemed to have been spontaneously carved out by the sheer force of the initial utterance return to that shape, using it now as a pre-existing mould in which to pour increasingly "metaphysical" variations on the opening statement.

This is not just a technical trick: in his best poems it is always psychologically and dramatically justified. "The Good-

177

Morrow," for example, enacts both a temporal progression and a persuasive movement of feeling, beginning with an exclamation of bemused incredulity about the unawakened life the lovers had led before they fell in love with each other, moving on to their present sense of being all-in-all to each other, and concluding with an assurance about the future. The first stanza deals with the past, the second with the present, the third and last with the future. And the increase in the ratiocinative element as the poem moves forward in time is psychologically justified by the emotional cycle which the poem acts out.

The opening question appeals directly to a universally shared human feeling, the sense that a profound new emotional experience has totally changed one's life, so that one looks back on one's life before this crisis with incredulous wonder at its emptiness:

> *I wonder by my troth, what thou and I*
> *Did, till we lov'd?*

This draws the reader at once right into the poem. It seems to me one of the most marvelous openings of any poem in the English language: we are *caught* by it, trapped inside the experience the poet is creating. And we need to be thus caught, thus trapped, if we are to stay with the poet during his later more "metaphysical" moments. Donne has in fact found a way (it seems simple, but it is the exquisite cunning of art) of making sure that his reader shares his own urge to enlarge his emotion by including a dimension of reason. We are taken so fully and irresistibly into the poem at its opening that we cannot quit when it becomes more difficult: we are carried on to share the speculations which give intellectual contours to the passion.

Part of this compulsion lies in the poem's psychological plausibility. The recognition of the presence of passion is fol-

lowed by the calm which results from the acting out of passion
and this in turn is followed by that affectionate intellectual
play in which confident love manifests itself in the contented
aftermath of sexual activity. So the "metaphysical" element in
the poem takes its place naturally in a little acted drama of
sexual love which might appropriately appear as an introductory (or a concluding) poem in a marriage-manual.

But let us consider the first stanza more carefully:

> *I wonder by my troth, what thou, and I*
> *Did, till we lov'd? were we not wean'd till then?*
> *But suck'd on countrey pleasures, childishly?*
> *Or snorted we in the seaven sleepers den?*
> *'Twas so; But this, all pleasures fancies bee.*
> *If ever any beauty I did see,*
> *Which I desir'd, and got, 'twas but a dreame of thee.*

The two lovers were infants before they fell in love with
each other. "Were we not wean'd till then?" puts the point with
half-humorous forcefulness. (Donne's union of thought and
passion is less characteristic than his union of passionate feeling
with intellectual playfulness.) Even if they were physically
grown up, they were children emotionally, and "suck'd on
countrey pleasures, childishly." I have little doubt that Donne
was being delicately coarse in talking of "countrey pleasures."
"Do you think I meant country matters?" Hamlet asks Ophelia
(*Hamlet*, act 3, scene 2) in the course of his deliberately suggestive dialogue with her. Any sexual activity they had indulged in previously was a purely physical matter and had
nothing to do with adult feeling. (Helen Gardner comments
that if we accept this overtone of meaning in "countrey pleasures" then "the lady, as well as her lover, had enjoyed such
pleasures." But I am not sure: Donne seems to be moving in-
sensibly in this first stanza from talking of them both to talking

179

of himself only: certainly, by lines 6 and 7 he is talking *to* her *about* himself.) In this former existence, they "suck'd," they "snorted" ("snorted," a better reading than the "slumbered" of some manuscripts): the verbs suggest both childishness and brutish insensibility. Generations of commentators have given us precise information about the "seven sleepers den," in which seven noble youths from Ephesus were said to have taken refuge from the persecution of Christians by the Emperor Decius and to have been miraculously preserved in sleep for nearly two hundred years. But the precise reference is unimportant either to the tone or the meaning of the poem. The phrase, with its suggestion of folklore, evokes at once a cave of deep magical slumber, and the Sleeping Beauty is really more relevant here than Gregory of Tours, the Emperor Decius, Theodosius II, or Gibbon's *Decline and Fall*, where "the memorable fable of the Seven Sleepers" is told and the sources cited in chapter 33.

Line 5 breaks off the discussion, almost with impatience. The sharp snap of the first two words provide the necessary air of decisiveness, of conclusiveness:

> *'Twas so; But this [i.e., except for this], all pleasures*
> *fancies bee.*

But the stanza does not end here: with sly humor Donne goes on to introduce the Platonic idea that any previous love of his must have been a "dream" of his present mistress:

> *If ever any beauty I did see,*
> *Which I desir'd, and got, 'twas but a dreame of thee.*

The Platonist begins by pursuing any person or object in which the idea of beauty is reflected, ascending by degrees to the state in which he apprehends directly the idea of beauty itself. Similarly, the lady to whom this poem is addressed is implicitly compared to the Platonic idea of beauty, while his former loves represented earlier stages in his search for the real thing. The lines mingle humor, wit, philosophy, confession and affection. He is using conventional Platonic philosophy to turn his confession of having had previous affairs into a compliment to his present mistress. Yes, he has had other girls, but they were part of his ascent to *her*. Note that he says "which I desired, *and got*": his relations with these earlier girls had not been (to use a paradox Donne would have liked) Platonic, even though Platonism justified them as necessary states in his progress to his present state of permanent and genuine love.

Even though the three stanzas mark a temporal and psychological progression, as I have noted, this first stanza itself progresses in mood and tone, from the simple exclamation, "I wonder . . ." to the affectionate teasing of the last two lines. Yet these lines represent more than teasing. They end with the wooing phrase "a dreame of thee," and on that final "thee" the poet, as it were, turns to the girl, and the pause that follows represents their union.

If the movement of the first stanza forces a pause at its end, the opening of the second stanza has the air of beginning after a pause, of starting over again on a new tack. It is morning. The lovers are awake, and they turn to each other after a night of passion. The slow-moving first line of the second stanza has an air of happy langour about it:

And now good morrow to our waking souls, . . .

The "waking" refers back to the first stanza, with its discussion of the period before they were in love when they were unawakened, but at the same time it also suggests a more literal kind of waking, a more literal "good morrow" after a night of love followed by sleep. "Waking" suggests "watching," and the two lovers are watching each other not out of fear (for since between them they comprehend the whole universe they have nothing to fear) but out of a love of exploring the universe which they two make up. The thought is playful, but persuasively grounded in psychological reality:

> *And now good morrow to our waking soules,*
> *Which watch not one another out of feare;*
> *For love, all love of other sights controules,*
> *And makes one little roome, an every where.*

Love prevents any desire on the part of the lovers to see anything or anybody except themselves and their immediate environment. And they and their environment represent the whole world anyway. This, of course, is the Elizabethan commonplace of the microcosm, but used originally, with that slightly quizzical touch that Donne was able to introduce so happily into the very heart of his passionate utterances.

The movement of this stanza is interesting. After the steady, slow pace of the first line, the second and third lines, where argument succeeds greeting, move more hesitantly, more ratiocinatively as it were: "For love, all love of other sights controules," with its repetition of the word "love" and the rationally necessary pause between the first "love" and the phrase "all love," suggests an actual thought-process in motion. The next line, however, "And makes one little roome, an everywhere," comes to rest in a smooth affirmative statement which sweeps on without a pause (for the comma is grammatical, not rhetorical): it both clarifies and sums up the preceding line. The final three lines of the second stanza elaborate this thought with teasing cosmological imagery, playful in tone, serious in meaning, affectionate in its happy combination of playfulness and logic:

Let sea-discoverers to new worlds have gone,
Let Maps to other, worlds on worlds have showne,
Let us possesse one world, each hath one, and is one.

The 1633 edition reads "other" in the second of these lines, and this reading is adopted by Grierson who also accepts "one world" from the same edition. But the most reliable manuscripts read "others" (which does not change the meaning but is more consistent with modern usage), a reading adopted by Helen Gardner, who also adopts from manuscripts "our world" instead of the 1633 reading "one world." "Our world" probably makes better sense: they are one, and possess their common world, "ours"; at the same time, there is the paradox that, being made one by love, they are also made four. Helen Gardner quotes Leone Ebreo: "each one being transformed into the other becomes two, at once lover and beloved; and two multiplied by two makes four, so that each of them is twain, and both together are one and four." Each *hath* one and *is* one: the emphasis here is on the two verbs "hath" and "is," not on the "one."

But the literal meaning, though of course we must understand it if we are to read the poem with any sort of appreciation, is less interesting than Donne's use of language in expressing it. Commentators have noted that the notion that the poet's love is more precious than anything brought back from newly discovered lands by exploring merchants is not uncommon in Elizabethan poetry (cf. Spenser, *Amoretti*, 15), but, as far as I am aware, nobody had commented on the oddity of Donne's use of a third-person imperative in the past tense. The sense is: "Let explorers have discovered new worlds, let maps have shown worlds on worlds to other people." This is a most unusual form in English, "Let *x* have done *y*," ordering, as it were, someone in the past to have done what they have done anyway. But of course the third person imperative in English, beginning with "let," is not a true imperative, and has over-tones of *dismissiveness*. The old Aberdeen University motto, "They say; what say they? let them say" illustrates this perfect-ly: the "let" is positively contemptuous. Latin and some other European languages would use a third-person subjunctive for this, but this way of forming a third-person imperative is more likely to sound a permissive than a dismissive note. The Rus-sian *pust'* comes nearest to the English usage, and can have a similar suggestion of dismissiveness. My point is that Donne needs the unusual form of a third-person imperative in the past tense beginning with "let" because he needs the tone of dis-missiveness which it sounds, a tone which reinforces his rejec-tion of everything in the cosmos except himself and his mis-tress, who in fact constitute the whole universe that matters.

The final stanza is the only truly "metaphysical" one in the poem. As the two lovers gaze at each other, each seeing the reflection of his face in the other's eye and the faces themselves reflecting the candor and openness of their mutual love, the poet gives a new twist to his cosmological imagery before rein-forcing it with a highly technical concept from Thomist phi-losophy, and this in turn enables him (one of the great triumphs of the poem) to turn the poem to a conclusion which affirms, in simple and ringing language, the eternity of their love.

> *My face in thine eye; thine in mine appeares,*
> *And true plain hearts doe in the faces rest,*
> *Where can we finde two better hemispheares*
> *Without sharpe North, without declining West?*
> *What ever dyes, was not mixt equally;*
> *If our two loves be one, or, thou and I*
> *Love so alike, that none doe slacken, none can die.*

The first two lines of this stanza give no notice of the developing intricacy of the thought: the language is straight-

forward and the situation described is immediately recogniz-
able. The truth about "true plain hearts" is expressed in true
plain language. Donne begins his slide into metaphysics with
a question which links up with the cosmological and carto-
graphical imagery of the preceding stanza: where can they find
two better hemispheres (than each other's eyes, into which they
are looking), for these, unlike the two hemispheres which make
up the world (of which no more than one could be visible at
once), lack the bitter cold of the north and the declining sun
of the west. The thought is still not difficult, though playfully
extravagant. But then, in one of the simplest lines in the poem
so far as language and syntax goes, he takes up from the over-
tones of the word "declining" to assert that "What ever dyes,
was not mixt equally." Grierson was the first to explain this
with reference to Thomas Aquinas, quoting from the *Summa*:
*Non enim invenitur corruptio, nisi ubi invenitur contrarietas;
generationes enim et corruptiones ex contrariis et in contraria
sunt.* ("For corruption is not found except where contrariety
is found; generation and corruption arise from contraries and
in contraries.") Therefore whatever is "mixt equally," whatever
is not made up of contrarieties but is entirely homogeneous
must be immortal. If their two loves are one, "mixt equally"
into a homogeneous unity, or if they are so alike that neither
slackens, then their two loves must be immortal. There is a
slight difficulty here on the level of straightforward meaning:
identity of their two loves is no logical guarantee of neither
slackening. As Theodore Redpath put it, in his note on these
last two lines in his *Editio Minor* of the *Songs and Sonets*: "on
the one hand, there seems nothing to prevent two precisely
similar loves both slackening to a precisely similar degree:
while, on the other, if 'loving so alike' necessarily excluded
that possibility, by precluding the possibility of slackening
at all, then the mentioning of slackening would be redundant
to the point of absurdity." Helen Gardner, in her note on the

lines, avoids the difficulty by paraphrasing it out of existence, for she takes the lines to mean: "If our two loves are wholly united in one love, or, if they are always alike and at the same pitch [but what Donne says is something rather different, namely, if they are so much alike that they will always be at the same pitch], neither can perish." Redpath solves the problem by adopting a reading that is not that of the 1633 edition but is found in a number of manuscripts:

> *If our two loves be one, or, thou and I*
> *Love just alike in all, none of these loves can die.*

This is clear enough, and Redpath thinks that it is "more conclusive in point of rhythm" than the 1633 reading adopted by both Grierson and Gardner. I myself feel that "none can die" is a much stronger ending than "none of these loves can die," and I feel, too, that the repetition ". . . none doe slacken, none can die" gives the necessary rhetorical weight to the final line of the poem. It sounds very much as though the clearer version represents somebody else's attempt to tidy up what he thought (with Redpath) was a not wholly logical statement. Yet it does not seem to me to be difficult to resolve the logical problem of the 1633 reading. The phrase "thou and I Love so alike, that none doe slacken" must refer back to "What ever dyes, was not mixt equally"; two loves "mixt equally" and so lacking contrarieties form an incorruptible unity. Donne is putting the matter in two alternate ways; *either* our two loves are one, *or* they are so perfectly identical that together they form an incorruptible unity: whichever of these two ways we state the case (and it is the same case whichever way we state it), we can prove the immortality of our love. But why, it might be asked, does he say *"none* doe slacken, *none* can die" when "none" implies "not any" (out of a considerable number)? I suggest that the unqualified "none" (unlike the qualified and more pedestrian "none of these loves") combines a strong negative force with a sort of echoing of the word "one"; it suggests, in fact, in this context, not multiplicity but unity. "If our two loves be *one*, . . . *none* can die." The "none" clearly echoes the "one." Further, these two lovers are a microcosm of the whole universe, since their little room is an everywhere, so any statement about them is a universal statement.

The interesting thing about these last lines is that, while it is true that we can see a possible logical difficulty if we look closely at the deployment of the argument, we have no immediate sense of this as we read with that heightened awareness and appreciation that comes with living through the poem, in the world which the poem creates. And the creation of a compelling world of psychological and chronological reality, a world of experience that actually works itself out in time within the poem, is Donne's greatest and most characteristic achievement. The explication of Donne's thought is a barren exercise if it does not lead us back to the living reality of a powerful and moving poem. I do not find the conceits extravagant or the arguments fantastic. The line of thought—we were unawakened until we fell in love; now that we are awake after love-making let us look at each other and talk, and realise that we are a microcosm of the whole universe; our mutual love is perfect, so it cannot die—is carried through the three stanzas in a progression that is psychologically satisfying, persuasive in terms of our own knowledge of human experience. The use of the intellect is playful at first, serious (but not solemn) at the end, and the slightly teasing note is bound up with the groundswell of affection which is the ultimate justification of everything in the poem. I do not use the word "affection" here as something necessarily less than "love," but as something less demonic, more relaxed and tender, more capable of wit as a playful overflow of the high spirits that come with mutually successful love-making. In some of his love poems, Donne gives perfect expression to a very remarkable aspect of the relation between the sexes. It is time to take him out of the hands of the professional explicators and restore him, if not to the "common reader," at least to those who read poetry because they find it humanly illuminating—not just a quarry for articles in learned journals.

The University of Sussex

ROSALIE L. COLIE

"ALL IN PEECES"

PROBLEMS OF INTERPRETATION

IN DONNE'S ANNIVERSARY POEMS

Problems of Interpretation

Some problems of interpretation are encountered by readers trying to make sense of Donne's pair of long poems, usually called the *Anniversary Poems*, which, together with "A Funerall Elegie" and two complimentary poems by another hand, were published to do honor to the memory of Elizabeth Drury, a girl dead before maturity, the daughter of Donne's patron.[1] After years of scholarly and critical neglect, the poems have latterly been interpreted and annotated by some of the most considerable scholars of English Renaissance literature with the curious result that, after all the explication of background and foreground, they still seem fundamentally unexplained.[2] Naturally, literary works that we come to call "great" are hospitable to many disparate but valid interpretations; the problem with the *Anniversary Poems* is that the various interpretations have seemed especially selective and difficult to modulate into a general understanding of the works. Perhaps that is why, in a lively reading innocent of scholarly apparatus, Carol Marks Sicherman has attempted to make sense of the poems by close-reading techniques, in terms of what the poems say and do.[3] Her essay follows, at least covertly, the model for criticism set by Georges Poulet, according to which the works of an author are seen as manifestations of his inner biography. Mrs. Sicherman reads the *Anniversary Poems* as Donne's attempt to come to terms, through his art, with a serious personal crisis of faith.[4] In them, she suggests, Donne wrote himself out of his disappointment and disgust with the mutable timebound world of materiality and appearances, and persuaded himself finally of the realities of a heaven securely designed to receive the Christian soul.

Mrs. Sicherman's essay has the merit of enlivening these often over-schematized poems, but the problems they raise are, I think, less confessional and more literary than her reading suggests. Tempting as it is to jettison all the scholarship on the subject as unsatisfactory and with sympathetic common sense to read the *Anniversary Poems* anew for students rightly impatient with literary scholasticism, the odd muddles of the criticism of these poems do in fact point to an interesting problem case in literary interpretation and in hermeneutics. For, although the criticisms deal with very different subject matters and offer markedly different solutions to "interpretation," the solutions offered seem even more irrelevant to one another than simultaneously valid readings usually do. For all that, several interpretations do seem "right," do "explain" aspects of the *Anniversary Poems*. Leaving Queen Elizabeth aside, Marjorie Hope Nicolson's demonstrations of the importance of the new science in the poems cannot be dismissed. "An Anatomie of the World" makes the most of *topoi* of the new science as well as of those of the old;[5] "Of the Progresse of the Soule" borrows metaphors and other literary devices from expositions, both descriptive and fanciful, of the modes of early modern natural philosophy. The first poem follows the topical order of the physico-theologies so common later in the century, and owes something to the encyclopedic surveys of the universe produced in the late middle ages. With her attention concentrated upon the scientific material in the poems, Miss Nicolson naturally stressed the first poem over the second, where scientific systematics is weaker; Louis Martz's near-classical reading of the poems in terms of traditional religious meditation favors the second poem over the first, naturally enough, since the second poem adheres more fully than the first to the meditative structure Mr. Martz used as his measuring-rod. According to Miss Nicolson, the first poem is brilliantly organized in a strict topical order. According to Mr. Martz, its rigidity, precisely in this respect, causes it to "break apart." Sooner or later, such critical disparities must be dealt with: both these views cannot be correct. George Williamson, discontented with Martz's assimilation of the poems to the meditative tradition and evidently unconcerned with science, old or new, pointed to their likeness both in topic and structure to the *quaestio* and *responsio* of medieval debate,[6] with their (consequent) reliance on the themes of *contemptus mundi* and *consolatio philosophiae*. O. B. Hardison has shown how the two poems exemplify and adorn the manifold traditions of epideixis: his rhetorical interpretation is particularly valuable in making Elizabeth Drury's place in the poem conventionally comprehensible. Frank Manley's edition of the poems stressed one local deity of the Johns Hopkins Renaissance interpreters, Sophia or Wisdom; for Manley, Elizabeth-Drury-as-Logos is a metaphor for organizing the poem according to the threefold nature of the soul, a solution neatly accounting for the material in both poems on memory, understanding, and will. Northrop Frye's original interpretation of "anatomy," with its implications of mixed genre and tone, responds to the encyclopedic nature of these poems. Frye associates "anatomy" with a cate-

191

gory of works he calls "Menippean satire"; this ghostly category, though useful for the first of our poems, by no means accounts fully for the second which, although "like" its partner in many ways, is far more visionary and even apocalyptic than "anatomical." Recently, Earl Miner has made some very helpful remarks on the poems, stressing the tension between their "satiric antagonism" and their "lyric affirmation," a tension he identifies throughout Donne's verse. Earlier, I tried to solve some problems of interpretation by assimilating the poems to a genre of philosophical (really, epistemological) poetry to be found in the Renaissance, an association which seems to me now to be valid enough, but also seems to raise a great many problems of tone and genre which I did not cope with there. My colleague Barbara Lewalski, at work on Donne's idiosyncratic use of imagery in his epideictic poetry, concentrates on the *Verse Letters* and the *Epicedes and Obsequies*, in order to clarify important aspects of the *Anniversary Poems*. Her forthcoming study should clarify a good deal about the place of meditative structure and of the device *figura* in Donne's poetry.

Now, all these critiques of the poems certainly explain elements of the poems' argument, imagery, doctrine, or structure—and yet the readings conspicuously do not mesh with one another in mutually valuable contributions to interpretation. One can recognize in some of the critics cited a strong effort to find in the poems "harmonious wholes,"[7] to read them as if they are, no matter what, harmonious wholes and thus to ignore or deplore those sections which do not manifest proper proportion or integration. This has meant, of course, that each critic reads the poems from a fixed point of view and ignores viewpoints at variance from his own. One thing does seem clear from the disparate readings themselves: these poems are very highly structured indeed, by one or another (or by one *and* another) system—as is, say, *Ulysses*, another work by a critical and self-critical craftsman. It is the question of "system"

192

that I want to explore—to suggest that the poems' hospitality to multiple readings is not a function of the author's sloppiness so much as of his rigorous inclusiveness.[8]

That inclusiveness comes, I think, from Donne's literary control, his mastery of forms of diction appropriate to, or normally domiciled in, different kinds of poetry. Literally, *kinds*: the poems exploit playfully and seriously, a great many literary genres available to the Renaissance poet. It is precisely this shiftiness that makes the *Anniversary Poems* so difficult for us to read, trained as we are to find unity of thought, structure, pattern and tone in the "good" poems we read; Mr. Frye's postulate of a genre of fragmented works inclusive of various styles was one way to get around, by nomenclature, the critical problem offered by the encyclopedic literary opus.

There is no longer serious doubt that the idea of genre was very important for Renaissance poetry and poetics: even in England (where no great generic quarrels raged such as the Italian battles over epic, romance, and tragi-comedy) critical practice demonstrates the pervasiveness of the habit of writing both within a genre and with reference to definite generic norms. In his *Defence*, Sidney ran through the genres he acknowledged, measuring English accomplishment against various typical models; Wilson and Puttenham, with their very different views of poetry, offered generic catalogs with appropriate rules of rhetoric and poetics. Most important of all, writers recognized (in the breach and in the observance) existing genres as normal modes of expression.[9]

And where there are genres, witness those Italian critical battles, there are mixtures of genres; nothing is more tedious, surely, than the "correct" formal poem so obedient to norm as to lack identity or an identifiable authorial "style," and no Renaissance student will deny that there are a great many such works in that long period of imitation and invention in literary creation. But in the Renaissance, too, there are won-

193

derful experiments with genre, experiments within a given genre, experiments beyond a given genre, experiments with *genera mixta*.[10] Another way of saying that "genre" is important in Renaissance critical theory and practice is to say that there was a great deal of anthological work published in the period. I do not mean just official collections (such as Tottel's) of lyric types or (like *England's Helicon*) of pastoral types, which we naturally call "anthologies"; but also such collections as Spenser's *Fowre Hymnes*, which offers variations upon the uncommon hymn-genre[11]; or his pastoral anthology; or his *Amoretti*, a celebration in several styles of literary love; or (most of all, really) *The Faerie Queene* itself, a conglomerate of literary forms under the mixed title of romantic epic. When one comes to think of it, much major Renaissance literary production is to some degree anthological. From Dante on, sonnet sequences are mixed; obviously collections of essays, following Montaigne's, are bound to be anthological. One can point to the medly of forms common to most Renaissance pastorals—Sannazaro's and Sidney's versions of *Arcadia* are remarkably mixed forms, as many long narrative and discursive works tend to be (e.g., *Gargantua et Pantagruel, The Anatomy of Melancholy*, to say nothing of *Don Quixote*). According to its theorists, pastoral invited the mixing of forms; so did the picaresque, obviously—but so could any form. Lyric forms interpenetrate one another; Marino called one collection *La Galeria*, because it was so ecphrastic and so varied. Andrew Marvell wrote a tiny but mixed gallery poem, and two of his major works, "The Garden" and "Upon Appleton House," are manifestly anthological.[12] Mr. Giamatti has pointed to the "pastoral" in epics, and Alarik Skarstrom has written on the "georgic" element of Renaissance epics.[13] Shakespeare worked constantly in *genera mixta*—the histories are comical-historical and tragical-historical, and most are comical-historical-tragical; *King Lear* may be seen as his anthological play *par excellence*, comical-tragical-historical-pastoral.[14] To speak of nondramatic mixtures, Shakespeare's early love-comedies are (naturally) strongly imbued with sonnet language, but without that sonnet language, he would have had difficulty in making the comic materials of *Romeo and Juliet* and *Othello* into the tragic structures they are.[15]

When one looks at Donne's poetical work, one can see at once that he too performed exercises in a received repertory. The *Songs and Sonets* and *Elegies* show his versatility and experimentalism with traditional forms of lyric verse. His satires are cast in very different tones; the five poems called *Satyres* are very different from the unfinished "Progresse of the Soule," and his satiric prose is altogether different again. Many passages in the parodic elegies and "libertine" love-poems are, as Professor Miner says, governed by the generic vocabulary of satire. The *Epicedes and Obsequies*, the *Verse Letters*, and the *Divine Poems* all show the range of Donne's generic control, both within specific genres and as cross-generic experiments. If one looks at the Elizabeth Drury poems, the elegy and the two anniversaries, as another collection within a genre, this time elegiac, a collection deliberately and openly written with reference to its generic resources, some of the interpretative difficulties associated with the poems may slightly recede.

It is a temptation to take "genre" as an answer—or even *the* answer—to a particular poem's problems, as a set of prescriptive rules to which individual works "must" or "should" conform. Of course, such a view of genre is entirely uncritical, though it might seem justified to modern readers deep in Renaissance treatises on poetics, where the notion is at least implied that a literary work is good insofar as it adheres to that genre's rules and displays its typical qualities. Other critics, innocent of Renaissance literary doctrine, also behave as if identifying the genre of a given work "explains" why it is as it is. With most works, especially good ones, that method does not lead far. Cervantes borrowed a great deal from the pica-resque novel, but he did not, for instance, borrow its generic hero; Shakespeare, similarly, wrote a revenge tragedy with a hero strayed in from an entirely different literary and psychological milieu.[16] To "identify" *Don Quixote* by calling it picaresque, or *Hamlet* by calling it a revenge-tragedy, is a poor substitute for criticism—let alone a poor substitute for reading. On the other hand, one can understand a great deal about Renaissance craftsmanship if one has some sense of what genres meant in a given country or culture, what Renaissance writers thought a given genre "implied" or "invoked." A writer's modifications of genre, like his choices among genres, can tell a great deal about his literary mastery, as well as about the modes of what we now call "communication" between a writer and his audi-ence. I doubt that criticism-by-genre, viewed as definitive (as occasionally E.D. Hirsch seems to imply, in his valuable book),[17] is a final method of reading literature, even Renais-sance literature; but I am as sure that to read Renaissance literature without some sense of what genre meant to writers is to falsify unnecessarily. Further, what might be called the *thematics* of genre is often useful, particularly in reading those works which elude definition both by Renaissance standards and by the prevailing modes of modern criticism. Works like the *Anniversary Poems*—or Burton's *Anatomy*, or *Paradise Lost* —have at the very least adumbrations of literary genres differ-ent from the "dominant" genre and at most whole sections ad-mittedly cast in a genre different from the dominant or official genre of the book. The case of *Paradise Lost*, mentioned on purpose, seems simpler to us than it is, I think, because in spite of pastoral and georgic interludes, hexaemeric narrative, theo-logical debate, cosmological debate, and psychomachy, we know that the poem "is" an epic, so sturdily does it adhere to what we recognize as the rules for epic behavior. But its text, its weave, has many individual patterns, which manage by some power of literary deployment and tact to be serviceable also to a larger (and, in this case, actually harmonious) whole.[18]

In the case of the *Anniversary Poems*, the matter is by no means so simple. We do not in fact know to what major genre, if any, these poems belong. Indeed, they may be "new" genres (as Mr. Frye suggests); the titles given them, "anatomy" and "progress," suggest that we are not supposed to read the poems against any normative generic set, but rather with other considerations in mind. "Anatomy" carries categorical and taxonomic implications and "progress" implications of an orderly picaresque; from the beginning, then, the poems pose problems and offer hints to their solution.

Certainly the two poems, and "A Funerall Elegie" as well, display passages from kinds other than elegiac. Meditative structure is important in both poems; particularly in the second, there are passages of "perfect" meditation. They are in important ways "like" other philosophical poems of the Renaissance (a recognized genre then if not now), as Henri Estienne's edition of ancient philosophical poetry attests[19]; the first poem is in part the physico-theology which Miss Nicolson's imaginative scholarship has identified. The poems display the proper elements of the poetry of praise, a mode crossing many generic boundaries; they utilize lyric and satiric language, to say nothing of the languages of religion and natural philosophy, which in other poets' work are not customarily found in funeral poetry. Indeed, the poems point so blatantly to their multiple formal origins that it is not surprising that scholars have in fact taken them apart ("as a sundred clocke is peece-meale laid") to look at fragments, segments, image lines, and so on which could be organized into a consistent system. What *is* surprising is that no one has addressed himself to this problem, that of the multiple systems in the poem; that no one has tried to put himself in the poet's place, save psychologically, to work at the literary reason for the many "peeces" of the poems. Why *are* they so oddly and so persistently disjunctive? Might they, their parts reexamined like the clock-parts in "A Funerall Elegie," "Re-pollish'd" be seen "without errour then to stand"?

If there are readings which actually see the poems whole, I do not know them; nor have I seen (though I cannot imagine why not) a stylistic analysis of the poems utilizing the notion of "voice" exploited by Anne Davidson Ferry in her reading of *Paradise Lost*.[20] Mrs. Sicherman's "gallinic" reading strikes at the poem's central meaning, but leaves aside considerations of art, or even craftsmanship. To look at the generic aspects of the poem has at the very least the merit of implied comparison: to think of "satyre" or "lyric" in relation to the *Anniversaries*, one must know some satires and some lyrics, by Donne and others. My interpretation of the poems, far from final, relies on the notion of genre as a set of scales, in different keys and in different modes, scales tempered and modulated by mutual compatibility; or on the idea of genre as offering a range of alternatives possible to Renaissance poets searching for languages for their particular poems. In no sense is the idea of "genre" here assumed to be dictatorial or predestinating—very far from it. Genre is taken to be a set of hints, suggestions, evocations, a range of implications borne by thematic language and structure (or ordering of language), which a given poet arranges to convey his meanings, his messages. This way, content and form are not seen as separate or separable elements in a work, still less as hostile elements: thematic language may be highly intellectual (or oriented toward content) at one time, highly emotional at another, but the linguistic devices are in each case not formally different. Sometimes a poet's messages are in shorthand (cryptic, "metaphysical"), sometimes they are explicit, but the messages are there, and are there to be read and deciphered. They are directed to auditors and readers assumed to be as aware as the poet of the state of the poet's art, directed to a reader experienced in literary schemata, *topoi*, customs, habits.[21]

琴

Generic Themes

In his *Epicedes and Obsequies,* Donne showed that he knew the difference between two principal kinds of funeral poem. An epicedium is traditionally spoken over a body still unburied, as George Puttenham tells us, "at the very burialls of the dead"[22]; those spoken later, "at monthes mindes and longer times, by custome continued yearely, when as they used many offices of service and love towardes the dead," were "thereupon . . . called *Obsequies* by our vulgare."[23] To Scaliger, poems in the second category were called, not obsequies, but anniversaries: of them, he says specifically that no one can continue to bewail the dead after two years, so that as anniversaries "progress," or go on, they should lose their qualities of lament and take on the character of a consolation or even, in some cases, of a rejoicing.[24] Certainly the three poems in the Drury elegiac collection observe the various literary funeral conventions. They move, as Scaliger prescribes, from hyperbolical lament to hyperbolical joy. The "Funerall Elegie" is properly an epitaph, the pronunciation over the body buried—in the poet's words, "in a marble chest," in "a Tombe," both the actual container of the dead body and the metaphorical container of the dead person, "these memorials, ragges of paper," the elegy's pretty room. As the two complimentary poems on Donne's verses (probably by Joseph Hall) make plain, the poems are also monodies, in which the poet speaks largely in his own voice, but with passages spoken as by a chorus; that is, passages of lament to which his hearers are assumed to subscribe.[25] In the *First Anniversary,* "An Anat-

omy of the World," the poet combines the official elegiac epitaph, spoken over the lady's buried body, with an epicedium,
spoken over the world's unburied body. In "The Progesse," the
whole point of the poem is that the bodies, lady's and world's,
have been left behind as soul(s), poet, and poem "progress" to
heaven, where all worthy souls dwell and to which their resur-
rected bodies, maintained in perfection, shall ultimately come.
This elegiac collection transcends elegy, but in terms familiar
to readers of Christian consolation.

Conventional and unconventional, these poems are obedient to old regulations about funeral poetry, but peculiarly
independent as well; they fuse styles and themes normally held
apart in separate poems. The titles of the *Anniversaries* are,
similarly, conventional and unconventional; as "anniversaries,"
the poems move from lament to paean, and insofar as they illustrate their own titles, "Anatomie" and "Progresse," they deal
in material perfectly irrelevant to elegiac content. Obviously,
the word "anatomie" has been given new currency by one aspect
of the new science; as the title of many different examples of
kinds of writing, the word was widespread in the period. It
often meant no more than "analysis," as Hardison notes,[26] and,
although it may have carried strong medical connotations, these
were usually metaphorical. Donne not only exploited the term's
medical application but built elaborate conceits on the idea of
dissection, the process of disassembling his "world" as Vesalius
had disassembled the different systems of the human body. The
governing metaphor in "The Anatomie of the World" is of
course that of the correspondence between the human body
(taken as microcosm) and the world's body (macrocosm), which
in the poem is both the body of the planet Earth and the body
of the universe, or known cosmos. As Miss Nicolson's chapter on
the poem shows, the first poem commemorates the idea, ob-
solescent in the seventeenth century, that the universe is an ani-

mate body composed of material elements like any other part of
the creation, and especially like the human body; like the human body also inspirited with a soul by its creator.

Though obviously this metaphor of correspondence has
its origin in the human body, extrapolated to "explain" the
world (man the measure of all things),[27] the hieratic conception
of the creation made canonical in the middle ages usually expressed the correspondence from the large to the small, from the
universe down to man: the cosmos, or the world, was the analogy's dominant figure, the human body described as if it were
designed in imitation of the cosmic order. By Donne's time, the
analogy was so common as to be used without particular sense
of its oddity, visual or intellectual[28]; it was not, then, a conceit
but a paradigm. What is interesting about Donne's use of the
common cliché is his taking the term "anatomy" so literally, his
unmetaphorical use of the common notion, expressed again and
again by preachers, moralists and satirists, that the world is in
decay, is "sick." Certainly the notion of the world's illness does
lead to the notion of its death (oddly enough, however, not a
common topic even among those who lamented its decay at
length),[29] thence to the notion of the world-as-carcass, thence to
the clever variation that as a carcass, the world is properly subject to "anatomy."

On the one hand, the anatomy-notion permits the poet
to demonstrate, one by one and category by category, the diseases and defects of the world, to show the world part by part,
member by member, "in peeces"; on the other, his function as
elegist permits the poet to deplore the ills of the world, to catalog the world's lack of health, integrity, value, wholeness. But
neither tradition dictates the radical metaphor[30] of the world's
soul as the "shee" lamented as the official subject of the poems.
That variation on conventional correspondence is the poet's
own.[31] What have we, then, in terms of literary thematics? The

girl's body, entombed, has been honored in "A Funerall Elegie"; the "Anatomie" celebrates, as it says it does, the first anniversary of her death,[32] yet it is an anatomy too, and as such it catalogs the world's ills as preacher or satirist might. The stress on pneumatology adds still another dimension to the poem, so that we are less surprised than we might be by the passages of doctrinal content; because of the systematic implications of the word "anatomy," we are ready for the considerable philosophical material intermixed with the rest. For all his flighty vocabulary, Northrop Frye is surely on the right track when he considers an anatomy to be an encyclopedic work of mixed materials; if the materials are mixed, then Renaissance decorum suggests that genre and tone are likely to be mixed as well.

The divisions of the poem's systematic content are marked by a refrain which fills another prescription of funeral poetry, the epigrammatic epitaph designed for incision on a stone, the briefest possible record of a dead person's value. "Shee, shee is dead" is such an epigrammatic epitaph, as well as the functional refrain marking the substantive categories by which the examination, the anatomy, is carried out. But in fact there is no special literary rule connecting the death of a woman and the death of a world—the cosmological and scientific analysis Donne lays out so engagingly is no natural pendent of the decision to write an elegy. The illness of this world, in the poem, is simply the happy extension of the implications of the title. It turns out, though, that the poet as anatomist, or as physician, is well domiciled in lament and satire, or more simply, in complaint. "This was a very necessary devise of the Poet and a fine [sic], besides his poetrie to play also the Phisitian, and not onely by applying a medicine to the ordinary sicknes of mankind, but by making the very greef it self (in part) cure of the disease."[33] Making the physician an anatomist brings the metaphor up to date and is, given the decision to exploit the possibilities of cosmic correspondence, tactically brilliant—but it remains entirely within the implications of the decorum of lamenting. John Peter has pointed out at length[34] that the complaint characteristically considers man's fallen state as a result of "home-borne, intrinsique harme," a topical preoccupation which brings the lament well into the area we associate with the genre of meditation, in which the Fall is also a major topic. Medieval complaint characteristically attacked the social categories of the fallen world, types of profession, sinner, and abuse: each category has its place in Donne's "Anatomie," which dutifully dissects the abuses of both social and political worlds.

The analogy of the state to the human body, both seen as corporate entities, is a classical commonplace everywhere in Renaissance political writing. Though it sometimes occurs in metaphorical parallel to "body," it is rare in those extended analogies between the human body and the physical world found in the philosophical and subphilosophical literature; here, it seems to me eminently to apply to the extended correspondences of the poem, especially when these are systematically laid out. The most overt statement of the correspondence between body and state is in "A Funerall Elegie," where different professions take their proper places as anatomical members of Leviathan's body (all quotations of poetry are from *The Poems of John Donne*, ed. H. J. C. Grierson [Oxford, 1912]):

> *The world containes*
> *Princes for armes, and Counsellors for braines,*
> *Lawyers for tongues, Divines for hearts, and more,*
> *The Riche for stomackes, and for backes, the Poore;*
> *The Officers for hands, Merchants for feet,*
> *By which, remote and distant Countries meet.*

> (ll. 21–26)

In the "Anatomie," there are several references, some quite slanting, to the goverance of the world and to political units parallel in organization (and in decay)[35]; further use is made of the analogy in the "Progresse."[36] In various ways, these passages of political and social commentary are made to conform with the poem's specific topics as well as with the general theme of decay. Furthermore, though some commentators have considered the satiric tone of these passages out of place in the "Anatomie," tasteless results of the poet's personal cast of mind, such images have their traditional place in the literature of complaint. As Minturno tells us, satires properly used the language of disease, both body and soul, to make vivid metaphors for social ills;[37] and the satirist's cathartic aims are prescribed from antiquity. Nonetheless, though disease-language was common to both complaint and formal satire, the notion of treating the macrocosmic world as a human body, literally subject to diseases usually treated metaphorically only, is the particular imaginative contribution of our poet, consciously marrying the conventions of many literary modes to unify and to increase the force of the metaphors and themes of his long cosmic lament.

By saying so much, in so many literary languages, the poet manages a literary pluralism appropriate to the encyclopedic notion of analyzing the world. But the problem of such pluralism, as of such encyclopedism, is precisely one of focus. We are made to consider a great many areas of reference, are forced to change our tempo as readers, because the poet calls up various generic and topical themes and moves us about from one generic tone to another. It is no accident that the following passage, from "An Anatomie," dealing with members of the body politic reminds us of the *Satyres*, or the satirical *Elegies*, and passages in "The Will," "The Indifferent," or "The Canonization":

> *. . . some Princes have some temperance;*
> *Some Counsellors some purpose to advance*
> *The common profit; and some people have*
> *Some stay, no more than Kings should give, to crave;*
> *Some women have some taciturnity,*
> *Some nunneries some graines of chastitie.*

(ll. 419–424)

Certainly the passage is an interjection from that field of feeling. But it fits the poem too, in its quick survey of social types with special pretensions to the responsibility, wisdom, and virtue with which the poem fundamentally deals. The passage gives us, in little, an anatomy of the social and political world, of society's corporate body, in parallel to the larger anatomical scheme of the whole poem. Of course, there is a flamboyance in this passage, notably different from the section of the poem in which it occurs (as can be said of so many passages in these poems). One is tempted to say, then, that this disjunction of tone and generic topic illustrates the fragmented style which to so many critics has seemed to harm the poems' effects and to deprive them of unity. As one examines these "separable" passages, though, they seem thematically or intellectually ever more related to the whole, as the poet uses the formal implications of theme to support his strategy.

These lines invite comparison with another passage, on harmony in the state, in the "Progresse" (ll. 359–375), which led Miss Nicolson and Marius Bewley to associate "shee" with the dead Queen Elizabeth. The poet runs through the duties of kingship, attributing them in perfect kind to the proportion-giving lady praised in his eulogies; "Shee" was a state, enjoyed royalties, made wars and made peace, distributed justice, pardoned, coined, protected against arrest; "Shee" was a church as well as a state. All these prerogatives were unquestionably

205

those of real sovereigns, Elizabeth Tudor and her forbears and descendants, her colleagues across the Channel and wherever monarchies remained. But these same things were said, metaphorically, hyperbolically, of many nonpolitical subjects of epideixis, as Curtius and Hardison have shown us.[38] So used, the praise, conventional though it was, was frankly hyperbolical, a display of hyperbole. That is all that can be said of the *topos* here, too—save that it too operates in a particularly intellectual way, as the poet seeks to make vivid the metaphor of incorporation common in the technical literature of politics. The healthy political world, neither diseased nor dead, with no use for an anatomy, was incorporated into the once-living body of the lady.[39] She was "all," a word which redresses the defects of the repeated "some" in the passage of similar subject-matter in the "Anatomie," and entirely alters the tone in which this political matter is cast.

Altogether, the "Progresse" passage is pure paean, more appropriate to what Puttenham calls "poeticall rejoycinges" than to lament. Its lamenting quality lies simply in the nostalgic tense, when all this wonderful condition "was" the world's. That tense is crucial, however, as the reiterated "made," "made," "made" turns the glories into elegiac memory. Other themes of lament, complaint, and satire, strong and incisive when passages are taken alone, modulate into the dominant key as well; the philosophical material, for instance, turns out to be generically appropriate. The satirist, Minturno tells us, is not supposed to *be* a philosopher, but he is supposed to *use* philosophy to turn people away from vice; the perturbations and illnesses of the soul can be allayed and corrected by a philosophical prescription or demonstration.[40] As George Williamson pointed out, the *Anniversary Poems* draw heavily on medieval philosophical traditions already assimilated in poetry organized in debate-form, *contemptus mundi* and *consolatio philosophiae*.[41] The debate is a genre which quite obviously

206

throws its shadow across our poems, in strongly "philosophical" shape. The scientific dubieties of the first poem are swept away in the wind from the cosmic excursion in the second; the episte-mological uncertainties of both poems are resolved in the celes-tial perfection promised the soul at the end of the second poem. Though the poems are not exactly *quaestio* and *responsio*, they do exploit the structural patterns of such deliberative formulae, and exploit them in the service of the lament and its dialectical concomitant, comfort and consolation. *Con-temptus mundi* is a topic not generically limited, of course; rather it is a theme, or set of themes, often found in debates, in meditations, and particularly in poems (sometimes they are debates or meditative poems) dealing with pneumatology, dis-cussions or debates of soul and body. In the case of Donne's poems, the body-soul debate is present, but we have to think to see how it works, with the soul in debate, not with the human body only, but also with the world's body, a piece of fancy planning that permits the fusion of traditions from several types of moral literature.

Philosophical though they are, the poems do not offer much consolation from philosophy, here taken not as a source of comfort but as one of the sheerly worldly things distracting the soul from her proper object, the heavenly state. The "Anat-omie" and the "Progresse" both reject the world, though they do their rejecting very differently. In the first poem, intellec-tual constructs commonly used to "explain" the world are rejected; in the second, modes of human understanding are rejected altogether. "Philosophy" goes down before theology, before pneumatology, in this curious debate of soul with mind. Philosophy, in short, does not console, but further contributes to human distress, offering the poet opportunity for human self-criticism and self-derogation. To say that, in the seventeenth century, major philosophers turned from the study of meta-physics to the study of epistemology (perhaps in some cases

207

even turned metaphysics into epistemology) is a truism. Donne was fully aware of the threat to metaphysics involved in a preoccupation with human understanding. Like Montaigne in the *Apologie,* he does away with the possibility of human knowledge: "Poore soule, in this thy flesh what dost thou know?" he asks, in the "Progresse," to answer discouragingly. For the purposes of Donne's poems, epistemology is one of the maladies of the world.

Nonetheless, *Consolatio est oratio reducens moerentis animum ad tranquillitatem,*[42] and Donne's poem gradually conforms to that regulation. To do so, however, the poet has to reject, along with the world, the usual sources of intellectual consolation in order to clear man's attention for revelation. No wonder Mr. Martz judged "Of the Progresse of the Soule" the better poem of the two by standards of meditative structure: its title tells us that this must be so. Not only does it exhibit more fully the formal strategies of private meditation in that marvellous passage of *compositio loci* where the poet exhorts his soul to "Thinke," "Thinke" its way into the grave and out again, it observes as well the full meditative "Progresse" from earth to heaven ("Up," "Up"), as "An Anatomie of the World," preoccupied with its titular subject, obedient to its titular method, could not be expected to do. In the "Progresse" the subject-matter "ascends," even in that contemporary flight of fancy by which, in a space-fiction, the doubts of the world are transcended. In the "Anatomie," the poet looted material from the new science, material cited normally as evidence of God's providence, to make absolute the need to reject the world; in the "Progresse," he raids it again, to permit the soul easy escape from the world's limitations. The consolations offered in the "Progresse," however, do not encourage men to "think" or to think well of the new cosmography, the new philosophy; they are entirely the comforts of faith and the true religion. The

mind gives way to the soul, philosophy to theology, since only
the soul can learn, can experience joy, can achieve reward in
heaven. Under our eyes, we see the metamorphosis of "shee"
from human person to soul—and the gender is right, for Elizabeth Drury, for *psyche,* and for *anima.*

The developing "Progresse" is as remarkable for its
climax as the "Anatomie" for its hyperbolical lamenting. In
the end, these poems do become "poeticall rejoycinges," the
preparative and the realization; the cause for lament becomes
the cause for rejoicing. "Joy" is dependent, for poet and readers
as representatives of mankind, upon the lady's death and resurrection. The exaggerated despair of the lament gradually turns
into an equally extreme rejoicing, as the second poem ends on a
formal catalog of distinguishable but fused joys awaiting the
Christian soul. Looking back across the poems, the reader can
find, amidst all the gloom, substantial hints in the first poem of
the joy to come in the second. Some of these hints bear literary names. In the birth of the lady's soul—"thy second birth, /
That is, thy death"—at the end of the "Anatomie," and the
soul's enfranchisement and enlargement in the "Progresse,"
we can recognize a pneumatological genethliac; in the absorp-
tion of that liberated soul as a saint into heaven, the glorious
predictions of the Messianic Eclogue are brought up-to-date as
the young ruler-soul enters her kingdom.

Again and again, we find linguistic incidents of praise associated with classes and types of poetry—the satiric misogyny
of the poems (women's painting, lovers' fluidity, woman's constant temptation to men) is more than balanced by the petrarchan language applied to the lady. In "A Funerall Elegie,"
we find chrysolite, pearls, rubies, and the Indies, standard love
compliments to a lady's beauty; in the "Anatomie," the West
Indies and the East too, as well as their spice and gold. There
is also the red and white of all lovely ladies, applied to our lady's

complexion, and the electrum, applied to her entire self. This lady is the epitome and purification of all ladies loved by poets ("The Idea of Woman"). The dean's complimenter, probably Joseph Hall, noted the right association in his "Harbinger to the [Donne's] Progresse," when he wrote "Let thy Makers praise / Honor thy Laura," a beloved woman who, like our poet's lady, was particularly celebrated and particularly effective *in morte.*

Honored by the language of secular love and ennobled by the *stilnovisti* habit (inherited and exploited by Petrarch) of likening a beloved woman to the Virgin or to the Deity,[43] our "shee" is called "blessed maid," "Immortall Maide"; her name is invoked like a saint's name in papist France; her virginity is like the virtue of the Wise Virgins ("A Funerall Elegie," ll. 73–76) as well as like that of the Virgin Mary. For those who believe that the lady is Queen Elizabeth, it is worth noting that, Protestant that she was, that Queen was nonetheless often celebrated by her subjects in the language Roman Catholics used to praise religious virgins and the Virgin herself. In other words, "virginity" is a *topos* in which complimentary likeness to Mary is normal. Typology works to praise this lady, whose perfect proportions make her a type of the Ark, and the Ark in turn becomes a type of her, not just because it was constructed according to human proportions, but also because (as all things did in her), all creatures lived in peace in the Ark ("Anatomie," ll. 317–321). More important still is the decorous analogy to Christ, an analogy made in terms of the poetic form, the anniversary, in which the poet is writing:

> *Some moneths she hath beene dead (but being dead,*
> *Measures of times are all determined) . . .*

> (ll. 39–40)

As human time is reckoned from the birth of Our Lord, so the poet's time is reckoned from the death of the lady, or, better, from the birth of her soul—or, her life-in-death.[44] In "A Funerall Elegie," Donne describes the process of *figura*, that is, how one reads present events as the fulfillment of an actual and symbolic event from the past, in terms of his dead maiden: the man who studied her early perfections as if he studied a sacred book, "measuring future things, by things before,/ Should turn the leafe to reade," and because she is dead, "reade no more." "History" is finished. In fact, Donne offers, in these poems themselves, a gloss upon that empty page, upon the significance of that abridged life. His "shee" is treated symbolically as the world's soul, typologically as involved in the world's history and in the development of each human soul. She becomes a type to be fulfilled in any Christian's experience; from her, all else can be inferred. She is the epitome; she is a true microcosm. To this extent, Ben Jonson, confessing a religion different from Donne's, was not altogether wrong in calling Donne's treatment of this lady blasphemous. Indeed, as many of the symbolized subjects in Donne's *Verse Letters* and *Epicedes and Obsequies* are also, this lady is a model for the Christian life, a model the Roman Catholic world would more naturally assume to be Christ or a saint. But this is a once living girl, raised to hyperbolical rhetoric to be the true model of human *imitatio*:[45]

> if after her
> Any shall live, which dare true good prefer,
> Every such person is her deligate,
> T'accomplish that which should have been her
>   Fate.
> They shall make up that Booke and shall have
>   thanks

Of Fate, and her, for filling up their blankes.
For future vertuous deeds are Legacies,
Which from the gift of her example rise;
And 'tis in heav'n part of spirituall mirth,
To see how well the good play her, on earth.

("A Funerall Elegie," ll. 97–106)

At the same time, this is the function of ladies secularly as well
as spiritually loved; in such terms Dante invoked his mediating
Beatrice, Petrarch his mediating Laura, whose future effect
must be felt in each case by means of the poet's "Booke."

There is a poetic type to which, I think, Donne's verse
aspires, though it does not conform to that type's conventions.
That is the hymn, named in the "Progresse." "These Hymnes,"
he says, "may work on future wits"; "These Hymnes" shall be
the lady's issue, until the Day of Judgment cut them off. Several sorts of hymn were known to Renaissance theorists, the
hymns of the gentiles praising their gods and the hymns of the
Christian in praise of his single Deity. The Psalms of David
were the major models for the Christian hymn, which therefore tended to be a subspecies of the poetry of praise; Spenser's
Fowre Hymnes manages to recapitulate, with a Christian cast
given the vocabulary, the high philosophical aims attributed
by Renaissance critics to ancient hymnodists.[46] In speaking of
the Christian hymn, Scaliger says that by its means the soul is
led from the prison of its body to the wide fields of contemplation, to which region the hymn's reader is also translated.
Chiefly, the hymn should make clear the great gulf between
God and man, and man made aware of his "imbecillitas."[47] Certainly this definition of the hymn is congruent with what Donne
does, and "imbecillitas" has its peculiar application in his
poems. But all the same, though this might be its theme when
handled by Christians, the hymn proper, with its supposed
classical models, was quite different, and dealt rather with the

descent of the soul to earth than with the (Christian) ascent of the soul to heaven. Donne borrows devices from the literary kind, indeed, as usual fused with other literary implications, such as the soul's flight and passage through the spheres; but Donne's poems, for all their arrival in heaven, begin on earth and take their measurements from human experience. Furthermore, the classical hymn derives from philosophical convictions, and his poems manage to undermine precisely these.

What can these poems be called? They are, in each case, what the poet called them—the first an anatomy, the second a progress, *ad hoc* forms pointing rather to theme than to structure, indeed named to suggest their formal independence and creativity. The first poem is an examination of the world dismembered into "peeces" and into smaller "worlds" of cosmology, intellection, and experience. Since the "Anatomie" is by definition future-oriented, looking to a later cure, it is no wonder that the poet fitted his material to that scheme, to lead toward the progressions of the second year, the *Second Anniversary*, far less unhappy than the first. The same sort of justification may be made for "Progresse," the name given to a sovereign's formal removal from one seat to another. Practically speaking, the term consolidates the recurrent imagery of statecraft and ruling ("When that Queene ended here her progresse time"); thematically, it stresses the movement forward from despair to hope, from decay to renewed health, from intellectual confusion to spiritual revelation. The lady's soul makes that progress, on its way fusing with the poet's soul, to carry him along, the first of her imitators, on a meditative passage to heaven. The medical "Extasie," the "Lethargie," from which the world and poet suffer in the first poem turns into the environmental ecstasy offered by heavenly experience; the condition of ecstasy is, then, normalized in the course of the poem.

To reach this ecstasy, bodies must, as we know from

Donne's other poetry, be cast aside. The dead lady's soul has as its midwife death, freeing it for its second birth; the world's body must have died and been anatomized before it can be knowingly rejected. From its anatomy, its systematic disassembly, comes understanding of the world's worth, without which the soul cannot reject the world. When the body of the world has "died" to the soul, then individual souls—the poet's, the readers'—can hear the trumpet of the Apocalypse; since his subject is "like" the book from which the lady takes her typological power, the poet can, at her death and the world's, play his part by being a "Trumpet, at whose voyce the people came" after, his poem the proclamation of her progress to her new seat, to her new reign. The imagery fuses various ranges of the poems' thematically different languages in an image to remind us of the fundamental "cohaerence" of Christian revelation, which can make "peeces" of a magnificent whole, at the Christian Apocalypse recomposing the separated bodies and souls of all human beings into one great experiential, inconceivable cosmic structure. By seeing into and wittily exploiting the various pieces of the literary repertory, Donne has forced them beyond their own limits, toward a new coherence unspecified in the textbooks of mankind.

Brown University

Notes

1. For biographical material relating to the composition of these poems, see R. C. Bald, *Donne and the Druries* (Cambridge, 1959); and R. C. Bald, *John Donne: A Life* (Oxford, 1970).

2. For discussions of this poem, see chiefly: Marjorie Hope Nicolson, *The Breaking of the Circle* (New York, 1960), chapter 3; Louis L. Martz, *The*

ROSALIE L. COLIE

Poetry of Meditation (New Haven, 1954), chapter 6; George Williamson, "The Design of Donne's *Anniversaries*," in *Milton and Others* (Chicago, 1965); Frank Manley's Introduction to his edition of the *Anniversaries* (Baltimore, 1963); O. B. Hardison, Jr., *The Enduring Monument* (Chapel Hill, 1962), Chapter 7; Northrop Frye, *Anatomy of Criticism* (Princeton, 1969); my *Paradoxia Epidemica* (Princeton, 1966), Chapter 13; and the forthcoming study by Barbara K. Lewalski of the imagery of the *Anniversary Poems* in the context of epideixis in general and of Donne's practice in his poems addressed to specific people and in his funeral sermons of praise.

3. Carol Marks Sicherman, "Donne's Timeless Anniversaries," *UTQ*, 39 (1970): 126–43.

4. Poulet's method, now powerful in American criticism, is admirably illustrated in his *Studies in Human Time* and *The Interior Distance*; the recent work of J. Hillis Miller and Geoffrey Hartman provide examples of the transfer to American modes of literary criticism Poulet's mode of extracting from literary works the inner biographies of their authors. Mrs. Sicherman's essay, by no means the programmatically organized study that Miller's and Hartman's are, nonetheless raises (as do the others) interesting questions about the relation of this new biographism to the critically discredited "old" biographies, of which Gosse's life of Donne is a notorious example. Though the method is very seductive, especially now, when the confessional theory of literary is dominant, it has remarkably anti-literary presuppositions, in its identification of literary products with the producer's mental processes. I note this new romanticism simply to make clear my own divergence from it.

5. Nicolson, *Breaking of the Circle* contains much new material and a far greater degree of systematization than the useful, stimulating study by Charles Monroe Coffin, *John Donne and the New Philosophy* (New York, 1937, 1958), especially chapters 6 through 9.

6. For notions on medieval debates, I am indebted to my colleague Michel-André Bossy.

7. For observations on the implications of this phrase, see E. H. Gombrich, "Raphael's 'Madonna della Sedia'," *Norm and Form* (London, 1966), pp. 64–80.

8. For a stimulating study of several different systems' working in single poems, see Stephen Booth, *An Essay on Shakespeare's Sonnets* (New Haven, 1969).

9. For some of my colleagues, "genre" needs no defense; for others, genre criticism is indefensible. All the same, I have made some effort to treat the place of genre in the work of one Renaissance poet and to formulate a concept of generic thematics there; *see* my *"My Ecchoing Song": Andrew Marvell's Poetry of Criticism* (Princeton, 1970).

10. *Genera mixta (mista)* is a subject many literary scholars write about without invoking its ugly name. For the Renaissance, at least, a good critical study of the subject is badly needed.

11. My colleague Sears Jayne has just finished an article on the genre of Spenser's *Fowre Hymnes,* with a substantial account of Renaissance hymn theory.

12. Colie, *"My Ecchoing Song,"* parts 2 and 4.

13. A. Bartlett Giamatti, *The Earthly Paradise and the Renaissance Epic* (Princeton, 1966); Mr. Skarstrom's work is in progress.

14. For material on *Lear* and *genera mixta,* see Sheldon Zitner's forthcoming piece.

15. In my work on Shakespeare and various Renaissance conventions, I deal with this subject, especially in relation to *Othello.*

16. Bridget J. Gellert's *The Voices of Melancholy* (London, 1971) and my study of *Hamlet* (as yet unpublished), very closely related to hers, deal with this specific mixture.

17. *Validity in Interpretation* (New Haven, 1967).

18. Actually, *Paradise Lost* could bear more study in this direction, for which the works of many scholars and critics (e.g., Martz, Giamatti, McColley, Nicolson, Williams, Samuel, Empson, Lewalski) all lay considerable groundwork; what we need though, is a critical study of the workings of genre and generic themes in the poem.

19. Cf. *Poesis Philosophica* (Paris, 1573), ed. Henri Estienne, who also published several other collections by genre of classical texts.

20. See Ferry, *Milton's Epic Voice* (Cambridge, Mass., 1963).

21. See (as always) E. H. Gombrich, *Art and Illusion* (London and New York, 1960) and his essay in *Norm and Form;* I have tried to adapt some of his method in my work on paradoxy and on Andrew Marvell.

22. Puttenham, *The Arte of English Poetrie,* ed. G. D. Willcock and Alice Walker (Cambridge, 1936), p. 48: cf. J. C. Scaliger, *Poetices libri septem,* ed. August Buck (Stuttgart, 1964), p. 52.

23. Puttenham, *Arte of English Poetrie,* p. 48.

24. Scaliger, *Poetices,* p. 168.

25. Puttenham, *Arte of English Poetrie,* p. 48; Scaliger, *Poetices,* pp. 52, 168.

26. Hardison, *Enduring Monument,* p. 171.

27. For material on this metaphor, see Nicolson, *Breaking the Circle;* Rudolf Wittkower, *Architectural Principles in an Age of Humanism* (London, 1962); Erwin Panofsky, "The History of Human Proportion as a Re-

flection of the History of Styles," *Meaning in the Visual Arts* (Garden City, 1955), and the bibliography there cited.

28. The metaphor was, in the work of writers in the occult tradition (Fludd, Dee, the Rosicrucians), remarkably "animate" as a metaphor and as a tenet of belief.

29. For material on the decay of the world, see Victor Harris, *All Coherence Gone* (Chicago, 1949); it is worth noting, too, that decay, with its odours, ("Nor smels it well to hearers"), was a standard meditative topic, especially in Catholic devotional literature. See Terence Cave, *Devotional Poetry in France* (Cambridge, 1970), pp. 40–41.

30. For much on the soul in this poem, I am indebted to Mrs. Lewalski.

31. For this reason, among others, Charles Coffin thought of Elizabeth Drury as a Christ-figure, if not as Christ. Mrs. Lewalski's work should go far to set the limits of verification for such interpretations.

32. It suggests her death at least poetically: Bald's dating suggests that the poet did not keep to the calendar.

33. Puttenham, *Arte of English Poetrie*, p. 47.

34. John Peter, *Complaint and Satire in Early English Literature* (Oxford, 1956), esp. pp. 60–80.

35. "Anatomie," ll. 215–217, 233–234, 322, 415ff.

36. "Progresse," ll. 78, 117–118, 236–238, 357–375.

37. Antonio Sebastiano Minturno, *De Poeta* (Venice, 1559), p. 421: "*Ut igitur corporis aegrotationes, ac vulnera medicinae materiam diceres, quod in his illa omnino vertatur, ita morbos animi, in quibus haec Satyrica poesis versetur, eijus facultatis materiam appellemus.*" As he says a bit later, the satiric poet "*amara potione curat.*"

38. E. R. Curtius, *European Literature in the Latin Middle Ages*, tr. Willard Trask (New York, 1953), Chapter 9; Hardison, *Enduring Monument,* and *see* Marius Bewley, "Religious Cynicism in Donne's Poetry," *Kenyon Review,* 14 (1952): 619–46.

39. The political matter is thus turned to both satiric and eulogistic uses; the passage cited is part of the eulogy which Martz praises in the second poem—but manifestly it is not on a meditative subject.

40. Minturno, *De Poeta*, p. 424.

41. Williamson, "Design"; Peter, *Complaint*; *see* also J. B. Leishman, *The Monarch of Wit* (London, 1957), pp. 238–50.

42. Scaliger, *Poetices*, p. 168.

43. Martz, *Poetry of Meditation*, pp. 223–30; Hardison, *Enduring Monument*, p. 173.

44. An important pun on "determined" is included.

45. *See* note 25, above: Mrs. Lewalski is concerned about showing the differences between Roman Catholic and Protestant meditative traditions and habits.

46. Cf. Jayne (Fowre *Hymnes*) on Spencer's hymns.

47. Scaliger, *Poetices*, p. 162.

DAVID NOVARR

"*THE EXSTASIE*"

DONNE'S ADDRESS ON THE STATES OF UNION

From thinking us all soule, neglecting thus
Our mutuall duties, Lord deliver us.
("A Litanie," ll. 143–44)

"We are at last becoming aware, in general, that our primary office for this poet is . . . to establish a full technical context, and to trace material sources." The words of Mr. A. J. Smith, written in 1958,[1] may serve to remind us that Donne scholarship has come a long way since the pioneering work done by Sir Herbert Grierson in his commentary on the poems (1912), by Mary Paton Ramsay in *Les Doctrines Médiévales chez Donne* (1917), and by Charles M. Coffin in *John Donne and the New Philosophy* (1937). The last decade or two have seen the publication of contextual and source studies even for individual poems, such work as that of Louis L. Martz, Frank Manley, and O. B. Hardison on *The Anniversaries,* Jay A. Levine on "The Dissolution," John Freccero on "A Valediction: forbidding Mourning," Robert Silhol on "A Litanie," and A. B. Chambers on "Goodfriday, 1613. Riding Westward."[2] The reconstruction of traditions and conventions, the explicitations of the course of ideas in history (especially in non-literary disciplines) have enriched the knowledge and deepened the understanding of Donne scholars. The studies have provided us with the climate of opinion in which Donne worked, and, with varying success, have illuminated poems or passages in poems. Our debt to them is immense.

But R. S. Crane has brilliantly pointed out some of the pitfalls of the study of the history of ideas,[3] and others are so readily apparent that we overlook them. It is perhaps worth reminding ourselves, for instance, that *zeitgeist* explanations are likely to be most useful when we are dealing with second-rate writers rather than first-rate ones. Again, though the thoroughness of the immersion of some authors in some ideas is not to be questioned, others have merely tested the temperature of the water from time to time. Donne has told us that he "survayed and digested the whole body of Divinity, controverted between ours and the Romane Church,"[4] and that "an Hydroptique immoderate desire of humane learning and languages"[5] diverted him from the law; Walton says that among the "visible fruits of his labours" in his study, Donne left "the resultance of 1400. Authors, most of them abridged and analyzed with his own hand."[6] The breadth of his interests and the extent of his learning are hardly in question, but his "voluptuousnes" toward languages did not make him a skilled Hebraist, and it is unlikely that he had the technical command of alchemy, astronomy, and philosophy often attributed to him by some modern historians of ideas who are proficient in particular disciplines. Moreover, even though we may have reservations about the dictum that "in poetry, all facts and beliefs cease to be true or false and become interesting possibilities," there is no one-to-one relation between a poet's learning and his use of it as he draws upon it and tempers it in a particular poem. *De Doctrina Christiana* is not *Paradise Lost,* and when Milton forces Adam to choose between the basic tenet of man's superiority and the equally basic tenet that Eve's will is free and must not be forced, interesting things start to happen.

About a decade ago, Professor Helen Gardner and Mr. A. J. Smith published major articles which combined the study of material source or technical context with a detailed reading of "The Exstasie."[7] More recently, Mr. A. R. Cirillo has published an article in which he says, "There is no need to prolong further the still unresolved controversy about the tone of that poem and its attitude toward human love. All I want to suggest is that the *topos* of the hermaphrodite is basic to its context, whether Donne was using it seriously or cynically."[8] Mr. Cirillo's interest in an idea for its own sake needs no justification; his candor in separating the idea from the uses made of it in the poem is commendable. Most students of literature are not willing, however, thus to compartmentalize their concerns. A close look at the approaches and interpretations of Professor Gardner and Mr. Smith, who have immeasurably increased our sensitivity to "The Exstasie," reveals a foundation upon which a resolution of the controversy about the tone of the poem and its attitude toward human love can be built, given three assumptions: that Donne did not research "The Exstasie" as he did *Biathanatos* and *Pseudo-Martyr*; that in "The Exstasie" he was not only interested in casuistry of love but even more interested in a poetic construct; that he was not only the first poet in the world in some things, but also that the level of his customary achievement is so high that "The Exstasie" is a fine poem.

Professor Gardner regards "The Exstasie" as "wholly serious in intention" ("The Argument," p. 284). "As the title tells us," she says, Donne's "subject is ecstasy. He is attempting to imagine and make intellectually conceivable the Neo-Platonic conception of ecstasy as the union of the soul with the object of its desire, attained by the abandonment of the body."

But, she continues, "it is the essence of ecstasy that while it lasts the normal powers of soul and body are suspended, including the power of speech, and the soul learns and communicates itself by other means than the natural." It is, then, the very nature of the experience which Donne is trying to render (ecstasy can only be spoken about in the past tense) which makes him choose a narrative form unusual for him; moreover, with "characteristic daring and a characteristic ingenuity," he attempts a hypothetical ideal listener "to render the illumination of the soul in ecstasy as a present experience" (p. 285).

Persuaded that Donne derived his conception of "amorous ecstasy" from Leon Ebreo's *Dialoghi d'Amore*, Professor Gardner says that "The Exstasie" originated in Donne's interest in Ebreo's long description of the semi-death of ecstasy and in the idea that the force of ecstasy might be so strong that it would break the bond between soul and body and lead to the death of rapture: "This death in ecstasy his lovers withdraw from, to return to life in the body. What they are concerned to argue, in the concluding section of the poem, is that the bond of the 'new soul' will still subsist when their souls once more inhabit their separate bodies, and that they have a function to fulfil in the world of men which justifies their retreat from the blessed death of ecstasy" (p. 295). According to Professor Gardner, the ecstasy of the lovers reaches its climax by line 48 of the poem, with the revelation that their love is immortal. "Unless they are to enjoy the 'blessed death' of ecstasy," she says, "they must now return to their bodies" (p. 300). The conclusion of the poem (ll. 49–76) justifies this return by reference to Ebreo's doctrine of the circle of love:

> The inferior desires to unite itself in love with what is superior; but equally the superior desires to unite itself in love with what is inferior. The inferior desires the per-

fection which it lacks; the superior desires to bestow its own perfection on what lacks it . . . The blood strives to become spiritual, to produce the spirits, or powers of the soul, which are necessary to unite the intellectual and corporal in man. Conversely souls must condescend to the affections and faculties of the bodies in order that man's sense organs may become rational . . . [A soul's] duty is to take 'intellectual life and knowledge and the light of God down from the upper world of eternity to the lower world of decay' and thus realize the unity of the Universe. A soul that does not perform this divinely appointed function is like a prince in a prison . . . If the soul does not thus animate the body in all its parts, it is imprisoned in a carcass instead of reigning in its kingdom [pp. 301–3].

The only "proposal," then, which she finds in the last section of the poem is "the perfectly modest one that the lover's souls, having enjoyed the rare privilege of union outside the body, should now resume possession of their separate bodies and re-animate these virtual corpses" (p. 283). She reads the last lines of the poem as a further justification for life in this world—the duty to reveal love to men (p. 303): "The final and, one must suppose from its position, the conclusive reason for such a return of the separated souls is not that it will in any way benefit the lovers; but that only in the body can they manifest love to 'weake men' " (p. 283).

If Donne's subject is "ecstasy," the structure of his poem is strange, though its proportions are symmetrical. The heart of the poem must be thought to lie in the central section, which, as Professor Gardner says, "contains illumination which the lovers received in their ecstasy" (p. 298). Since these twenty lines are flanked by a 28-line "prelude" (p. 295) and by a 28-line "conclusion" (p. 300) justifying a return to bodies, the illumination, central though it is, seems foreshortened. But, she thinks

that Donne's poem originated in his interest in Ebreo's description of the semi-death of ecstasy, and we should look for evidence of that aspect of ecstasy in the poem. The climax of the
ecstasy of the lovers, as Professor Gardner sees, is reached with
revelation that their love is immortal (p. 300). As she says, the
central section of the poem describes "the union of their intellectual souls, or spiritual minds": "This union is indissoluble
because it is a union of perfect with perfect, or like with like. It
is only those things which are unequally mixed which are
subject to decay or mutability" (p. 299). Now, this kind of
emphasis on immortality and indissolubility perhaps carries,
suppressed beneath the surface, the seed of the idea of the
semideath of ecstasy, but Donne's focus and perspective seem
at odds with the concept of death. In "The Exstasie," the idea
of death is at best implied in two places: in the "sepulchrall
statues" of line 18 and in the "great Prince in prison" of line
68. Nowhere does Donne make explicit the idea of rapturous
death. Had he done so, he must certainly have done so at the
beginning of his last section. But the culminating words of the
second section are "no change can invade"; in their emphasis
on permanence, perfection, immortality, these words seem to
preclude rather than to include the idea of death. Professor
Gardner then, reads the last section of the poem as an alternative to a proposition which is not stated, a proposition to which
Donne does not direct us but from which he diverts us.

When Professor Gardner asks how successfully Donne
has achieved his purpose in "The Exstasie," she finds the
poem remarkable among Donne's lyrics for its lack of metrical interest and variety. She finds fine lines and fine passages in
it, but thinks that "it lacks, as a whole, Donne's characteristic
élan, and at times it descends to what can only be described as
a dogged plod" (p. 303). She finds, moreover, that "there is
a tone of argument throughout the lovers' speech which is out
of keeping with the poem's subject. . . . The essence of any

224

illumination received in ecstasy," she says, "is that it is immediate and not arrived at by the normal processes of ratiocination," and Donne's lovers seem far from the holy stillness, the peace of union, the blissful quiet characteristic of ecstasy. She rightly feels that the tone of the poem is that of "an ordinary dialogue in which points are being made and objections met" (p. 304), and she would explain this by saying that in "The Exstasie," Donne is "too tied to his source. It smells a little of the lamp" (p. 306). "When Donne was inspired by the *Dialoghi d 'Amore* to write a poem showing the achievement of union in love, he caught from his source that tone of persuasion which has misled readers. The poem sounds as if someone is persuading someone. The defect of 'The Ecstasy' is that it is not sufficiently ecstatic. It is rather too much of an 'argument about an ecstasy' " (p. 304). But she goes further: "I do not believe that Donne was very deeply moved by the conception of ecstasy. He too often in his sermons disparages the idea of ecstatic revelation for me to feel that it had never a strong hold on his imagination." She points out, however, that Donne was profoundly moved by the conception of love as union, and she would in some measure attribute the deficiencies of "The Exstasie" to the fact that it was one of Donne's earliest poems on love as union, written as a result of his recent discovery of Ebreo (p. 304).

In the last paragraph of her essay, Professor Gardner reiterates, notwithstanding what she has so candidly said of Donne's general lack of sympathy for the conception of ecstasy, her opinion that he is here writing seriously about ecstasy. She is concerned to defend his artistic and intellectual integrity against the critics who so exalt his wit that they "deny that ideas had any value to him as a poet except as counters to be used in an argument." She holds, quite correctly, that "no poet has made greater poetry than Donne has on the theme of mutual love . . . The poems which Donne wrote on the subject

of love as the union of equals, such poems as "The Good-
morrow," "The Anniversary," or "A Valediction: Forbidding
Mourning" are his most beautiful and original contribution
to the poetry of human love; for poets have written very little
of love as fullness of joy" (p. 304). Since she finds in "The
Exstasie" "the key to Donne's greatest love-poetry" (p. 304),
she finds it important to read the poem as "wholly serious in
intention" in order to protect Donne's integrity and sincerity.
She is willing to grant that "the language of the first twelve
lines is 'pregnant' with sexual meanings," that the lovers are
young and fit for all the offices of love; she has no objection
to M. Legouis' suggestion that, although hands and eyes are
so far the only physical means the lovers have employed, they
will soon enjoy bodily union (p. 296). She is even right to
insist that the *main* meaning in these lines is that so far the
lovers' only union is "through the corporal sense of touch and
the spiritual sense of sight" (p. 296).[9] When she shows that
Ebreo sanctions what has been called "Donne's metaphysic of
love"—that bodily love is not incompatible with spiritual love,
and that spiritual love can exist after bodily love has been
satisfied—she grants that the words of Ebreo which she cites
makes the same point "as it has been assumed [by others] that
Donne was making in his poem: that lovers who are united in
soul must, in order that their union should be complete, unite
also in body." But, she insists, in this particular poem this conclusion is not being argued for, "although it is implied" (p. 295).
She does not wish to deny that the poem "implies the lawfulness
and value of physical love," but she denies that "the poem is in
the least concerned to argue to this particular point"; it is
merely a corollary to its main line of thought (p. 284). Professor
Gardner makes it quite clear that she is aware of the sexuality
in the poem, but at the same time she works heroically to free
it from the charge of libertinism. She seems to feel that unless
Donne is serious about ecstasy in this crucial poem, the pre-

226

cursor of the great love poems, he has somehow compromised the integrity of his basic belief about love. To that we may answer that it is frequently the committed man who dares to explore and exploit alternatives and that it in no way undercuts a man's integrity if he choses to be witty about a subject that matters to him.

Mr. A. J. Smith reads "The Exstasie" as a witty poem which has its context not only in Ebreo's metaphysic of love but also in the theories of other sixteenth-century Italian writers. To establish the full technical context, he demonstrates the range of these theories, from Ficino's pure idealism, which emphasized the essential independence of the soul from the body, to the modified empiricism of commentators who, building on the ideas of Aristotle and Aquinas, made the perfect love of souls inseparable from or dependent upon the love of bodies. Whether or not Donne actually read Ficino, Ebreo, Speroni, Varchi, Tullia d'Aragona, Betussi, Tasso, and others, Mr. Smith says, he was exposed to "a varied and malleable body of public material." Donne, he thinks, used this material eclectically, and his "individual contribution to the theory of love in this poem is, to all appearance, not great": "one's attention is on the whole less usefully directed to what he used than to how he used it. In other words, it is in that measure a typical piece of witty writing" ("The Metaphysic of Love," p. 370).

Mr. Smith is, I think, right. He concludes that "The Exstasie" is a "remarkably 'witty' " poem (p. 375); still, he does not seem to find the wit very remarkable when he discusses it. Part of the difficulty stems from the fact that, for all he has to say about Italian love theory and Donne's eclectic use of it, he is disposed to attribute to Donne a position which Donne does not hold in the poem.

The "stereotyped and emblematic" situation with which the poems begins, Mr. Smith finds "tricked out with every convenient quirk of current poetic wit" (p. 370). He speaks of the

227

"little play" on the stock Petrarchan properties by which Donne describes the ecstatic posture of the lovers in order to show the depth and fixity of their trance. He sees the "erotic motivation" provided by "Pillow" and "Pregnant banke," he starts to enunciate Donne's general attitude toward love when he says that the coupling of contemplating eyes "would have satisfied an Aristotelian only as a preliminary," and he finds that in the first dozen lines Donne "unambiguously motivates his later position": "A deft exploitation of the even more Petrarchan play of the picture in the eye enables him [Donne] to refer to the normal end of physical union, and the whole extent of the present deficiency is shown. Moreover, his 'as yet,' in line 9, promises a remedy." He mentions the "comic literalness" of the description of the emanation and coupling of souls, and calls attention to the cleverness by which Donne has the souls as armies not contend against each other, but augment themselves by the closest alliance, the perfecting power of the ecstatic union (p. 371).

Though Mr. Smith is content to describe the hypothetical listener as "an amusing and also a pointed devise," he explains admirably the function of the listener in the poem:

> Donne is able at once to claim that there is a kind of arcanum of love, a soul-language for initiates, and, to assert the perfect oneness of these loving souls. But he has another point too, no less neatly made. This bystander is an initiate, and some way advanced in the mystery—besides being 'refin'd' by love, he has by his good love 'growen all minde.' Yet if he listens carefully here he will learn much; will indeed take 'a new concoction' ('the acceleration of anything towards purity and perfection,' Johnson says), and 'part farre purer then he came.' But the lovers who grew all mind in the process, spurning the body, were the strict Neoplatonists. Donne is certainly not condemning them. He only sug-

gests pleasantly they have still a great deal to learn, and
that he is about to show them what it is.

(pp. 371–72)

Mr. Smith has little to say of the five stanzas which describe the
knowledge granted to the lovers in their ecstasy, "the climax
of the first half of the poem." Like Professor Gardner, he states
that this knowledge lies in an awareness of the fusion of souls
and a realization of eternal fidelity. Where wit is concerned, he
merely says that Donne "dresses up" the "one and four" of the
theorists by an analogy from Plotinian metaphysics (p. 372).

Of the last section of the poem, Mr. Smith says, "One
is not unprepared for Donne's return to the incompletely united
bodies. . . . His concern now, in this latter part of the poem, is
to develop the assertion that the lovers' state cannot be perfect
while their bodies remain in unsatisfied singleness." He considers the treatment in lines 51–56 of the notion that the body is
the instrument of the soul "not remarkable," and he continues,

> What is curious is to find Donne all but compromising
> his argument, and certainly reducing its possible effec-
> tiveness, by his apparent adoption of the Augustinian—
> and Ficinian—dichotomy in this section: 'They are ours,
> though they are not wee.' This is much more like Ficino's
> 'the soul is the man' than Speroni's figure of the centaur,
> and Aquinas's assertion that the man is neither body nor
> soul alone, but a complex of both. It is, I suppose, with
> the analogy of 'intelligences' and 'spheres,' capable of
> bearing a Thomist construction. 'They are not wee'—we
> are no more bodies alone than we are souls alone. But
> there would seem a maladroitness in that way of pre-
> senting it unlooked for in so accomplished a rhetorician
> [pp. 372–73].

Donne is not, however, compromising *his* assertion but one
which Mr. Smith has pushed on him. He is not in the last

229

section of "The Exstasie" stating that "the lovers' state cannot be perfect while their bodies remain in unsatisfied singleness." In no way does he undercut the perfection of the ecstatic union of souls; he wishes, rather, to demonstrate conclusively the interrelations of souls and bodies in order to make a persuasive case for the propriety of physical love. Mr. Smith says that the very end of the poem "seems" to be "an assertion that the lovers' resort to their bodies now will mean no debasing of their love, or sundering of their eternally faithful souls" (p. 375). It *is* such an assertion, and the reason Mr. Smith finds the conclusion of the poem "somewhat enigmatic" is that he has pushed Donne too far into the Aristotelian camp.

Of Donne's use of spirits intermediary between body and soul, Mr. Smith says, "his metaphysics are ordinary in doctrine as in production": "He has merely made a pleasant (or perhaps tendentious) figure of that physiological explanation of the hypostatic union" (p. 373). He works hard to show that Donne may have used the figure of "a great Prince in prison" with originality, but his suggestion that Donne may be saying that the joint soul of lovers has not attained its full prerogatives until their joined bodies release it through physical intercourse (p. 375) seems far-fetched. The last lines of the poem Mr. Smith treats as a "winding-up, chiefly by means of the comic pretence of the arcana of love": "The idea that bodily union might be desired 'as sign of the primary conjunction' is deftly dressed, the body becoming love's book wherein he reveals his spiritual mysteries to uninitiates. We have, again, the point that the speech of the loving souls is intelligible only to another lover— with the weak joke added that it has been a 'dialogue of one,' a novel and mysterious sort of *dialogo d'amore*" (p. 375).

If Mr. Smith's statement about what Donne wishes to assert in "The Exstasie" is too extreme, his statement about its conclusion puts him in the ranks of most critics, excepting Professor Gardner, who, as she says, "take it for granted that the main point of the poem is a justification of physical love as not incompatible with the highest form of ideal love" ("The Argument," p. 283). But neither her dissatisfaction with Donne's achievement in the poem nor Mr. Smith's account of the wit of the poem vindicates the fascination it has had for scholars, anthologists, and readers. The critics are right, I think, about the intent of the poem, but I think too that some aspects of its wit have not been sufficiently emphasized. I shall now try to underscore aspects of the wit which have been in some degree neglected or misinterpreted.

"The Exstasie" opens with the description of a strange, an extraordinary experience.[10] The situation is imprecise, full of ill-sorting details, mysterious. The oddness of the condition of the lovers is emphasized, the extent to which they are abstracted from nature and reality. The first stanza seems to show us two lovers who are sitting with their backs against a bank. We revise this picture when we learn that they sit facing each other, staring into each other's eyes, their fingers intertwined. But, it turns out, "sit" may be wrong, for we find out that they have been lying all day "like sepulchrall statues." Did they first sit, and then shift position so that they are on their backs, gazing at the heavens? Or have they been leaning, even reclining, on the bank, facing each other, their hands intergrafted? We cannot be sure, but we are sure that we have been projected into an unusual situation, and its strangeness is intensified when we are told that the lovers' souls have left their bodies, to hang in mid-air between the bodies in order to "negotiate." Puzzled by lovers who are sitting or lying, by lovers "cimented / With a fast balme" and entranced by twisted eyebeams (who yet make us aware explicitly of propagation), by unspeaking bodies and articulate souls, we are not surprised to learn that only a very special listener will be able to comprehend the negotiation. The negotiation, in fact, is also puzzling, for the souls have no differences of opinion; they speak as one.

231

The situation is, then, a highly rarified one. Quite suddenly, certainly without the careful step-by-step procedure we are familiar with in discourses about love, we have been taken to the top of the ladder of love. We are face to face with ecstatic rapture; we have ascended "to the lofty mansion where heavenly, lovely, and true beauty dwells, which lies hidden in the inmost secret recesses of God, so that profane eyes cannot behold it."[11] Donne starts where Bembo ends. He *assumes* that glorified state of love which the philosophers and courtiers seek to reach. By a wonderful turn of wit, he has placed us in a position where we shall not hear about the gradual attainment of spiritual love from the lips of a virtuoso or from the dialogue between a lover and his beloved, but where we shall learn about love from the most highly qualified of all commentators—the "abler soule" which has divined all mysteries.[12]

The voice of the "abler soule" is, of course, authoritative. Having achieved the acme of the experience of love, the "abler soule" is perfect, immutable, at one with itself, and it soliloquizes. The "dialogue of one" is not a "weak joke." It is the keystone of Donne's arching wit. The "abler soule" has no doubts as it speaks; it knows. Its certainty lies in the metrical regularity of "The Exstasie," in the patness of its stanzaic form.

In five stanzas, the "abler soule" describes its exalted state. If, as C. S. Lewis says, most of Donne's love poetry is "less true than that of the Petrarchans, in so far as it largely omits the very thing that all the pother is about,"[13] so his ecstasy is less "true" than that of the Neo-Platonists. If the love poetry is *Hamlet* without the prince, the ecstasy lacks the soaring rapture of Bembo, himself almost inebriated as he envisions "that inexhaustible fountain of contentment that ever delights and never satiates."[14] In "Satyre III," Donne had said that it is easy enough to apprehend mysteries: they "are like the Sunne, dazling, yet plaine to all eyes"; but they are difficult to comprehend: the mind must extend itself to reach "hard knowledge."

As Professor Gardner says, "Donne's "abler soule" is not ecstatic as it speaks of ecstasy; refined by love, it has "grown all minde," and is tries to make its experience comprehensible. Therefore it speaks logically, dispassionately: its aim is explicatory.

Its first statement defines the nature of love by telling what it is not: "Wee see by this, it was not sexe." Since the situation of the lovers has already made this abundantly clear, the statement seems almost superfluous; indeed, like the earlier descriptions of intergrafted hands and propagating eyes, it seems to intrude sexuality at the same time that it denies it. And what does the hypothetical listener, so exquisitely refined by love that he is able to understand the language of souls, so purified that he has "grown all minde," learn from such a statement which would give him additional insight into love? Indeed, what lessons can so devoted a believer in spiritual love learn from anything the "abler soule" says in the five stanzas describing ecstasy? He may be edified, he must get immense pleasure in being reassured of his own beliefs, not by a fellow Neo-Platonist, but by the "abler soule" which has attained the heights of spiritual love; however, the doctrine of the mixture, interanimation, and perfection of lovers' souls is not new to him.

If the refined listener hardly needs to be reminded that it was not sex which led to ecstasy, if what he learns in the five stanzas which elucidate the state of ecstasy is merely confirmatory, why should it be necessary for the "abler soule" to indulge in the analogy of the violet in order to enlighten him? "Like a modern scientist, trying to explain some scientific mystery to laymen, Donne refers to something rather similar in nature to the union which love effects in souls" (Gardner, "The Argument," p. 299).[15] Professor Gardner's analogy, though faulty, is provocative. The "abler soule" is, to be sure, in the position of a modern scientist who reports his findings. The listener, however, is not a layman but another qualified scientist, an expert in the same field. Given his special qualifications, he surely does not need a simplified or popularized or analogized explanation. But, like many experts, he has so specialized that he needs to be reminded of the relation between pure science and life. The burden of what the "abler soule" as scientist has to tell his proficient listener about the experiment he is describing has precisely to do with its relation to nature. The description of ecstatic union which Professor Gardner calls a "scientific mystery" is not a mystery to the listener; this he knows. The mystery is in the violet, the link between spiritual and natural phenomena. The violet, here linked to the soul, had in the first stanza been juxtaposed to the lovers' bodies. Like the earlier mention of "sexe," the reference to the violet also serves as a reminder of the physical world in the midst of a spiritual experience. The middle section of the poem, then, like the first section, has in it elements which serve not only to define the situation and experience, but which also, at the same time, point away from them, beyond them.

Mr. Smith has noticed that in concluding the first section of "The Exstasie" Donne has unambiguously motivated his later position and that the "as yet" in line 9 promises a remedy. "One is not unprepared," he says, "for Donne's return to the incompletely united bodies. But his transition is dramatic, and the rhetoric of memorable cadence" ("The Metaphysic of Love," p. 372). He is quite right. Still, the "abler soule," that most competent exponent of spiritual love, having quickly and dispassionately summarized the state of ecstasy, surprises us and the listener when, instead of providing answers, it asks a question. The question is rhetorical, to be sure, but the lines "But O alas, so long, so farre / Our bodies why doe wee forbeare?" are the only ones in the long speech which are infused with feeling. Certainly, the question must stir the listener. If he has to this point merely received corroboration of his opinions, if he has thus far learned nothing new, he can hardly "part farre purer than he came." Now he is about to hear the ablest, the most authoritative of all speakers instruct him not on the love of souls but on a question so urgent and important that it preempts the larger part of his discourse (seven stanzas, as compared to the five which have preceded). That question concerns the role of the body in love, and the doctrine announced must, of course, given the nature of the speaker, be definitive.

What the listener hears, what it is that allows him to part far purer than he came, is a justification of physical union, and this is made clear in the first argument which the "abler soule" propounds:

> *They [our bodies] 'are ours, though they're not*
> *wee, Wee are*
> *The 'intelligences, they the spheare.*

The lines contain a textual difficulty: the manuscripts have "spheare"; the editions, "spheares." Herbert Grierson and Helen Gardner prefer "spheare"; and Grierson explains, "The bodies made one are the Sphere in which the two Intelligences meet and command."[16] Mr. Smith finds this gloss "attractive," but he would justify "spheares" on the ground that the use of "spheare" is "an anticipation of Donne's argument" (p. 373). It is precisely this anticipatory quality of "spheare" which assures its rightness; it looks forward to rolling all strength and all sweetness into one ball just as other seemingly obtrusive details in the poem have done. Moreover, the argument which the "abler soule" is making also depends on the singular "spheare," for it is an inversion of a mystery which the "soule" has already described: in the same way that the lovers have been refined into the union of an "abler soule," souls too may interact so as to bring their power to fruition in bodily union. Since the listener believes that the ecstatic doctrine of the "abler soule" is right and authoritative, he will certainly find persuasive the "abler soule's" conception of the role of the body, new and startling though it is to him.

The "abler soule" proceeds not to denigrate but to dignify bodies. It starts by expressing gratitude and appreciation to bodies for their role in making ecstasy possible. Since the bodies were responsible for conveying the souls to each other, they are not "drosse" to souls, but "allay"; not the scum thrown off from molten ore or metal, but a less valuable metal added to one more valuable in order to provide it with qualities of worth it would not otherwise have. Unlike the conventional Neo-Platonic advocate who is anxious to divorce body and soul, to leave the body behind so that he may focus on soul, the "abler soule," in its infinite wisdom about love, makes it clear that it is concerned not merely with soul, but with *man*, and the word appears three times in the last five stanzas:

> *On man heavens influence workes not so,*
> *But that it first imprints the ayre.*

The basic doctrine here, that heavenly influence works not directly but through an intermediary, is used to explain the intermediary function of the body in the union of souls, and the two ideas are developed in the next three stanzas. The "abler soule" assumes the truth of the doctrine that man reaches wholeness by aspiring to spirituality: the blood produces intermediary "spirits" which unite the corporal to the intellectual. Its special concern is, however, to announce that the inverse of this is equally true, and the "abler soule" enunciates with authority the doctrine that if man is to be whole, souls, too, must work through intermediary "affections" and "faculties" (passions and functions) in order to "reach and apprehend" sense: that is, in order to affect and inform the activities of the body.[17] For the "abler soule's" major assumption about heaven's influence working by indirection, Donne could have relied on several classical sources,[18] but he probably had in mind also the dangers expressed in Exodus 33:20 about the direct apprehension of God: "And he said, Thou canst not see my face: for there shall no man see me, and live."[19] The "abler soule" in a state of ecstasy has looked directly on the face of God, but God reveals himself to *men* through acts, signs, words, and laws. Only an "abler soule" can perceive directly the mysteries of love which grow in souls; men, who are weak,[20] can perceive these mysteries not directly, but only as they are made manifest in the body. The soul is subject to direct revelation; man learns the same truths by relying on the scripture of the body.

The "abler soule," having described the nature of the union of souls in ecstasy, takes great pains to make it clear that there is little to choose between the love of souls and the love of bodies. The listener to the "abler soule" of the lovers "will not be aware of much difference between their union when 'out of the body' and *their union* when they have resumed possession of their" bodies. (Gardner, "The Argument," p. 303; the italics are mine). Their emphasis is a little different from Professor Gardner's insistence that the proposal in the last part of the poem is "the perfectly modest one that the lovers' souls, having enjoyed the rare privilege of union outside the body, should now resume possession of their separate bodies and reanimate these virtual corpses" (p. 283). To be sure, the last lines of the poem do not so much point directly to physical intercourse as do other earlier lines; they are, rather, directed to clarifying the relation between souls and bodies. Still, there is little doubt about Donne's direction throughout the poem and about its end doctrine: a justification of bodily love as not incompatible with spiritual love.

But, Professor Gardner says, the fact that an ideal lover is invited to "marke" the lovers when they are "to bodies gone" "surely makes the notion that the poem culminates in an 'immodest proposal' absolutely impossible." "It is one thing," she explains, "for a narrative poet to describe two lovers in passionate embrace oblivious of a bystander, as Spenser does at the original ending of Book III of the *Faerie Queene*; it is quite another for lovers themselves to call for an audience at their coupling." And, she continues, "M. Legouis himself thought it particularly shocking that 'the hypothetical listener of the prelude re-appears and turns spectator at a time when the lovers as well as we could wish him away' " (p. 284). It is, of course, possible to defend Donne by asserting that the ideal listener and voyeur is hypothetical, not real. He is, in fact, not present to hear the words of the "abler soule" or to view the union of bodies; his presence is imagined. This defense is not, however, necessary. If the proposal at the end of the poem is considered "immodest," the wit in the poem leads us to insist that the immodesty is in the eye of the beholder. Who are we, who is the ideal listener, to doubt the authority and the propriety of what is proposed by the "abler soule"? Can we deny the truths which it has propounded about the relation between soul and body? The conclusion of the poem follows logically and wittily from what has preceded. We must be strange believers indeed if we find it immodest to read Scripture. The chief stroke of wit in "The Exstasie" is Donne's tactic of having the "abler soule" make the case justifying the role of the body in love and educating not "the layetie" but the refined Neo-Platonist who must be persuaded of the prerogatives of the body. This listener has no use for the softnesses of love; he will be persuaded only by the nice speculations of philosophy. In the amorous verses of "The Exstasie," Donne affects the metaphysics so that nature may reign.

What of Donne's "sincerity" in "The Exstasie"? All we can say is that he is here concerned about making a case for physical love; here he asserts, above all else, the prerogatives of the body. Is his justification seriously meant? If it is not, it is hard to see why Donne would have bothered to write the poem; he means seriously what he says about the role of the body in love. Does he, in fact, believe what he propounds about spiritual love, about ecstasy? There is no reason to deny his belief in the situation and doctrine he sets forth. We must admit, however, that the first sections of the poem are used to point toward and reinforce the last section, that it is most useful for Donne, indeed crucial for him, in this poem to assume the validity and value of the ecstatic experience so that he can through his speaker make the most authoritative and convincing statement possible about the role of the body to a listener who has "grown all minde." But is the whole argument intentionally sophisticated? This question seems to imply that, if Donne was not a firm believer in ecstasy as he described it, there is something immoral, lacking in integrity, in his feigning such a belief. We must judge intent by performance and we must not confuse literature with life. The whole of Donne's argument is coherent and effective; the argument itself is not sophisticated, whatever his own beliefs and motives may have been. Is somebody being "led up the garden path"? This question begs a question, or two. Is it wayward to sing the Song of Songs? May it not be therapeutic to impart the wisdom of Solomon to a congregation grown all mind?

"The Exstasie" is not a moving celebration of mutual love like "The Good-morrow" or "A Valediction: forbidding Mourning." It is not so great a poem about love as "The Canonization," for, because of the kind of poem Donne wanted to write, it lacks feeling except in the communication of the mystery at its beginning and in the two lines which introduce the last section. Its doctrinal content contains no startling truths or insights for the modern reader, who, in fact, must acquaint himself with the subtleties of ideal long since outmoded[21] in order to understand what Donne is saying about spiritual and

239

physical love. But the arid air of refined doctrine provides a fertile atmosphere for crisp argument and dry wit. No one will deny that Donne was profoundly moved by the concept of love as union; however, the concept took not one shape but several in his poetry. If "The Exstasie" holds the key to Donne's greatest love poetry, it opens only the door of his subject matter, not of his feeling. For all that, I agree with Professor Gardner that "it is a wonderful poem and a poem that only Donne could have written" (p. 304), the inventive, cerebral, imperious Donne who ruled as he saw fit the universal monarchy of wit.

Cornell University

Notes

1. "The Metaphysic of Love," *RES* 9 (1958): 363.

2. Martz, *The Poetry of Meditation* (New Haven, 1954); Manley, *John Donne: The Anniversaries* (Baltimore, 1963); Hardison, *The Enduring Monument* (Chapel Hill, 1962); Levine, " ' The Dissolution': Donne's Twofold Elegy," *EA*, 28 (1961), 301–15; Freccero, "Donne's 'Valediction: forbidding Mourning,' " *ELH*, 30 (1963), 335–76; Silhol, "Réflexions sur les sources et la structure de *A Litanie* de John Donne," *Etudes Anglaises*, 15 (1962), 329–46; Chambers, "Goodfriday, 1613. Riding Westward: The Poem and the Tradition," *ELH*, 28 (1961): 31–53. *See also* my "Donne's 'Epithalamion made at Lincoln's Inn': Context and Date," *RES* 7 (1956): 250–63. (All quotations of poetry are from *The Poems of John Donne*, ed. H. J. C. Grierson [Oxford, 1912].)

3. "The Houyhnhnms, The Yahoos, and the History of Ideas" in *Reason and the Imagination*, ed. J. A. Mazzeo (New York, 1962), pp. 231–53.

4. *Pseudo-Martyr* (London, 1610), sig. B3^r.

5. *Letters to Severall Persons of Honour* (London, 1651), p. 51.

6. Izaak Walton, *The Lives of Dr. John Donne . . .* (London, 1675), p. 60.

7. Gardner, "The Argument about 'The Ecstasy' " in *Elizabethan and Jacobean Studies Presented to Frank Percy Wilson* (Oxford, 1959), pp. 279–306; Smith, "The Metaphysic of Love," *RES* 9 (1958): 362–75. I single these out because they are most relevant to my purpose here. Among other major studies, those of Merritt Y. Hughes are invaluable: "The Lineage of 'The Extasie,' " *MLR* 27 (1932): 1–7, and "Some of Donne's 'Ecstasies,' " *PMLA* 75 (1960): 509–18.

8. "The Fair Hermaphrodite: Love-Union in the Poetry of Donne and Spenser," *SEL* 9 (Winter 1969): 90.

9. There is, of course, no necessary contradiction between this statement and those which Professor Gardner makes in Appendix D (p. 262) of her edition of *The Elegies and the Songs and Sonnets* (Oxford, 1965): "I do not know why it is always assumed that so far they have only loved chastely"; " 'One another's best' at least implies that there has been no question of one refusing the other." Still, in the edition, she glosses "sexe," in the line "Wee see by this, it was not sexe," as "all the desires and impulses that arise from differentiation of sex," not as "indulgence in physical intercourse." I think she is right. The "all our meanes to make us one" of line 10, like the reference to "sexe," seems to describe the lovers' general relation to this time, not merely the isolated experience described in the poem.

10. Whether or not the modern reader approaches the poem with the "convention" delineated by Professors Croll and Williamson in mind (George Williamson, "The Convention of The Extasie" in *Seventeenth Century Contexts* [London, 1960], pp. 63–77), it is fair to say that the convention probably did not exist for Donne's first readers. If the opening reminded them vaguely of poems about a springtime dialogue of love, reminiscence would serve only to set "The Exstasie" apart from the usual shepherd and his lass in a pastoral setting.

11. Baldesar Castiglione, *The Book of the Courtier*, trans. Charles S. Singleton (Garden City, 1959), p. 355.

12. To be sure, the ecstasy described by Bembo arises from his perception of the idea of beauty. Donne's ecstasy arises from an ecstatic union of lovers. Ebreo's discussion of ecstasy arises from Philo's experience of an ecstatic union with the idea of Sophia's beauty. As Professor Gardner says, he is still in the process of wooing her, and they have not reached the state of Donne's lovers, in which each is equally lover and beloved ("The Argument," pp. 290–91). The point I am trying to make, however, is that Donne is less interested in the method of attainment of ecstasy than in what is to be learned from having attained it.

13. "Donne and Love Poetry in the Seventeenth Century" in *Seventeenth Century Studies Presented to Sir Herbert Grierson* (Oxford, 1938), p. 81.

14. Castiglione, *The Book of the Courtier*, p. 356.

15. Professor Gardner's use of "Donne refers" indicates that she is looking at the passage not in terms of its speaker and listener, but in terms of the poet and his audience. There is no question that the poet's analogy aids his readers to comprehend the mysterious union being described by referring to seventeenth-century horticultural speculations about transplantation and "commixtion of seeds," though her informed account of this speculation shows that Donne was clarifying a larger mystery by a somewhat smaller one ("The Argument," p. 300). But Donne has been very careful to define the speaker and the listener in his poem, and *their* points of view are crucial to the intent of the poem.

16. *The Poems of John Donne* (Oxford, 1912), 2: 43.

17. In the lines "So must pure lovers soules descend / T' affections, and to faculties, / Which sense may reach and apprehend," Professor Gardner emends "Which" to "That"; she reads "sense" as subject of "may reach and apprehend," and thinks a purposive clause is needed, not a relative one (*The Elegies and the Songs and Sonnets*, p. 187). I agree with René Graziani ("John Donne's 'The Estasie' and Ecstasy," *RES* 19 [1968]: 134–35) that it is not necessary to emend; "Which," referring to "affections" and "faculties," is subject and "sense" an inverted object. My paraphrase differs very little from Professor Gardner's.

18. Grierson (*Poems*, 2: 44) quotes a passage from Du Bartas which refers to Pliny, Plutarch, Plato, and Aristotle. Professor Gardner cites a passage from Paracelsus (*The Elegies and the Songs and Sonnets*, p. 186).

19. Merritt Y. Hughes ("Some of Donne's 'Ecstasies,' " p. 514) quotes Donne's opinion that in this world we can see only through a glass darkly: "neither *Adam* in his ecstasie in Paradise, nor *Moses* in his conversation in the Mount, nor the other Apostles in the Transfiguration of Christ, nor S. Paul in his rapture to the third heavens, saw the Essence of God, because he that is admitted to that sight of God, can never look off, nor lose that sight againe. Only in heaven shall God proceed to this patefaction, this manifestation, this revelation of himself" (*The Sermons of John Donne*, ed. George R. Potter and Evelyn M. Simpson [Berkeley, 1953–1962], 8: 232). Donne utilizes the idea in his epithalamion for Somerset; he tells the bride, "Pouder thy Radiant haire, / Which if without such ashes thou would'st weare, / Thou, which to all which come to looke upon, / Art meant for Phoebus, would'st be Phaëton."

20. Professor Gardner's reading of the lines "To 'our bodies turne wee then, that so / Weake men on love reveal'd may looke" makes for difficulties. The introduction so late in the poem of a second audience, "weake men" or "layetie," not only makes diffuse the focus and point of view which Donne has carefully established, but it also assumes that the refined listener will be moved by an argument which calls for consideration of and generosity toward "prophane men." Moreover, the reading introduces a purpose

which has no intrinsic value for the lovers, which will in no way benefit them, but which calls upon their magnanimity and sense of duty.

Professor Gardner's reading depends too much on her recognition that "in his 'Platonic' poems Donne's lovers often speak as if they had a kind of mission to the world, to impart a glimmering of 'love's mysteries' to the 'laity' in love . . . . Donne's lovers always assume their superiority to the rest of mankind; and these have just given proof that they are extraordinary." She finds it impossible that the lovers should include themselves among "weake men" (*The Elegies and the Songs and Sonnets*, p. 261 n. 1).

Donne has in "The Exstasie" underscored the extraordinary nature of the ecstatic experience. The "abler soule" is uniquely qualified to speak about love. What is surprising about its speech is that it is not content to exalt souls in ecstasy, but that it still cares about bodies. It recognizes, refined as it is, its link to the body and it holds that man ("weake men") is composed of body as well as soul. It recognizes, too, that ecstasy is customarily beyond a mortal's share, reached only by casting the body's vest aside, and it therefore justifies man's cultivation of a garden less pure and sweet than the landscape of heaven.

21. They too are probably outmoded for many of Donne's contemporaries. Merritt Y. Hughes says ("Some of Donne's 'Ecstasies,' p. 515), "Donne wrote for an audience which had rejected its faith in ecstasy as Aquinas understood it." He holds that "by the end of the sixteenth century, if ecstasy in any of its meanings was to be taken seriously," it had to be used imaginatively or ingeniously by a poet.

JOHN T. SHAWCROSS

ALL ATTEST
HIS WRITS CANONICAL

THE TEXTS, MEANING AND
EVALUATION OF DONNE'S SATIRES

Despite their apparent contemporary popularity, the satires of John Donne have only seldom been treated as a group of poems significant in their contribution to an understanding of his poetical career. Texts and dates of composition have been discussed but unacceptably in certain specific instances. Their interpretations have likewise erred, and their techniques have at times been condemned through ignorance of what Donne intended to do. An examination of all matters related to these satires and an evaluation of them as poems and as documents in the biography of a major poet are long overdue.

The five satires generally accepted into the canon of John Donne's poetry begin as follows: "A way fondling motley humorist" (1); "Sir; though (I thanke God for it) I do hate" (2); "Kind pitty chokes my spleene; brave scorn forbids" (3); "Well;

I may now receive, and die; My sinne" (4); and "Thou shalt not laugh in this leafe, Muse, nor they" (5).[1] These poems appear in the above order, which is followed by H. J. C. Grierson in his two-volume edition of 1912 (Oxford: Clarendon Press), in the editions of 1633–68, in Group I manuscripts[2] (H49 omitting the fifth), and in some manuscripts that are related to Group III manuscripts.[3] Probably derived from a Group III, or a related manuscript, is C4, which has the first two satires in order; H51, which has the first three,[4] is probably descended from a Group I manuscript. Also related to Group III manuscripts are A25 and Cy.[5] A25 pulls the long fourth satire out of order, placing it first: 4, 1, 2, 3, 5: and Cy reverses 3 and 4, while omitting 5: 1, 2, 4, 3.

On the other hand, Group II and Group III manuscripts and certain related ones rearrange Satire 2. Group II manuscripts[6] place the second following a spurious "sixth" satire: 1, 3, 4, 5, "6," 2; the other manuscripts[7] reverse Satires 1 and 2: 2, 1, 3, 4, 5. Similar in arrangement are the two related and coeval manuscripts O and P,[8] which separate the second from the rest, O placing it after the main group as in Group II manuscripts and P placing it before as in Group III manuscripts; however, 4 and 5 are also reversed:

O 1, 3, 5, 4, (other poems), 2, (prose)
P 2, prose, 1, 3, 5, 4, (other poems)

L74,[9] adjunct to Group II, gives 2 immediately after 3, 4, 5, but gives 1 later after an intervening poem and the spurious satire. The oddest order occurs in the remaining Group III manuscript, Dob:[10] 1, 5, "6," 4, 2, 3.

The satires are thus best arranged on the evidence of all the texts: 1, 2, 3, 4, 5. William Drummond implies this order in a note in HN. Although this arrangement is standard, no full discussion of the foregoing manuscript evidence has previously been offered. Significant in the arrangement may be the dates of composition and the relationship of subject and style from one to another. For example, N. J. C. Andreasen argues largely on the grounds of subject but partially on the grounds of the nature of each satire that 1 and 4 are related, that 2 and 5 are related, and that 3 stands independently between the two groups.[11] We might note that 4 and 1, and 5 and 2 are contiguous in only one manuscript each, and that 3 is initial only once and final only twice (in one case the omission of 5 places it last). What Mrs. Andreasen is suggesting, of course, is a formal balancing of the five satires.

As a group the satires appear first in Group I manuscripts (except C57), Group II manuscripts, W, JC, D17, S, K, S96, and L74. They are found after various poems in 1635–69 (immediately after the epithalamia), A23, Hd, C4, A25, Cy, S962, O and P; and after at least some of the divine poems (and others) in 1633 (but here at the end), C57, Lut, O'F, and Dob. Most unusually, then, the satires are placed first to introduce the collected poems, perhaps because they had circulated as a unit and thus perhaps because of their reputation. If the Group I manuscripts are derived from a collection which Donne had had made around 1614 before his ordination, which seems likely, then we have further reason to arrange the five in the usual fashion and to place them in initial position in a volume of collected poems.

Wesley Milgate has provided a stemma describing the apparent transmission of versions of the satires (*Satires, Epigrams, and Verse Letters*, p. lxi). Basically there seem to be three groupings of text. That of Group III and associated manuscripts (Dob, S96, Lut, O'F; Hd, JC, D17, S, K, Q, D16, Cy, C4, A25, S962, O, P, Ash 38, and PwV 191) is characterized by "challenging" (1.1); "departest hence" (1.63); and "Sleydan" (4.48). However, Dob changed "Surius" to "Sleydan," indicating some kind of intermediary position in transcription. Milgate does not note the significance of this change. Dob is the only manuscript with this specific combination of these variants in its basic text. The combination of part of Group I manuscripts and others (H49, D, SP, W, B, H51, HN and Wed) is characterized by "challenging," "departest from hence," and "Surius." Some of the Groups I and II manuscripts 1633–54 (derived from a cognate of C57 and Lec, C57; TCD, N, and L74) read "fondling," "departest from me," and "Surius."[12] Further significant variants are "prove," (3.104), and "ask" (5.68), which occur in all manuscripts except for parts of Group I and Group II, 1633–54; Lec, and C57 give "do," (3.104), and "lack," (5.68);[13] "do" also appears in the 1669 versions, TCD and N.

Milgate makes much of the omission of Satire 5 from H49 and he believes that Donne revised the texts of the satires. But Satire 5 is the only poem in D that is not also found in H49, even though the text and arrangement of poems in H49 is different at some points later on from those in other Group I manuscripts. The satires and the poems immediately after them are the same in H49 and D. To conclude that the progenitor of H49 "must have contained only the first four" (Milgate, ed., *Satires, Epigrams, and Verse Letters* p. xliii) and that the compiler of the progenitor of other Group I manuscripts or the compiler of D added the fifth satire, therefore, seems questionable. The Group I manuscripts come ultimately from some common source but not directly from the same source. The fact that Lec and C57 have a different text of the first four but a similar text for the fifth (and thus the conclusion that D and its copy SP must have added the poem) is made less significant by remarking (1) that the text of Lec and C57 is sometimes distinct from that of D and SP in other poems (e.g., "The Perfume," 1.40, "my" H49, Lec, and C57, but "mine" in the others) though at most times quite similar, and (2) that Satire 5 does differ in D and SP in three important places. D and SP give "ask" (1.68), rather than "lack"; "mayne" (1.46), not "meane" as C57 has it; and "warnes" (1.2) rather than "warmes," a seem-

248

ingly trivial reading yet one occurring also in Q. It is certainly possible that the scribe of H49 simply omitted this one poem or that wherever Lec and C57 acquired their text for the satires the fifth satire was simply not much different from that in D. We should note that Cy also omits Satire 5 although it is a manuscript related to Group III.

The assumption that Donne revised the texts rests for Milgate on variants like "Sleyand" and "Surius." Such collections as Q may represent the earliest text of the satires; the variants preserved in Group III or its related manuscripts for all the poems also suggest those texts as earliest. This would mean that "changeling," "departest hence" (four syllables), "prove," "Sleydan," and "ask" constitute the first stage of text. The next stage would then be "changeling," "depart'st from hence" (with elision in the first word), "prove," "Surius," and "ask." The possibility that "departest hence" was read as three syllables may account for the addition of "from," a useless word here. Such a variation, in any case, should not be assigned to authorial revision. The third stage would be characterized by "fondling," "depart'st from me," "prove" and later "do," "Surius," and "ask" and later for some manuscripts "lack." "Fondling" may be thought to replace the somewhat tautological "changeling" as Milgate suggests, but whether this is Donne's alteration is far from positive. Indeed scribal writing as it is could account for someone's guess that "fondling" was what was meant; for "changeling" might not have made sense to one reading "an elfin child" or "evil spirit" rather than "changeable" or "fickle person." Although "fondling" has become the standard reading, I would urge that it has less meaning than "changeling" for the line and that it was thus probably not Donne's word. The replacement of "hence" by "me" seems merely a refinement to rid the line of an infelicity of expression created, if the preceding is correct, by "improvement" of a supposedly defective line. The change to "do" and "lack" are unacceptable: the first because it voids a meaningful word by a colorless one, the second because it almost reverses the meaning. This leaves only "Sleydan" / "Surius" to consider, and here Milgate writes: "only Donne could have substituted the name of a particular Catholic historian, Surius, for that of the Protestant Sledian" (p. lvii). The evidence of Dob may mean that "Surius" was an intentional authorial change since otherwise it retains the allegedly earliest text.

I cannot, however, accept the speculation that Donne revised the text of his satires at a specific time and for a specific person (the Countess of Bedford) because of the lack of evidence. Such alterations as those in Satire 3, lines 79 ff., can be explained variously despite Milgate's statement that "few of the more than eighty characteristic readings of this version can reasonably be ascribed to accidents of copying or to scribal interference" (p. lix). A tissue of inference leads to positive phrases like "Donne's final revisions," but saying it does not make it so. Of these supposedly authorial alterations not all are accepted or acceptable into the text.

The texts of the satires, like those of Donne's other poems, are not definitive: a diplomatic text drawn from various printed and manuscript sources seems to be the best that can be achieved in view of the lack of authorial materials.

The dates of composition of the five satires are uncertain and debated. H51 assigns its three to 1593, a questionable date as references in 1 and 2 seem to evidence. Milgate speculates that Satire 1 should be so dated and that the date was attached to it in the copy used by the H51 scribe. However, the first is dated after 1594 because of its reference to Banks' theatrical act involving an elephant and an ape (lines 80–81) and before 1598 when Everard Guilpin published *Skialetheia,* which borrows from this satire. The second is dated after 1594 also if there is a reference to the sonnet sequence *Zepheria* in the name Coscus; but also after 23 July 1597 if line 59 alludes to a contemporary event in mentioning "ten Sclavonians." The satire should date before November 1598, the year of Elizabeth's quadragesimus; Coscus says (line 50) that he has been in love since her "tricesimo," that is, 1588. Q gives this date as "37°," that is, 1595, suggesting that the satire was written later than 1595. Satire 4 is dated after 1594 by notice of *Mercurius Gallo-Belgicus,* which began to be published in that year (line 112); after 1595 by the possible allusion to Raleigh's report of the expedition to Guiana (line 22); after March 1597 because of Donne's citing of the fall of Amiens (line 114) and perhaps before September 1597 when it was regained by the French. But the line does not require that Amiens still be in Spanish hands. Possibly Dob's note to lines 56–57 concerning "two reverend men / Of our two Academies" is significant. The manuscript cites Lancelot Andrewes, Master of Pembroke College, Cambridge (1589–1605), and John Reynolds, President of Corpus Christi College, Oxford (1598–1607). Drummond dated this satire 1594, an obvious error. The date of the fifth satire is conditioned by lines 31–33, which refer to Donne's employment as secretary by Sir Thomas Egerton. This began at the end of 1597.

Certain allusions, one can argue, are not pertinent or may have been added with a later revision of a poem. But to place the satires over the years 1593 for 1, 1594 for 2, 1594 or 1595 for 3, 1597 for 4, and 1598 for 5 is to spread them over too long a period. It makes them incidental or even occasional poems, in the sense of being provoked by some specific reason for writing at just that time. Rather if they were written in this order as a comment by Drummond implies, they all may have been written in the years 1597–98 when Donne was first in Egerton's employ. The two verse letters to Sir Henry Wotton beginning "Sir, more then kisses" and "Here's no more newes, then vertue" satirically treat similar subjects and attitudes. And these are dated, respectively, before April 1598 by an allusion in Thomas Bastard's *Chrestoleros*, entered 3 April 1598, and 20 July 1598, the date given in various manuscripts. The belief that the satires would have pleased his fellow wits at Lincoln's Inn (1592–95) or on one of the expeditions with Essex (1596 and 1597) does not recognize the seriousness of the vignettes presented or the interrelationship of types who are the subjects of his work. The difference in tone between them and such poems as "The Storme" and "The Calme" written during the expeditions is also thus discounted. There are commentators who have dismissed the satires as not being charged with real concern, but forgetting their satiric techniques for the moment, we can discern a coverage of five outstanding areas of man's life which have tied him to falseness, show, meaninglessness, injustice, the deadly sins, manipulation by others, and so on. For some readers, the second satire may be a spoof on Donne's fellow would-be lawyers, who have wasted their time in poetic rivalries or amorous billets-doux, but one wonders whether Donne would have written this while he too was a prime target. To me the satire looks back on such experience and Donne's apparent rejection of just such a life as he jaundicely depicts. The fourth and fifth satires have also the ring of rejection of their life styles, possibilities for Donne during the years of secretarial service on the periphery of the court life. And the first and third are universal problems that man must solve for himself.

The five satires pillory five universal dilemmas besetting man: the opposing concerns of body and soul, lawyers and the law courts, religion, would-be nobles and their world, and those who subject themselves to the world's greed.[14] The first four move about through the streets or through various interrelated scenes, introducing characters and dramatic situations. The last is more reflective and not really humorous: "Thou shalt not laugh in this leafe, Muse," Donne begins, "nor they / Whom any pitty warmes" (lines 1–2). The ridicule and humor in the satires lies in exaggeration, puns (some obscene), unusual rhyme or versification, and ambiguity. The ultimate aim is reform through awareness and disgust and pity; but the satire is not personal or invective. Juvenalian, these satires are of the nature of most in the Elizabethan age, though they do not have the typically snarling quality, and their vignettes are not dissimilar to the "characters" which would prove so popular a few years later.

Satire 1 is a kind of debate between man's body ("thou") and his soul ("I"), seen within doors (lines 1–12, though they do not leave until line 52), in the street (lines 67–105), in his love's chamber (lines 106–110), and at home again (lines 110–112). The questions debated are: "Shall I leave all this constant company, / And follow headlong, wild uncertaine thee?" (lines 11–12) and "Why should'st thou . . . / Hate vertue, though shee be naked, and bare?" (37–41). The body is foolishly pampered, subject to the four humours—happiness, indifference, anger, melancholy. The soul is constant and wishes to escape from this bodily prison. It would remain the house's library ("this standing wooden chest"), likened to a coffin, for it would still be imprisoned here in death. Here the soul can consort with the paths to heaven, with philosophy, with statesmanship, with history, with literature. These are constant; it is body who is wild and uncertain. Urged to accompany the body out-of-doors, the soul wants to be assured that it will not be left behind in public, should they meet "some more spruce companion" or a captain who has defrauded "forty dead mens pay" or "a briske perfum'd piert Courtier" or "a velvet Justice" with a great retinue (lines

253

15–22). The body is obviously impressed by position, clothes, wealth, and appearances. The body "in ranke itchie lust" desires and loves "the nakednesse and barenesse" of its "plumpe muddy whore, or prostitute boy"; but virtue, never (lines 37–41). Still the body, "like a contrite penitent," seems to repent, and the soul is tricked into leaving the chambers. At first the body (being the weaker) is hemmed into the wall by the soul and "cannot skip forth now to greet / Every fine silken painted foole we meet" (lines 71–72); but soon he is able to deny the soul's prior requests in turn (lines 82–103). The shifting characters and scenes and bits of dialogue lend immediacy and drama to the monologue. Finally body sees "his love" in a window, she apparently beckoning him to join the many others awaiting her services. Sexually spent, and unable to attain more time with "his love" even by fighting, the body returns to the soul "hanging the head" (with its obvious double entendre).

The soul, in good conscience, will always hope that repentance can be sincere and that the love of virtue can be learned; but the body is not trustworthy. It is external and inconstant and thus loves external and inconstant things. It will always be "violently ravish'd to his lechery": only for a while (though then constantly) must it stay in bed. Though Donne is not resigned to accept only these crumbs, he shows little belief in the soul's ever changing the body to a prolonged virtuous course.

Satire 2 has been most often discussed because of supposedly difficult textual readings, but these problems disappear with analysis. Donne's concern is corrupt lawyers, who constitute that "one state / In all ill things so excellently best, / That hate, toward them, breeds pitty towards the rest" (lines 2–4).[15] He also lampoons various kinds of poets and musicians (lines 5–30) and others (lines 31–38), who punish themselves. The poetry which sustains his criticism may be a sin itself, but it serves to "catch men." He is justified by the reform which his original, witty writing may achieve: "Pistolets are the best Artillerie" (line 20). The involved pun suggests, first, that little guns, rather than rams and slings, are today the best ordnance, that they subtly will devastate the opponent; second, that Spanish money will "move Love" best in the eternal war of love; and third, that punning proves the most successful art. The writer who chews others' wits and spews them out half-digested is the worst kind of author; still such excrement is his own (lines 25–30). And the playwright who gives idiot actors the means to enliven the scenes he labors over, thereby becoming immortals of the stage, Donne will not be, for the playwright is like a wretch under trial, who, so guilty that his death is mandatory, nonetheless saves another by prompting him what to say, since the latter cannot read and thus cannot receive benefit of clergy. Rather, it is Coscus, the lawyer, who breeds Donne's "just offence";[16] the name was often contemporaneously used for a court pleader, but it also suggested itself as the anonymous author of the vapid sonnet sequence *Zepheria*. Coscus had been "of late / But a scarse Poët" (lines 43–44), and was thereby "sicke with Poëtrie, and possest with muse / . . . and mad" (lines 61–62). He uses his title of barrister and the language of the court room to woo every wench he meets, and we hear him pleading in such terms with his lady, who asks him to spare her. "Men which choose law practice for mere gain," the poet remarks, "are esteemed worse than embrotheled strumpets who prostitute themselves."

Turned down, for lawyers do lose some cases, Coscus pursues his legal money-grabbing ("his hand still at a bill"). Among other things, he is like the lower die of an anvil as used in Roman coinage ("a wedge"); he must press against the upper die ("the bar"), producing identical coins ("Bearing like Asses"). That is, the lawyer acquires money over and over again by twisting testimony as he pleads at the bar of law. In this he shows himself to be an ass and two-faced (since the *as* pictured Janus, the two-faced god). And he must lie to the grave judge more shamelessly than do whores rounded up and transported to court in a cart. (As whores, the embrotheled strumpets of line 64, lawyers also "wring" to a different—obscene—kind of "bar," bearing their posteriors which are similar to whores'. The nouns of lines 74–75 iterate their being strumpets, "bastardy"; their being greedy, "simony"; and their baring of their posteriors, "sodomy.") The lawyer's corruption has spread from north to south, from west to east, throughout England; he wrests land piecemeal through writing up lengthy writs and assurances. Trickily, he sells or changes ownership of land by omitting the phrase "his heirs" in agreements so that the land will not devolve upon the new owners' progeny but will default to the lawyer. The woods that used to forest the lands which the lawyer has filched have not been used for building or for warmth (lines 103–104); instead they rot, being owned by so few. If only the *via media* would again exist! But it seems that no one within the vast reach of law is drawn by Donne's words to reform or to force reform of this "one state / In all ill things so excellently best" (lines 111–112).

Perhaps the major difficulty of life that Donne has recognized here is change, change which has brought corruption and decay and disutility through opportunists, imitators, and venal hypocrites. Time, he observes, rots all things and develops minor illness (botches) into wasting disease (syphilis). The law, so fear-inducing and difficult of correction by the people, has been perverted into an instrument of the few to swindle the many. Its use to achieve sexual alliance exposes its debasement.

Satire 3 makes clear both man's retreat from religion and also his confusion.[17] No longer does "our Mistresse faire Religion" receive our soul's devotion: we will not now join our father's spirit in heaven, where he has met the faithful, blind philosophers of the age before God's enlightenment, for we shall be damned. Man shows courage (he thinks) in war, but it is "courage of straw." Man has left the "appointed field" of

battle with the real foe, "the foule Devill"; he loves the world,
"a wither'd and worne strumpet," now "in her decrepit wayne";
and "last, / Flesh (it selfes death) and joyes which flesh can
taste," he loves: the Devil, the World, and the Flesh, the triple
equation of temptation. (The waning of the world reflects the
argument concerning the decay of nature so current in the
seventeenth century and resulting in deistic principles a century later.) Man should rather "seeke true religion," but where
it can be found is confused. Mirreus (not finding it in England)
seeks it in Rome because Roman Catholicism existed there a
thousand years ago. Crants seeks it in Geneva because Calvin-
ism is so "plaine, simple, sullen, yong, / Contemptuous, yet un-
hansome" (lines 51–52). Graius remains in England, following
Anglicanism because it is his father's faith and he is led to believe only it is perfect by the preachers, who are "vile ambitious
bauds." Phrygius atheistically rejects all religions, "as one, /
Knowing some women whores, dares marry none" (lines 63–64).
Graccus eclectically embraces all faiths, for women are women
no matter how they are dressed to accord with their divers countries' styles.

Donne's advice is to seek truth. "To stand inquiring
right, is not to stray" (line 78). Truth stands on a huge hill,
which is cragged and steep—the mythical, magical mountain of
Hesiod, of Zion, of Shakespeare's Belmonte, and of Mann. "He
that will / Reach it must turn around and around" (lines 80–
81), instancing the long, circuitous route up the mountainside,
fraught with back-sliding, with precipitous falls, with sore feet
and broken bones. But implied also is the constant moving upward, if not quite always forward. One goes upward, spiritually,
if he follows Donne's admonishment: "Keepe the 'truth which
thou hast found" (line 89). The soul should not be tied to man's
religious laws, but to God's, for those are the laws of trial at
Judgment Day. One should not follow Philip II of Spain or
Pope Gregory XIII (Roman Catholic); Henry VIII of England

or Martin Luther (Protestants). These men may claim power from God, but once the bounds of such power are known one's allegiance becomes idolatry. One should trust God himself, as a blest flower dwelling at the calm headwaters of a rough stream, which may be likened to power, for those caught up in the rough stream are "almost / Consum'd in going, in the sea are lost" (lines 107–8). The blest flowers "thrive and do well." Rebuffed are the religious proselyters, the schismatics, and the bigots: religion is personal; it is seeking after God's truth; it is hard deeds and body's pains. But simply to will implies delay (line 85): one must do, for "I must work the works of him that sent me, while it is day: the night cometh, when no man can work" (John 9:4).

Donne's message is unmistakable: we must have faith, we must follow virtue (but not the translated meaning of "power"), and we must bind ourselves, like the philosophers of old, by looking directly at the dazzling sun (God), which is there for all plainly to see, in order to perceive the mysteries of life (lines 87–88).

Satire 4 immediately sets a satiric tone with its metrics by the extreme enjambing of lines 1, 2, 3, with such odd end-of-line words as "in" and "is." The breaking of a word between two lines ("forget- / full," lines 13–14; "egge- / shels," lines 104–5), wrenched rhymes ("Sir," "Westminster," lines 73–74; "spit," "Yet," lines 109–110), another odd end-word ("A," line 215), and altered metrics (for example, "I shooke like a spyed Spie; Preachers which are / Seas of Wits and Arts, you can, then dare," lines 237–38) continue the trenchant wit. The court and its "huffing braggart, puft Nobility" (line 164) are ridiculed in such pejorative language as "A thing more strange, then on Niles slime, the Sunie / E'r bred" (lines 18–19); "A thing . . . / Stranger then seaven Antiquaries studies, / Then Africks Monsters, Guianaes rarities" (lines 20–22). This "thing" wears strange, coarse, black, bare clothes, and a sleeveless jerkin that had been velvet, but is now well worn; it speaks no real language because it mixes up "all tongues / . . . Made of th' Accents, and best phrase of all these" (lines 35–38). Its tongue "can win widdowes, and pay scores, / Make men speake treason, cosen subtlest whores, / Out-flatter favorites, or outlie either / Jovius, or Surius, or both together" (lines 45–48). Stopping the poet, the "thing" counsels that if he knew the good of court life, he would not be always alone. "I" answers that what is learned by observing vice does not dissuade from vice. Since princes' courts have been mentioned, the "thing" has opportunity to speak of kings and to praise the French.

Changing the subject momentarily, he asks, "What news?" The poet tells him of new plays, but he guides the discussion back to "triviall houshold trash":

> *He knowes*
> *When the Queene frown'd, or smil'd . . .*
> . . . .
> *He knows who loves; whom; and who by poyson*
> *Hasts to an Offices reversion . . .*
> *He knowes what Ladie is not painted . . .*

(lines 98–108)

He talks of the wars; he libels each great man as an accepter of graft or maintainer of lucrative war; he notes "Who loves Whores, who boys, and who goats" (line 128). The only way that "I" can get rid of the "thing" is to bribe him as ransom.

Now back in his home, informed of the court's puffed nobility, the poet envisions those at court like unto those Dante saw in hell. Vanity "swells the bladder of our court" (line 168); the nobles, in clothes as fresh and sweet as "The fields they sold to buy them" (line 181), flood in from the stables, from games, from the dinner table, and from the brothels. (But the clothes

259

are sold next week and new ones purchased secondhand in Cheapside.) The ladies arrive, weak ships painted red (symbol of prostitution and the Whore of Babylon, as well as of despair), and the men, like pirates, board them, one group praising the other for beauty or for wit. Glorius next enters to plague both man and woman. His rough carelessness is good fashion; his face is ill, like one scourging Christ. He spits out ill words and jests like a licensed fool. But all pay heed.

What is needed to drown the seven deadly sins of this place are preachers, "Seas of Wits and Arts." The poet, "a scarce brooke," can hope only to wash the stains away, not sink the painted ships and their now-commanders. With Maccabees he says, "I too will here conclude my account. If it has been well and pointedly written, that is what I wanted; but if it is poor, mediocre work, that was all I could do" (2 Macc. 15:37–38).

The last satire written by Donne has lost some of the spleen of the others and is almost pervaded with pity. The misery of those who must beg for sustenance is too great for jest, although lines 79–89 are particularly contemptuous of such fools, who have brought on their misery. Officers (of the law, acting as agents for supposed justice) are vast, ravishing seas that drown the suitors, who are springs (now full, now shallow, now dry) running to them (lines 13–16). These officers are a devouring stomach which consumes all the nutriment the suitors may possess and then voids the residue, the suitors themselves (lines 16–19). Yet men are to blame for allowing, even for helping, these officers to make them indebted. The suitors are gamesters who having lost their money seek justice before the court of law, but obtain none. The queen cannot know of these circumstances any more than the headwaters of the Thames can know what lands are inundated by its eastward flow or its branches. Sir Thomas Egerton, Lord Keeper after 1596 and Donne's employer at this time, is addressed to determine and extirpate "this enormous sinne" (line 34). Astraea, goddess of justice, had forsaken the world at the beginning of the Age of Bronze because of the corruption of men, and now the present age, the Age of Iron, has grown rusty. There is no appealing to the courts or to the judge; they may think themselves gods, but they are pursuivants, reached only by coins (angels). Law has made some officers, some pleaders of legal suits (line 73); she scratches the latter with her "foule long nailes." Following the metaphor through, obscenely making his point, Donne comments: "Officers stretch to more then Law can doe, / As our nailes, reach what no else part comes to" (that is, our posteriors). Man is subservient to officers, even doffing his hat to them, even baring his posterior to them to be scratched (line 79). For people are fools: they buy wrong over and over, then "hungerly" beg for right (lines 81–82); they try to put the supposed magic of law to the proof. These fools dramatize Aesop's fable of the dog carrying meat, who seeing his shadow in the water and thinking it another dog, drops his own meat, dives after the other dog, nearly drowns, and loses all. Their greed, which has brought on their plight, has become proverbial.

Donne attacks the lack of justice, the venality of the officers of law, the steady decline from bad to worse ("now full, now shallow, now dry," line 15) suffered by man, but also the foolishness of man and his greed which is at the root of his difficulty. Although a wasteful war is fought against man by other men, man himself fights in that war against himself (lines 24–25). "Faire lawes white reverend name" is "strumpeted, to warrant thefts" (lines 69–70). What is to be done? Nothing, probably, except to be aware of the cause and results before becoming entangled and except for the righteousness of such men as Egerton who may aid in rooting out these weeds.

As stated before, the five satires pillory five universal dilemmas besetting man. They proceed from man's relationship with himself to his control by law to his control by religious belief to his control by the artificial world of society to his succumbing to greed or its effects in others. The satires pose the constant duel between the id and the superego, the problem of change in this world, the need for a guiding philosophy of life, the pride man shows in externalities, and the avaricious nature of man. There is no sure means out of any of these dilemmas, although the "I" of each suggests that by recognition of their existence and their evil, man will be better able to withstand their assaults upon him. Within the five spheres of action they depict lies a full range of deadly sin.[18] But Donne does not really see man extricating himself from such human failing. A chosen few may see the light, but most will be cosened by shadows. He writes in Satire 4 that "yet some wise man shall, / I hope, esteeme my writs Canonicall" (lines 243–44). This does not mean that the canon will be followed and mankind reformed, rather he hopes his satires will at least be recognized as proposing true doctrine for the world of moral men. There seems little hope that the world will change, that the moral life will prevail. No, as one looks at the world of men in Donne's time or our own, one sees that the types are everpresent: they attest his analysis and they attest its canonical worth. But man just doesn't learn or change his spots.[19]

Part of Donne's satiric technique in these poems rests in the prosody, part in the style. Jonson was reported by Drummond as saying that Donne should be hanged for not keeping accent, but in the satires the alteration of meter has such definite and appropriate effect that—at least generally—such alteration seems deliberate. Defective lines seem to be: 1.13; 4.62, 104, 128, 176, 183, 222, 223, 238, 239, 241; 5.11, 66, 73. But note the following considerations: 1.13—"earnest" may be three sylla-

bles; 4.104—"iron" may be two syllables; 4.183—"Theatre" may
be three syllables. Hypermetric lines seem to be: 1.8; 2.24, 43;
3.32, 38, 107, 4.5, 140, 143, 197, 199, 217, 240, 242; 5.6, 39, 40,
56, 57, 59, 67, 71, 76, 81, 83, 90. But note the following possibilities: 4.140—"Toughly 'and stubbornly' I beare this crosse; But
the 'houre"; 4.242—"modestie" may be only two syllables: 5–6—
"wreched" may be only one syllable; 5.71—is there some elision
in "Destiny on," either "Dest'ny on" or "Des ti ny'on"?; 5.76—
"So in" may be elided. In any case there are defective and hypermetric lines which some manuscripts (e.g., O'F) attempted to
"correct" in various ways in certain instances. In addition a
number of feminine endings occur, some final syllables being
catalectic, some really being accented for rhyme although normally unstressed. Such endings appear in 1.8, 13; 3.53–54; 4.47–
48, 101, 177, 201; 5.32, 63–64, 75, 84–85. Odd final stress for
rhyme is also found in 1.20, 4.21, and, according to meaning,
4.212. The effect of these prosodic anomolies is generally a more
conversational, normal expression, for the lines, read normally,
do not artificially end-stop. The final passage of Satire 4 is a
case in point: of eight lines three are regular, three are defective, and two are hypermetric. There is almost full compensa-
tion for the defective lines in the hypermetric. Five lines are
strongly enjambed, and two others require their succeeding
lines to complete their verbs. Of course, such run-on construction is typical of Donne's poetry in the satires, but the point is
that as one reads, any sense of defective or excessive syllables
disappears. Coupled with this are the unusual line breaks in
Satire 4, noted before, to which should be added 3.68–69: "and
this blind- / nesse too much light breeds."

The metric which Jonson objected to, however, was apparently the very frequent use of trochees and spondees and
pyrrhics. Note in 2.91–96 the inter-mixture of standard iambic
lines with lines containing variety in feet:

These hee writes not; nor for these written payes,
Therefore spares no length; as in those first dayes
When Luther was profest, He did desire
Short Pater nosters, *saying as a Fryer*
Each day his beads, but having left those lawes,
Addes to Christs prayer, the Power and Glory clause.

The reversed foot which begins line 91 is finally reversed again with a symmetrical pattern of a spondee, a pyrrhic, and a spondee in between; the reversed feet of line 92 are continued over a strong medial pause but then reversed by what appears (but is not) a pyrrhic; lines 93–95 are regular; and line 96 also begins with a reversed foot but the spondee that follows allows the brief passage to end regularly. The "feel" of the passage is of common speech, but the important words for the point being made—like "writes," "written," "length," "Addes," "Christs prayer"—are stressed partially by an iambic pattern, partially by alterations in the metric.

What Donne gains by his practice is an enhancement of the naturalness afforded by language and idea, plus an unavoidable emphasis on the words and ideas that are important (e.g., 3.49: "Crants to such brave Loves will not be inthrall'd") and an ambiguity on occasion which is significant for the context (e.g., 4.192: "Why good wits ne'r weare scarlet gownes, I thought," where one must decide whether "good" is stressed, whether "wits" or "ne'r" is stressed, and, if the former, whether "weare" is to carry stress and thus sarcasm). It is certainly possible that the text of the satires that we have is not in every detail the text that Donne thought he wrote, but the received texts and the diplomatic text, which we must base our observations upon, do allow for the conclusion that Donne's alterations of prosody were deliberate. There is a higher number and thus percentage of hypermetric lines in Satire 5 than in the others, but to conclude therefore that this is evidence of a flagging of ability or of interest in that poem is not justified. In each of these lines a combination of enjambment and rhythm within the line nullify any sense of prosodic disruption which one otherwise might feel. For example, line 39 of this satire has a strong medial pause after two briefer pauses, and thus the unaccented and extra syllable immediately before it has only the effect of an easing-off such as feminine lines yield: "All demands, fees, and duties; gamsters, anon." Or line 81, a six-foot line, does not pull us up short as an anomoly amongst regular pentameters because immediately before in line 79 the line has broken into two with the last three syllables attaching themselves to line 80, as we read the passage in context, and because line 81 enjambs with the first foot of line 82, after which again there is a strong break. In a way these lines (and so many others like them) are an embryonic drawing out of the sense from one verse into another that Milton was to develop for himself some fifty or sixty years later.

Inherent in a discussion of prosody, but also meaning, lies an awareness of style. Milgate sees Donne consistently adopting the techniques and tones of Roman satire while not succumbing to the harsh, snarling, obscure, prurient, uncouth methods of his contemporaries. He notes that Donne's wit and humor add to the dispassionate quality of the satires, although such humorous touch deserts him in the last. The style is a function of the technique of realistic detail and epitome of an attitude; it depends on the materials used and on the fact that one detail is added to another without a narrative structure developing. There is some movement toward a time development (as in the second), or toward a logical development (as in the third), or toward a spatial development (as in the fourth), but only Satire 1 seems to combine them all. Even so, we do not have a real narrative. The authorial point of view in the satires is one of observation which is recorded by often unrelated detail and through a perspective that allows humor to enter as a light source. The speaker of the satire can stand back and observe as a superior being recognizing the ridiculousness of human behavior and thought; only in the last satire does the "humor" become sardonic and lose its distance of observation.

The style is low, as expected of satiric writing, for its language is low, its mode is conversational, its allusions are commonplace and of the human world rather than of the world of knowledge, its effect is not uplifting and its aims are directed toward ordinary men. The style of Donne's satires seems different from others' because of the satires' techniques, their humor, and, beneath the jibes, their compassion for man.

The satires have generally been viewed, it seems, as Donne's personal reactions to the facets of man's life which are their subjects. They become what *he* wants to say, as if getting something off his chest that has been nagging him. Yet aside from the references in the last satire to Elizabeth and Egerton (lines 28–34) there are no direct, no personal touches. Even these lines are generalized: he is talking about a prevalent evil and notes that Elizabeth can do nothing about it but that in his position as lord keeper, Egerton may be able "now [to] beginne / To know and weed out this enormous sinne." For the sin in Satire 5 has its gestation in governmental hierarcies and laws, although its inception lies in man. There seems to be little thought that Donne may be reacting as poet-thinker to evils around him or problems which man, by his nature, encounters (witness Satire 1). There seems to be little thought that Donne is a poet in control of his materials, planning what organization, image, and detail there is. For example, Milgate (p. xix)

talks of "the use of ironic or illustrative allusions to things not strictly relevant to the main subject of the satire."

This is not to say that the term "private" for the modal character of Donne's poetry is not appropriate. Earl Miner argues for such modal terminology for so-called metaphysical poetry on the basis of the author's aesthetic distance from his surrounding world. The metaphysical is not concerned with public aims and externalities, and he draws substance from his relationship with his own mind rather than with others' way of thinking. Certainly there is little of the metaphysical as normally defined in Donne's satires, yet they exhibit Donne's poetic approach rather than Joseph Hall's or Thomas Lodge's or Ben Jonson's. What must be remembered in using such terminology, however, is that it describes mode, not substance, and that it is not equivalent to "personal." The materials which Donne uses are anecdotal; they are often details; but they all unite together—not in a real cohesion or narrative—to impress the reader with an attitude, an awareness crystalized in an image or allusion. Image or allusion crowds upon other images or allusions, producing a full panorama of the evil Donne sees about him.

And of course this is the etymological meaning of *satire*: the filled-to-brimming pot, the container replete with all manner of ingredients. Donne's satiric technique unlike that of some of his contemporaries is clearly to fill his container (the poem itself) with all manner of ingredients to show the prevalence and nature of this evil which exists. Those who find Satire 4 overlong would do well to heed this, for the courtier and the court cannot be confined in their pervasive influence to just an image or two. Those who find Satire 5 a failure (partially because of the lack of humor in it) would do well to recognize that the evil exposed is deeper, emboldened by the fabric of man's impoverished life and hopes of extrication through financial improvement. It is far from humorous, and its images are more

267

circumscribed. It does not have the multiple facets that the courtier's life has.

The satires are dialogues spoken by one person, who may, as in the fourth, quote others. In the first the soul-speaker and body-nonlistener are obvious; in the second the auditor is not defined (he is everyone), but we are aware of his presence after the opening lines by such statements as "the insolence / Of Coscus onely breeds my just offence" (lines 39–40); in the third, as Mrs. Slights shows, the auditor is a back-slider (aren't we all?) in religion; in the fourth he is again the undefined any-one; and in the fifth the auditor disappears entirely, for the "I" reflectively addresses his muse as well as the suitors who fall prey to officers through their own greed. (The seeming direct addresses to Elizabeth and Egerton are not, of course, actually being spoken to them.) Perhaps it is this reflectiveness which reduces the sense of directness and on-the-spot conversation that has caused Satire 5 to be generally criticized.

According to Milgate, Satires 2 and 4 fall apart, and 5 is filled out by a series of spasmodic efforts. I suggest that a demand for organization and structure lies behind these condemnations. Satire 3 may be analyzed as a triple structure within a limited area of subject matter, but this should not, I protest, be a basis for finding fault with other poems. If one considers the technique of the other satires as a "filling up of the poet," they succeed. Satire 3 as a delimited case of conscience *should* be more closely argued, *should* be organized, *should* adhere closely to the theme. But why must we demand this of the others? We have the artifacts which are the poems, and these are what we should evaluate.

The biographical implications of the satires depend on their dates, our interpretation of them, and the way in which we see Donne involved. If we read them as personal statements or as poetic rivalries from the days when Donne was at Lincoln's Inn, we call them either psychological manifestations of

Donne's disgruntledness with difficulties he has encountered in making a name for himself—in "getting somewhere" or "being somebody"—or not essentially meaningful and thoughtful treatments of the problems they pose. I do not want to accept either alternative. I see them as being written within a short time of each other, after his return from service and during his employment by Egerton, employment which held out a number of hopes of "getting somewhere" or of "being somebody." I read them as the products of a thoughtful mind viewing some of the evils of this world; progressing from the problem of self to the problems of law courts and lawyers (which and who still thwart real justice) to the problems of religious belief to the problems of the aristocratic world of his day (and we still are impressed by a glimpse of a movie star or the latest public scandal) to the problems which greed breeds in both the haves and the have-nots. Not that he envisioned all of these as a set when he began to write, or during their writing span; and not that more were conceived. But they do expose five basic universal problems. They propose no real solutions, for all taken together say that such dilemmas find their root in man and his nature.

The biographical implications of the satires, so read, present us with a Donne whose concern is with mankind, not with self and not with public adjustments, a Donne whose personal life is resolved enough for him to contemplate the world around him analytically, a Donne whose future will contain a direct means of showing his concern with mankind and a re-examination of his self as a result of the loss of security. The psychological proportions of this Donne—not a Jack Donne by any means, nor yet a Dr. Donne—lie outside a study of the satires only, but the direction of such a study is inherent, I believe, in the foregoing view which the satires depict.

Bloomfield, New Jersey

Notes

1. All quotations come from my edition of *The Complete Poetry of John Donne* (New York, 1967).

2. Group I Manuscripts: H49, British Museum, Harleian MS 4955; D, Bodleian Library, Dowden MS, MS Eng. Poet. e. 99; SP, St. Paul's Cathedral Library, MS 49 B43; *Lec*, Goeffrey Keynes, Leconfield MS; C57, Cambridge University Library, Add. MS 5778 (c). A manuscript adjunct to Group I (H40, British Museau, Harleian MS 4064) omits the satires. A23, British Museum, Add. MS 23,229, transcribed lines 203–244 of Satire 4 and all of Satire 5; apparently Satires 1, 2, 3, and lines 1–202 of Satire 4 were also transcribed but are now lost. The text in A23 derived from Lec and would seem to be in the hand of the same scribe; *see* W. Milgate, ed., *John Donne: The Satires, Epigrams and Verse Letters* (Oxford, 1967), p. xlii n. 2. Professor Milgate also prints the order: 1, 2, 3, 4, 5. The stemma of these manuscripts was established by Helen Gardner, ed., *John Donne: The Divine Poems* (Oxford, 1952).

3. These are: Hd, Harvard University, Norton MS 4620, Eng. MS 966.7; W, Berg Collection, New York Public Library, Westmoreland MS; JC, Arents Collection, New York Public Library, John Cave MS; D17, Victoria and Albert Museum, Dyce Collection, MS 25, F17; S, Harvard University, Stephens MS, Norton MS 4500, Eng. MS 966.6; K, James H. Osborn, Raphael King MS; Q, Queen's College, Oxford, MS 216; D16, Victoria and Albert Museum, Dyce Collection, MS D25, F16.

4. C4, Cambridge University Library, MS Ee. 4.14; H51, British Museum, Harleian MS 5110. Q, D16, and perhaps H51 are brief collections of the satires primarily, indicating that they were circulated as a group as Ben Jonson's Epigram XCIV: "To Lucy, Countess of Bedord, With Mr. Donne's Satires" also attests.

5. A25, British Museum, Add. MS 25, 707; Cy, Harvard University, Carnaby MS, Norton MS 4502, Eng. MS 966.1.

6. TCD, Trinity College, Dublin, MS G. 21; N, Harvard University, Norton MS 4503, Eng. MS 966.3. N is a copy of TCD. Three other manuscripts in this group omit the satires which begin TCD.

7. Group III Manuscripts: S96, British Museum, Stowe MS 961; Lut, Geoffrey Keynes, Narcissus Luttrell MS; O'F, Harvard University, O'Flaherty MS, Norton MS 4504, Eng. MS 966.5. Related MSS: B, Huntington Library, Bridgewater MS, MS EL 6893; S962, British Museum, Stowe MS 962. S96 omits 3 and 5.

8. O, James H. Osborn; P, Bodleian, Phillipps MS, MS Eng. Poet. f. 9.

9. L74, British Museum, Lansdowne MS 740.

10. Dob, Harvard University, Dobell MS, Norton MS 4506, Eng. MS 966.4. A partial version of Satire 4 in prose was added before the satires by another (later) hand.

The fourth satire is also found in Ash 38 (Bodleian Library, Ashmole MS 38); in HN (National Library of Scotland, Hawthornden MS XV, Cat. MS 2067), to which William Drummond added Satire 2 as an afterthought; in Wed (National Library of Scotland, Halkett of Pitfirrane Papers, Cat. MS 6504), which also transcribes Satire 2; and by itself (University of Nottingham Library, MS PwV 191), having been ripped out of some larger collection. Lines 18–23 of Satire 4 were quoted by Joseph Wybarne in *The New Age of Old Names* (London, 1609), p. 113. Wed, a recently discovered manuscript, is described by Alan MacColl in "A New Manuscript of Donne's Poems," *RES*, N. S. 19 (1968): 293–95. It shows close relationship with HN.

11. *See* Andreasen, "Theme and Structure in Donne's *Satyres*," *SEL* 3 (1963): 59–75.

12. O'F changed "Sleydan" to "Surius"; A25 spelled "Snodons"; and TCD changed "fondling" to "challenging." 1669 gives "changeling," "departest from me," and "Surius." Milgate did not report Hd, C4, PwV 191, or (of course) Wed.

13. A23 has "lack," 5.68, and would undoubtedly have had other variants found in Lec.

14. Aside from more generalized books on Donne and his poetry, the reader may wish to compare Mrs. Andreasen's article and two by Sister M. Geraldine, "John Donne and the Mindes Indeavours," *SEL* 5 (1965): 111–31, and "Donne's *Notitia*: The Evidence of the Satires," *UTQ* 36 (1966): 24–36. Mrs. Andreasen sees the dilemma of Satire 1 as the opportunism and lechery of a young rake. My discussion will make clear that I consider such a view not only circumscribed but essentially wrong.

15. The one state is not the state of love, provoking poetry as Milgate would have it in his edition, for Donne says, "Even though poetry is a grevious sin, yet it is poor and disarmed and not worth hate." He is using the vehicle of love pleaders and their function in poetry to satirize the court pleader and his fiction. The name Coscus (*see* below) epitomizes this. The subject of the satire is lawyers and the law courts, not poetic amorists. (The opening lines of Satire 5 should also be compared with the opening lines here.)

16. Roger Bennett (*The Complete Poems of John Donne* [Chicago, 1942]) gives "great offense," the reading of a number of manuscripts; but "just," the reading of the editions and a number of other manuscripts, is more meaningful for the subject of this satire. The crucial text in line 72 should be "Bearing like Asses" (without a hyphen) as the ensuing explica-

271

tion of the phrase makes clear. The hyphen, which has found its way into some printings of the satire, was an editorial change made by Grierson, who apparently did not understand what Donne was saying.

17. In a forthcoming article in *SEL* entitled " 'To Stand Inquiring Right': The Casuistry of Donne's 'Satyre III'," Camille Slights persuasively evidences that "In the third satire Donne assumes the person of a casuist addressing a young man whose confusion over the complexities and contradictions of institutionalized religion is apparently leading to cynicism." The case of conscience thus seen is, as Mrs. Slights notes, a rather early English example of an important subgenre for seventeenth-century writing. Mrs. Andreasen's contention that Satire 3 is a soliloquy conducted in meditative isolation is simply not borne out by the universality of Donne's theme or its treatment.

18. Mrs. Andreasen ("Theme and Structure in Donne's *Satyres*," p. 59) says that "they are all concerned with presenting an idealistic defense of spiritual values against the creeping encroachment of sixteenth-century materialism." Such a view denies the universality of themes and compound subject; and it somehow misses the tone of frustration and the lack of real hope for reform, though the aim is ultimately such reform.

19. In attempting to make valid the modal epithet "private" for Donne's poetry, Earl Miner seems to nullify the universal in Donne's satires: "The Donne of the satires constitutes himself as a personal, unloyal opposition to the Establishment, angry with the world for its indifference to him, and angry with himself for his partial involvement with it. When we come to consider the motives for such private response, we must not forget such partial involvement or the seemingly first-hand experience the satires record" (*The Metaphysical Mode from Donne to Cowley* [Princeton, 1969], pp. 10–11). The term "private" has its use in literary criticism (*see* later), but too frequently its modal relationship seems to be forgotten for the meaning "personal," and we read lines susceptible of misunderstanding like "He attacks what he purports to have seen" (p. 11) and "[His reactions show] retreat to the integrity of the private self" (p. 11).

Milgate, who seems not to like the *Satires* at all, asks whether Donne was actually concerned with the vicious life at all; he sees the subjects as stock and trite.

JOSEPHINE MILES

＊

IFS, ANDS, BUTS
FOR THE READER OF DONNE

Questions asked about Donne a generation ago by editors like
Grierson, poets like Eliot, and influential textbook makers like
George Potter were questions about his effect upon his readers:
what does he mean to us; why do we like him so much; what has
he got to tell us? Since then, the inquiries have turned more abstract and definitional: what is the essence of Donne; what is his
school, his group, his type? Joan Bennett's *Four Metaphysical
Poets* steadily stirred skepticism with its assumptions of grouping, and year upon year of students have read and re-read the
Songs and Sonnets trying to trace a pattern of figurative language, or a philosophical bent, or a violent yoking of ideas,
which would yield up the very heart of Donne's matter and also
provide a clue to his bonds with his contemporaries, in the
often disconcerting presence of Cowley and Cleveland.

 Under the impression that the hand is sometimes quick-
er than the eye, I have wondered whether certain patterns of
usage in Donne's writing might underlie both ostensible effects
and analytical categorizations; that is, whether a discerning of
basic materials and structures in the work might help separate
what the writer contributes to the transaction from what the
reader contributes to it. Our word *characteristic* often means

more characteristic of our interest in the author than characteristic of his own emphases; therefore an abstractive process,
which subordinates the actualities and complexities of a quali-
tative reading to the simplicities, even over-simplicities of a
quantitative and structural analysis may do something to show
the reader on what firm ground of actuality in the text some of
his reactions may rest.

Consider, for example, the simple content and the major
vocabulary of the *Songs and Sonnets*. Professor Hanan Selvin
and I have tried to see what a factor analysis would do to help
the eye in noting the steady recurrence of main terms of reference from poem to Donne poem and from poet to Donnian
poet.[1] *Man's heart, love, soul, name* occur and recur and are
constant for his time; *man's death, fear, tear* are, along with
negative adjectives *bad, false, poor* more especially limited to
Donne and a small group; and concepts of *time* in *new, day,
year* are even more definingly limited in their occurrence. So
too with basic actions: *love, make, see* are common to almost all,
while verbs of *knowing, telling, thinking* are more Donnian, as
are the active reciprocal *find, keep, give, take*. Not characteristic
of Donne are the early and late century Jonsonian classical and
moral terms *friend, fate, god, grace, nature,* the *grow* of Herrick
or the religio-aesthetic mid-century *fair, bright, high, heaven,
earth* and *night* of Sandys, Crashaw, Marvell, Walter, and Milton. The classical and the biblical traditions were not his, nor
were the moral or the aesthetic traditions. His was rather a
vocabulary of concept distinguished by its concern with time,
cognition, and truth, positive and negative. It links Donne early
to Wyatt and Sidney and later to Herbert and Cowley, more
than to the religious poets usually placed with him. His strong
use of the terms of formal logic—conjunctive *and-but*, alternative *either-or*, consequent *if therefore, though yet*—links him
also to Wyatt, Sidney and especially Jonson, while his powerful

descriptive relative clauses and active prepositions relate him also to his predecessors.

Factor analysis indicates a very high relevance of grouping by form as well as content, syntactic as well as lexical. In these terms, no poet in the seventeenth century is so participative in its poetic process as Donne. His are the extremes of the century's norms. More than any other poetry, the seventeenth century's was a poetry of predication, of strongly used verbs in sentences both short and long; and more than any other poet, Donne was the poet of verbs and the clausal connectives for verbs.

The growing tendencies in the century toward emphases on substantives and on adjectives were ignored by Donne; he worked not toward compromise or modification or moderation as Shakespeare did, but rather from what could be called the Wyatt-Sidney tradition and that of the Jonsonian sons like Herrick, Carew, Shirley, Suckling, Cowley, who were nearly as propositional as he, toward a dashing and imperious excess of what was central in his time. Where most poets before and after him used about a verb in every line, ten in every ten, Donne like Sidney and Jonson used a couple extra in every ten. Where others used twelve to eighteen connectives in ten lines, Donne used twenty-four, far more than other English poets of any time. This special structural combination of verbs and connectives means a special clausal structure. It both separates Donne from all other poets by its singularity and also affords a scale of approximations for affinities, by which we may see Jonson, Herrick, and later Coleridge as closest to him.

While vocabulary and structure provide two different scales of comparison, they come close to Donne's poetic focal point by indicating how the specialization of his structure in subordinative propositions and the specialization of his reference in cognitive terms makes a bond which relates sixteenth century poetic substance of Wyatt and Sidney to the seventeenth century poetic grammar of Jonson and Herrick, Carew and Cowley, and goes beyond it all to an inencompassable realm, where it is no wonder no one follows.

Some of the chief non-poetic seventeenth-century structures suggest that this realm of subordinate clausal is a realm of prose. The combination of many verbs and connectives is to be found in Donne's prose and in Hooker, Dekker, Jonson, Bunyan, Addison, Hazlitt, Russell, though it occurs most often in Donne's poetry. Characteristic of the thoughtful and familiar style, this combination is more dramatic in its energy than classically balanced. In some ways it is helpful to see the relation of Donne's poetry to such a style; it shows how he was able to enfold into poetry, as no other poet has, the complexities of logical argument inherent in a passionately active prose.

If Donne is a poet of thought and argument as his interpreters tell us, then readers should be able to receive directly the qualities of the "prose" in the poetry itself, the recurring poetic shapes and the sense of his characteristic line of thought, the structure of his argument. I think a reader can easily have such a sense, because Donne is an actively assertive, deeply repetitive poet who makes plain the pattern he works with. Begin the *Songs and Sonnets*, and after the first few you will be hearing underneath the substance the rhythm of a repeated process: *Goe, and catche . . . Get with child . . . Tell me . . . Teach me . . . If . . . If . . . Yet . . . Though . . . Though . . . Yet.* Or again: *Send home . . . Which . . . Yet . . . Send home . . . Which . . . Which . . . Yet send . . .* Or again: *I do not . . . But; . . . Then feare . . . But . . . O how . . . But . . . ; When . . . when . . . If . . . Let not . . . But.* In poem after poem, early and late in his career, in satires, letters, songs, sonnets, divine poems, Donne addresses, exhorts, argues, and then counters his own arguments.

Of the fifty *Songs and Sonnets,* the majority begin with

an imperative or a superlative or a question that needs to be supported, and then often is controverted in a stable and persistent structure based upon disjunction of thought and doubleness within the form. Imperatives resemble each other: *Goe and catche; Send home; Come live with me; So, so, breake off; Take heed; Marke, let me breathe; Oh doe not die; Let me powre forth; For Godsake hold your tongue; Stand still; do not harme nor question much.* Similarly questions—*Will he not let us love?*—and superlative statements—*If yet I have not all thy love, | Deare, I shall never have it all*—are controverted, as in this last example, by the counterstatement—*Yet no more can be due to mee, . . . Or if then thou gav'st mee all . . . But if in thy heart, . . . Yet I would not have all yet. If thou canst give it, then thou never gav'st it: | Loves riddles are, that though thy heart depart, | It stayes at home, and thou with losing sav'st it.* This pattern, and its resultant feeling, the loving support of a strong and even excessive demand by a resolving of all the exigencies, and a saving resolution by a shift into human terms, constitute a metaphysic.

But this metaphysic is not merely a characteristic of genre, of sonnet or meditation. Donne's first Satire, a hundred lines of iambic pentameter couplets, begins, *Away thou fondling motley humorist, | . . . Here . . . ; and here.* Line 48 begins the next section:

> *But since thou like a contrite penitent,*
> *Charitably warn'd of thy sinnes, dost repent*
> *These vanities, and giddinesses, loe*
> *I shut my chamber doore, and come, lets goe.*

The last section begins, *Now we are in the street;* and the active dialogue proceeds from there: *And so . . . Yet . . . As . . . till . . . him whom . . . why . . . Why . . . At last.*

In *Satire* II, the disjunction is built into the beginning:

> *Sir; though (I thanke God for it) I do hate*
> *Perfectly all this towne, yet there's one state*
> *In all ill things so excellently best,*
> *That hate, toward them, breeds pitty towards the rest.*

Then at line 25, an extension to a superlative *but*: *But hee is worst*, and at line 39, the consoling consequence, *But these punish themselves.* So the Satires move, by hyperbole which gives a second thought to another side or another attitude. Donne counters the hyperbolic extremes, believing that "means" are blessings:

> *Carthusian fasts, and fulsome Bachanalls*
> *Equally I hate; meanes blesse . . .*
>   *But (Oh) we'allow*
> *Good workes as good, but out of fashion now, . . .*

Similarly, "The Progresse of the Soule" begins, *I sing the progresse of a deathlesse soule*, and then in XII, *But snatch mee heavenly Spirit from this vaine / Reckoning their vanities . . .* ; then comes a narrative sequence—*Next . . . , next . . .* — and in conclusion *There's nothing simply good or ill alone, . . .*

Of the Verse Letters, "To Mr. T.W." and many others are good examples: the reasons are given first, and then the petition; in "To Mr. R.W." the argument and counter-argument come after the petition as they do in but one of the many to the Countesse of Bedford, with its central turn from *Beeing* and *seeming is your equall care . . . But as our Soules of growth and Soules of sense / Have birthright of our reasons Soule, . . . toward your whole wisdom and religion.*

The *Divine Poems*, maintain the basic structure exemplified by the progression in "La Corona": *Deigne at my hands . . . But doe not . . . ; Salvation to all . . . Which cannot sinne, and yet all sinnes must beare, . . . Immensitie cloysterd*

*in thy deare wombe . . . But Oh, for thee, for him, hath th'Inne
no roome? . . . With his kinde mother . . . But as for one; . . .
By miracles . . . But Oh! . . . Moyst with one drop . . . But
made that there, of which, and for which 'twas; . . . Salute the
last, . . . But first hee, . . .*

Donne's use of connectives is also exemplified in the Holy
Sonnets, published in 1633: *As due by many titles . . . Why doth
the devill then; . . . Oh my blacke Soule! . . . Yet grace . . . ; This
is my playes last scene . . . But my'ever-waking part . . . ; At the
round earths imagine'd corners, blow . . . But let them sleepe
. . . ; If poysonous mineralls . . . But who am I . . . ; Death be not
proud, though some have called thee . . . nor yet . . . ; Spit in my
face . . . But by my death . . . ; Why are wee . . . But wonder . . . ;
What if this present . . . No, no; but as in my idolatrie . . . ;
Batter of my heart . . . But is captiv'd . . . ; Wilt thou love God . . .
But, that God should . . . ; Father, part . . . Yet such are those
laws . . . ;* The mediations added in 1635 show the same kind of
poetic progression: *Thou has made me, . . . But our old subtle
foe . . . ; I am a little world . . . But blacke sinne . . . ; O might
those sighes . . . No ease . . . ;-If faithfull soules . . . But if our
mindes . . .* And from the Westmoreland MS: *Since she whome I
lovd . . . But why should I . . . ; Show me deare Christ . . . or
which rob'd . . . ; Oh, to vex me, contraryes meete in one.*

I have extended these quotations of connective links in
order to make clear not only the stability and persistence of the
structure of thought, and not only its likeness to that of the
Songs and Sonnets, but also the basic feeling, the play over address and the disjunction of thought, the doubleness of feeling,
within the form. In many of the poems, the break comes at the
sonnet sestet; sometimes it comes immediately at the beginning,
sometimes not until the end, sometimes it is embedded within a
sub-argument, and some few times, as in the last example, it is
explicit in the substance.

A break in the pattern comes for Donne in the late

hymns. In the "Hymn to God my God, in my sicknesse," the introductory *since* and *whilst* lead to *I joy*; and *the thoughs* and questions are overriden by the concluding *so* and *therefore*. In "A Hymn to God the Father," the petitions to forgive have no alternatives. Yet here, even, the implication of alternative lies in the poem itself—the *yet* latent in *hast done* and *hast not done*, up to the resolving *having done*.

As a norm, for example, we may look at the whole of the famed Holy Sonnet, "At the round earths." Not all are so vividly countered as this, but all are figured by it.

> *At the round earths imagin'd corners, blow*
> *Your trempets, Angells, and arise, arise*
> *From death, you numberlesse infinities*
> *Of soules, and to your scattred bodies goe,*
> *All whom the flood did, and fire shall o'erthrow,*
> *All whom warre, dearth, age, agues, tyrannies,*
> *Despaire, law, chance, hath slaine, and you whose*
> *   eyes,*
> *Shall behold God, and never tast deaths woe.*
> *But let them sleepe, Lord, and mee mourne a space,*
> *For, if above all these, my sinnes abound,*
> *'Tis late to aske abundance of thy grace,*
> *When wee are there; here on this lowly ground,*
> *Teach mee how to repent; for that's as good*
> *As if thou'hadst seal'd my pardon, with thy blood.*

The poem calls upon angels, in Donne's common imperative, to wake infinities of souls, in an octave of examples. Then comes a sestet of a changed mind—*But let them sleepe, Lord*—or it will be too late for me there; *here* teach me to repent. The *But* takes the poem from the accepted glorious to the truly personal. The following sonnet is also a good example of the break in Donne's pattern:

If poysonous mineralls, and if that tree,
Whose fruit threw death on else immortall us,
If lecherous goats, if serpents envious
Cannot be damn'd; Alas; why should I bee?
Why should intent or reason, borne in mee,
Make sinnes, else equall, in mee, more heinous?
And mercy being easie, and glorious
To God, in his sterne wrath, why threatens hee?
But who am I, that dare dispute with thee
O God, Oh! of thine onely worthy blood,
And my teares, make a heavenly Lethean flood,
And drowne in it my sinnes blacke memorie.
That thou remembered them, some claime as debt,
I thinke it mercy, if thou wilt forget.

The octave disputes with its *if . . . why*; the sestet self-disputes, and then calls for a heavenly Lethean flood; it moves from personal to vast, as the preceding sonnet moves from vast to personal. As the other substituted repentance for pardon, this substitutes forgetting for remembering, moves away from God as the other moves toward him. The pattern is in the motion, toward or away, the metaphysical sides of *if-then, and-but.*

The many critics of Donne write a good deal about this procedure as metaphysical, yet they seem to me often to talk about parts rather than wholes. They do not seem to refer to the guiding lines, the chief emphases of the poet. To note what a number of critics have to say is to note a number of converging approaches.

Is this poetic structure singular or shared? In his essay on "The Metaphysical Poets," T. S. Eliot re-stated the inquiry: "The question is to what extreme the so-called metaphysicals formed a school (in our own time we should say a "movement"), and how far this so-called school or movement is a digression from the main current."[2] He called attention to the yoking of ideas and feelings—"A thought to Donne was an experience."[3] He emphasized fusion in figure and sensory unities quite alien to the consciously labored logic we have been observing.

C. S. Lewis too has stressed Donne's dramatic argument, his dandyism, and astringency as they suit the present day, his constancy to the themes of parting, secrecy, falseness, fickleness, miseries of love—a limited series of passions: "Donne's love poems could not exist unless love poems of a more genial character existed first . . ."[4] He says that Carew's "When thou, poor Excommunicate" or Lovelace's "To Lucasta, going beyond the seas" are built up on Donne's favorite plan, but both lack his energy in favor of beauty: and that nothing could be more like Donne than Marvell's "Coy Mistress."

Cleanth Brooks illustrates Donne's use of paradox in "The Canonization"—the gain by losing, the world in sainthood. Helen Gardner explains Loyola's meditative practice by means of resignation—the place, the petition, the will; the rhetoric of proposition—consequence—conclusion. Louis Martz, too, draws attention to religious visualization, theological annalysis, and eloquence of will. And Stanley Archer makes a tripartite sequence of drama, reason, petition, or strophe, antistrophe, epode, and of meaning, understanding, will. Less programatically, Joseph Mazzeo has traced all sorts of possibilities for influence, from Ramism, baroque styles, emblem techniques to Renaissance interest in universal analogy.

Each critic makes a different emphasis: L. I. Bredvold on Donne's scepticism like Montaigne's—"I study my selfe more than any other subject. It is my supernaturall metaphysike, it is my naturall Philisophy . . . I had rather understand my selfe well in my selfe, then in Cicero."[5] Paradoxically, Donne was pro nature, anti-book, as well as the opposite! So Joseph Duncan and F. O. Mathierson help us see Donne as self-conscious rebel, Hamlet, for the nineteenth century. S. L. Bethel is especially revealing in his study of metaphysical wit in the traditions of Gracian and Tesauro—seeing dialectic as connecting terms as rhetoric adorns them; seeing both dialectic and rhetoric in art to seek beauty, a harmonic correlation, a symmetry of proportionate correspondence, implying truth through fiction and fallacy. So too Unger emphasizes complexity, Williamson negative figures like *ironia* and *catechresis*, Alvarez and Peterson on the plain, harsh, personal style, very different from the craftsmanly Sidney circle, based less on conceit and argument than on a realism of the intelligence. Especially clarifying is Arnold Stein's full discussion in *John Donne's Lyrics* of the lyricism of absent things made present by rhetoric and of things that do not exist nevertheless made to seem as though they did by poetry. The stress is on *differences,* the binary and ternary forms of these. "A characteristic movement of his mind is the energetic pursuit of a limited theme"[6] by witty inversion, through tempering reconciling, exhausting. The drive toward consciousness, gay and grim, compels Donne's negatives with his positives.[7] "Donne uses the old patterns of the mind's experience as other poets use myths, to be built upon, varied, and revealed by art."[8] *Ergo* and *igitur* were subdued, as Fraunce said, to illustrative substance, yet survived to be mocked by Pope's *The Dunciad.*

Closer to Donne's procedure are the guiding suggestions of earlier critics. For example, Grierson says in *Metaphysical Lyrics,* "Donne, moreover is metaphysical not only in virtue of his scholasticism, but by his deep reflective interest in the experience of which his poetry is the expression, the new psychological curiosity with which he writes of love and religion . . . the peculiar blend of passion and thought, feeling and ratiocination."[9] The most famous words are Johnson's in "Cowley": "The most heterogeneous ideas are linked by violence together; nature and art are ransacked for illustrations, comparisons, and allusions; their learning instructs, and their subtlety surprises . . . As they were wholly employed on something unexpected and surprising, they had no regard to that uniformity of sentiment, which enables us to conceive and to excite the pains and the pleasure of other minds . . . Nor was the sublime more within their reach than the pathetic . . . sublimity is produced by aggregation, and littleness by dispersion. Great thoughts are always general, and consist in positions not limited by exceptions, and in descriptions not descending to minuteness. . . . To write on their plan it was at least necessary to read and think."[10] Johnson named Donne, Jonson, Suckling, Waller, Denham, Cowley, Cleveland as those whose minds were exercised less by direct or general impression than by recollection or inquiry. Best of all in realizing the implications of such definition was Coleridge. Of "The Canonization" he wrote, "One of my favorite poems. As late as ten years ago, I used to seek and find out grand lines and fine stanzas; but my delight has been far greater since it has consisted more in tracing the leading thought thru'out the whole. The former is too much like coveting your neighbor's; in the latter you merge yourself in the author, you *become He*."[11]

Donne's leading thought is embodied in "The Canonization": *For Godsake hold your tongue, and let me love, Or chide . . . flout . . . improve, Take . . . get . . . Observe . . . Contemplate; what you will . . . So you will let me love. Who . . . Who . . . Who is harmed or even influenced by my love? . . . Call us what you will, wee'are made such by love.* Or—if we do not live by love, we can die by it—if not for tomb, or chronicle, for sainthood. Thus he advises us to invoke from such intensity of earthly love a pattern as from heaven. By the use of an imperative, many inspired possibilities, positive and negative, more and more hyperbolic and conditional, he focuses on love in its intensity. These were what Dryden called in his essay on *Satire* the "nice speculations of philosophy": they concerned as Donne himself told Jonson of "The Anniversarie", the "Idea of a woman and not as she was."

This is the heart of Donne that makes him different from

the rest: the *idea,* and not as she was; the positions limited, exactly as Johnson said they should *not* be, by exception. Here are poetic values not of atmosphere and observation, not of actuality, but of possibility. And here the simplest dictionary definitions of *metaphysical* help us: "concerned with abstract thought or subjects, as existence, causality, truth, etc., concerned with first principles and ultimate grounds, as being, time, or substance." Note the way the principles proceed in the beginning of Aristotle's *Metaphysics: All men naturally have an impulse to get knowledge, . . . From memory . . . now experience seems . . . Nevertheless, we believe . . . since . . . These then . . . Hence . . . Yet.* And at the end: *One might also raise the question . . . And if all things . . . But how . . Some also say . . . However . . . These, then . . . But . . .* Whether from this involved old tradition from the schoolmen, or new novelty, as Johnson thought, Aristotle's principles provided a world of poetry for Donne far more fully and consistently than for the other religious poets of his time.

> *Take heed . . . not that . . . but if . . . take heed*
> *Take heed . . . or . . . not that . . . and if . . . but then*
> *Yet . . . so . . . because . . . or . . . so . . . yet . . . take heed.*

Donne's colleagues are far stronger in atmosphere than in argument. Herrick's *Hesperides* begins "I sing of brooks, of blossoms, birds, and bowers" and goes on with these *ofs* for fourteen lines. In "When he would have his Verses Read," the sequence of *whens* stands out: in "Upon Julia's Rosemary," he uses imperatives with *and* or *or*; in "The Frozen Heart," an *if* against love; in "To Perilla," the *when* and *which* of foretelling; in "No Loathesomeness," subjunctives as substitutes for *ifs.* The imperative *Get up!* of "Corinna" is followed by manners of *how, while, before, so.* His later religious poems in *Noble Numbers* are similar in an exclamatory *Look,* or *Forgive,* with the appropriate modifiers: *My God! look on me ... with thine eye/ Of pittie, not of scrutinie.* Crashaw hails *Sister Springs*, and asks *What bright soft thing is this.* Herbert cries, *Oh, all ye who pass by ... Oh, King of Grief, how shall I grieve ... Lord, how I am all ague, when I seek.*

In Marvell, *See how*, and *when*, are very strong. In Vaughan, there is a more narrative structure: *Here I repos'd; we scarce will set; ... Oft have I seen ... But mists and shadows ...* Jonson does seem closest to Donne, an analysis has shown. In *The Forrest* he addresses and argues, *Thou art not*, Penhurst, ... *Let us prove ... But if we lose ...* The imperative of his famous song, *Drink to me only with thine eyes/ And I will pledge with mine*, also shows his closeness to Donne. But just as everybody said in their day, it was Cleveland and Cowley who were the closest to Donne. See, for example, Cowley's "To the Duchess of Buckingham," or "The Grasshopper" or the ode "Of Wit", or all of "The Mistress". See Cleveland's "Upon the King's return from Scotland": *Return'd? ... But the Crab-Tropick must not now prevail ...* Or "Upon a Miser" *—Nor 'scapes he so; ... But are we Tantaliz'd? ... But stay awhile; ...* or *Smectymnus? ... But doe the Brotherhood?* Cleveland, and Cowley in "The Mistress" submit all to the process of thought. Seldom is a setting established for the sake of atmosphere, rather only for intellectual point. So Donne seldom, despite his bracelet of bright hair, really relaxes into a tone of description.

More useful in the search for likeness is to look back to early norms. Here is Petrarch's procedure in the first sonnet: *O ye that hear ... the sighing On which ... I turned from fears ... to hopes ... If ever ... Pity, and pardon me this crying!/ But Well I know how I must walk derided ...* This octave is a plea for sympathy, and a sestet of self-scorn. In the second sonnet, octave *courage* and sestet *Thrown off guard ...* In the third, there is more of a parallel between the two: *I fell a cap-*

tive and *Love caught me naked.* So also in IV there is a progressive *He who . . . so* construction, while V returns to a seventh line adversative in *But Tacit peace prevents the end.* In the first ten sonnets, half use a more or less disjunctive form, with *buts* or negatives; the others work, rather, cumulatively, catching up contrasts into a resolving whole.

In Wyatt's "Ten Sonnets", there is a similar pattern. In the first, octave and sestet are parallel in *Who so list . . . Who list*, though within the sections Wyatt's personal negative, *But as for me,* appears. Most of the rest of the sestets make a turn with *Therefore farewell, And yet, Nother, But as for me, But since, But since.* In one or two, where a bare statement or a contrasting material, is negative, the sestet simply adds evidence.

It is not merely sonnet structure that establishes the pattern of thought. A simple epigram is a model, too.

> *The fruit of all the service that I serve*
> *Despair doth reap, such hapless hap have I.*
> *But though he have no power to make me swerve,*
> *Yet, by the fire, for cold I feel I die. . . .*

The three stanzas of *They flee from me . . . Thankt be Fortune, it hath been otherwise . . .* and *It was no dream; I lay broad waking:/ But all is turn'd . . .* gives another version of the pattern. The lively variations in subtle disjunction or negative implication seem unending in their surface forms.

Shakespeare's first sonnet establishes the adverse early, and then goes on to positives. *From fairest creatures we desire increase . . . But thou . . .* Sonnet 2, rather, takes a step forward in degree: *How much more praise . . .* Sonnets 3, 4, 5, 6, 8, 9, 10 support and explain, with connectives *for* and *then,* and extension of degree, and imperatives. But sonnet seven works in the Wyatt way, or more closely in the Petrarchan—as in the three stages of the sun's progress, the third is contrasted

to the other two. Shakespeare in these early sonnets is persuading to action; often sestet and couplet move toward this positive
end, with a tone quite different from the *But yet* dismays of
Wyatt and Donne. Of the last sixty sonnets in the sequence,
possibly the most argumentative, about a dozen, or one in five,
uses the counter-sestet mode, and then with modification. The
But at my mistress' eye of 153 is the phrasing of a minor conceit,
while in the final, 154, the sequence of action goes—*The Love-
god laid by . . . But the votary took up,* and *healthful remedy
. . . but I not cured,* leading to the final paradox, *Love's fire
heats water, water cools not love*—a characteristic sonneteering
antithesis, yet not fully stressed by, rather subordinate to, the
octave-sestet structure. There is a true "Shakespearean sonnet"
quality in the avoidance of the main structural break. The adversatives, if present, are largely disposed of step by step in the
three quatrains.

It is Sidney whom a simple list of conjunctions has shown
to be most like Donne, and it is Sidney in fact whose sonnets
move, though with simpler thought, in the way Donne's move.
Almost every sonnet makes its simple shift: I, *I sought fit words
. . . But words came halting out . . .* ; IV, *Let dainty wits cry
on the Sisters nine, . . . For me, in sooth, no Muse but one I
know . . . ;* CVI, *O absent presence! Stella is not here! . . . But
here I do store of fair ladies meet . . .* These are actual literal
contrasts where Donne grows more conceptual; but they provide his poetic frame for thought.

Sometimes Donne does use the simple literal sensory
materials of all of these others, but even then he complicates
them. In "The Computation" he explains why it is best to re-
hearse parting as the sun does: *For the first twenty years, since
yesterday, | I scarce beleev'd, thou coulds't be gone away* coun-
ters the simple declarative statement with the hyperbole of time.
"The Will" shows a rarely simple parallel structure. "Twicknam Garden" begins with unwonted descriptiveness: *Blasted*

*with sighs, and surrounded with tears, | Hither I came to seeke
the spring.* "A Nocturnall upon S. Lucies Day," starts with the
atmosphere of *'Tis the yeares midnight, and it is the dayes, |
Lucies, who scarce seaven hourse herself unmaskes, | The Sunne
is spent, and now his flasks/Send forth light squibs, no constant rayes.* But these, like the rest, go on to counter-arguments.

Donne's way is not to narrate, not to set scenes and atmosphere in any thorough way; no more by substantive vocabulary than by connectives does he present and expatiate. As his
chief connectives are *and, but, that, to,* in disjunction, relation,
and direction, and the rest of his connectives support mainly
the logic of alternatives or consequences, so his substantive vocabulary also establishes a world of arguable inference. Looking
back to his chief terms of reference, we remember that *good* is
encountered by *bad, true* by *false* in a way rare in English poetry; seldom are negatives so dominant. Of his nouns, *death,
fear, tear* too have their negative force; the only potentially
objective noun is *sun.* Of his chief verbs, most of them abundantly repeated, none are unusual to his time, but again the
presence of opposites is strong in *come-go, give-take-keep*; and,
though deictic *show* is present, stronger are the more verbal
know, tell, think. No *bright, fair, sweet* of Shakespeare or Jonson, no *rose* of Herrick, no *dust* and *stone* of Herbert, nor *cloud*
and *star* of Vaughan, no *bring* or *call* or *grow* or *hear* or *kiss* or
sing or *feel* or *shine* or *sleep* of Herrick, Herbert, Vaughan, are
used by Donne, at least not with their basic recurrences. Nor
are there many, in parallel, of their stronger adverbial construc-
tions of place and manner. So we have in Donne's *Songs and
Sonnets,* and in his art at large, a persistent characterizing
abstract structure. Farthest from the illustrative and substanti-
ating modes of classicism and from the qualifying modes of
Spenserian and Miltonic sublimity, far even from the natural-
izing progressive variations of the colloquial style, and far
even, in its extremes, from its basic contexts in the counter-

structures of Petrarch, Wyatt, Sidney, Jonson, Herbert, and the men of faith in doubt, Donne was singular both in his extreme personal concentration upon one plan and form and also in his sharing of that plan and form with his whole time. The number . 9 in correlation with Donne's usage in comparison with that of others comes to be seen as the figure of the most intense individualism, the most intense participation.

Why is it hard for readers to see and feel so vivid a correlation? Why are our reading critics worried more about complexities of the metaphysical than they are about responding to its simplicities? I think it is because their own assumptions, their own simplicities from their own times, stand between them and the poems. This is one valid meaning of the process of interpretation—standing between poem and reader, and making connections, relevances, for both. But simple reading and response in the poem's terms is something else again, richer in time. Our own impositions are those of sense impression, or what Donne calls the phantasie, and the fear of reason. Donne is aware of this very contrast and mocks it, as for example in "The Dreame":

> Deare love, for nothing lesse than thee
> Would I have broke this happy dreame,
>   It was a theame
> For reason, much too strong for phantasie,
>   Therefore thou wakds't me wisely; yet
> My dreame thou brok'st not, but continued'st it,
> Thou art so true, that thoughts of thee suffice,
> To make dreames truth; and fables histories;

" 'Tis not all spirit, pure, and brave," says Donne, "Thou com'st to kindle, goest to come." It is this mixture of physical in metaphysical that constantly necessitates the shifting of ground, the involving of negatives, alternatives, and hypotheticals of logic as reason to humanize substance by thought. There's no harm in calling this *felt thought* as Eliot does in effect, but in so doing, the relation gets stood on its head. To ask how Donne feels his thought is to seek unsuccessfully, as we have long been doing, for sustaining patterns of figure, or even imagery, in poem after poem; rather to ask how Donne thinks his feeling is to seek and find the pattern of exuberant superlative questions and imperatives compellingly tempered by conditionals, adversatives, and straight denials; a pattern that emerges as a simple downright statement of the actuality of language and of life.

University of California at Berkeley

Notes

1. *The Computer and Literary Style*, ed. Jacob Leed (Kentucky, 1966); all quotations of poetry are from *The Poems of John Donne*, ed. H. J. C. Grierson (Oxford, 1912).

2. Eliot, *Selected Essays* (New York, 1950), p. 24.

3. Ibid., p. 247.

4. "Donne and Love Poetry in the Seventeenth Century" in *Seventeenth Century English Poetry*, ed. William R. Keast (New York, 1962), p. 107.

5. "The Naturalism of Donne" in *Discussions of John Donne*, ed. Frank Kermode (Boston, 1962), p. 53.

6. Stein, *John Donne's Lyrics* (Minneapolis, 1962), p. 163.

7. Ibid.

8. Ibid., p. 161.

9. Grierson, *Metaphysical Lyrics* (London, 1921), pp. xiii–xxviii.

10. *Rasselas Poems and Selected Prose*, ed. Bertrand H. Bronson (New York, 1961), pp. 470–72.

11. *Coleridge's Miscellaneous Criticism*, Lecture x, ed. T. M. Raysor (London, 1936), p. 137.